Charting an Asian Trajectory for Literacy Education

Weaving outwards from a centripetal force of biographical stances, this book presents the collective perspectives of literacy researchers from Brunei, China, Hong Kong, Malaysia, Singapore, the Philippines and Taiwan. It represents the first all-Asian initiative to showcase the region's postcolonial, multilingual and multicultural narratives of literacy education. This book provides a much-needed platform that initiates important conversations about literacy as a sociocultural practice in a region that is both challenged and shaped by sociocultural influence unique to Asia's historical and geopolitical trajectory. Driven by the authors' lived experiences of becoming literate as well as their empirical research work in later years, each chapter brings decades of biographical narratives and collective empirical research findings to bear. Within the book are negotiations about literacy across and within home and school contexts; transactions of literature, text and reader and considerations of the literacy policy–practice nexus. These trajectories, while divergent in their issues, come together as shared lived experience located in local contexts considered through global perspectives. As Asia looks set to become the 21st century's new economic and labour force, the need to understand the sociocultural milieu of this region cannot be understated. This book on literacy education in Asia contributes to the larger narrative.

Su Li Chong is Senior Lecturer at the Department of Management and Humanities, Institute of Self Sustainable Building, Universiti Teknologi PETRONAS (UTP), Malaysia. She is also Head of UTP's University Social Responsibility (Education Pillar). She obtained an MPhil and a PhD in Education from University of Cambridge, UK, where she was the recipient of St. Edmund's College Dean's Award (2014). Her research interests are in literacy and language education, particularly in the intersections of multilingualism, multimodality and meaning-making.

Routledge Research in Literacy Education

This series provides cutting-edge research relating to the teaching and learning of literacy. Volumes provide coverage of a broad range of topics, theories, and issues from around the world, and contribute to developments in the field.

Recent titles in the series include:

Dialogic Literary Argumentation in High School Language Arts Classrooms
A Social Perspective for Teaching, Learning, and Reading Literature
David Bloome, George Newell, Alan Hirvela and Tzu-Jung Lin

Engaging Teachers, Students, and Families in K-6 Writing Instruction
Developing Effective Flipped Writing Pedagogies
Danielle L. DeFauw

Charting an Asian Trajectory for Literacy Education
Connecting Past, Present and Future Literacies
Edited by Su Li Chong

Supporting Student Literacy for the Transition to College
Working with Underrepresented Students in Pre-College Outreach Programs
Shauna Wight

For a complete list of titles in this series, please visit https://www.routledge.com/Routledge-Research-in-Literacy-Education/book-series/RRLIT.

Charting an Asian Trajectory for Literacy Education
Connecting Past, Present and Future Literacies

Edited by Su Li Chong

Routledge
Taylor & Francis Group

LONDON AND NEW YORK

First published 2021
by Routledge
2 Park Square, Milton Park, Abingdon, Oxon OX14 4RN

and by Routledge
52 Vanderbilt Avenue, New York, NY 10017

Routledge is an imprint of the Taylor & Francis Group, an informa business

British Library Cataloguing-in-Publication Data
A catalogue record for this book is available from the British Library

Library of Congress Cataloging-in-Publication Data
Names: Chong, Su Li, editor.
Title: Charting an Asian trajectory for literacy education : connecting past, present and future literacies / edited by Su Li Chong.
Description: Abingdon, Oxon ; New York, NY : Routledge, 2021. | Includes bibliographical references and index.
Identifiers: LCCN 2020046941 (print) | LCCN 2020046942 (ebook) | ISBN 9780367856281 (hardback) | ISBN 9780367751791 (paperback) | ISBN 9781003013983 (ebook)
Subjects: LCSH: Literacy—East Asia. | Literacy—Southeast Asia. | Reading—East Asia. | Reading—Southeast Asia. | Language and languages—Study and teaching—East Asia. | Language and languages—Study and teaching—Southeast Asia. | Education and state—East Asia. | Education and state—Southeast Asia.
Classification: LCC LC157.E18 C53 2021 (print) | LCC LC157.E18 (ebook) | DDC 374/.95—dc23
LC record available at https://lccn.loc.gov/2020046941
LC ebook record available at https://lccn.loc.gov/2020046942

ISBN: 978-0-367-85628-1 (hbk)
ISBN: 978-0-367-75179-1 (pbk)
ISBN: 978-1-003-01398-3 (ebk)

Typeset in Galliard
by Apex CoVantage, LLC

MIX
Paper from
responsible sources
FSC FSC™ C013985
www.fsc.org

Printed in the United Kingdom
by Henry Ling Limited

We dedicate our writings and our life's work to our families—past, present and future.

Contents

Figures

Tables

Contributors

Editor

Su Li Chong is Senior Lecturer at the Department of Management and Humanities, Institute of Self Sustainable Building, Universiti Teknologi PETRONAS (UTP), Malaysia. She is also Head of UTP's University Social Responsibility (Education Pillar). She obtained an MPhil and a PhD in Education from the University of Cambridge, UK, where she was the recipient of St. Edmund's College Dean's Award (2014). Her research interests are in literacy and language education, particularly in the intersections of multilingualism, multimodality and meaning-making. She can be contacted at chong_suli@utp.edu.my.

Authors

Chin Ee Loh is Associate Professor and Deputy Dean (Research) at the English Language and Literature Academic Group at the National Institute of Education, Nanyang Technological University, Singapore. Chin Ee's research focuses on literacy and literature education at the intersection of social class and globalisation. Her current projects examine the design of learning environments and role of technology in supporting equitable access to reading. She can be contacted at chinee.loh@nie.edu.sg.

Dahlia Janan is Associate Professor of the Malay Language and Literature Department in the Faculty of Languages and Communication at the Universiti Pendidikan Sultan Idris, Malaysia. The United Kingdom Literacy Association awarded her the Student Research Prize in 2012 (Best Literacy Thesis Award). She was appointed Adjunct Professor of the School of Asian Language at Zhejiang Yuexiu Universit: Shaoxing, Zhejiang, China (2017–2019 and 2020–2021). She has published chapters and articles on aspects of literacy, especially readability, in the Malay and English languages. She is currently researching innovative approaches to assessing readability and comparative study of reading and literacy. She can be contacted at dahlia@fbk.upsi.edu.my.

Faye Dorcas Yung is Assistant Professor at the Open University of Hong Kong. She teaches English language curriculum and pedagogy, literature in English, and children's literature. She received her PhD in education from the University of Cambridge, studying children's literature criticism. Prior to her postgraduate studies, she taught English language in secondary school for four years. Her passion in promoting reading opened the door to children's literature, paving the path for her later research direction. Her current research interests include children's literature publishing, cultural representations in children's literature and literacy and reading promotion in developing countries. She can be contacted at fdyung@ouhk.edu.hk.

Jia Wei Lim is Senior Lecturer in the Department of Language and Literacy Education, Faculty of Education, University of Malaya, Malaysia. Since receiving her doctorate degree from Cambridge University, UK, where she researched post-secondary literature education development in the Malaysian context, she has been actively involved in research projects related to literacy, reading and language education. Apart from lecturing and supervising students in TESL and literature education, she has also published articles in journals such as *Literacy*, *Asia Pacific Journal of Education* and *Innovations in Education and Teaching International*. She is a lifetime member of Asia TEFL and MELTA. She can be contacted at jwlim@um.edu.my.

Lalaine F. Yanilla Aquino is Professor at the Department of English and Comparative Literature, University of the Philippines (UP), where she teaches children's literature, stylistics and language and cognition. She has been given the UP Centennial Professorial Chair Award, the UP International Publication Award and the ONE UP Professorial Chair Award. She has presented her studies in more than 17 countries, including the International Research Society for Children's Literature (IRSCL) conferences in Hungary, Netherlands, United Kingdom and Canada, and the AILA World Congress in China and Australia. Her studies on children's literature, language and literacy have been included in anthologies published by Routledge, Gale Cengage, Multilingual Matters and Palgrave Macmillan. She can be contacted at lyaquino@up.edu.ph.

Malai Zeiti Sheikh Abdul Hamid is Assistant Professor at the Centre for Communication, Teaching and Learning and Wellness Research Thrust Leader at the Universiti of Teknologi Brunei (UTB). She graduated with a doctorate from the UK (Bath University), specialising in English Language and Literacy Education, and a Teaching Certificate in Higher Education (Harvard University). She also completed the Women's Leadership Development Programme (University of Oxford). Dr Zeiti was recipient of the US-ASEAN Fulbright Scholarship Program and Visiting Scholar at the Harvard Graduate School of Education (HGSE), US. She is currently attending her postdoctoral fellowship at Harvard University. She can be contacted at zeiti.hamid@utb.edu.bn.

Mukhlis Abu Bakar is Associate Professor in Linguistics and Language Education at the National Institute of Education, Nanyang Technological University, Singapore. Trained as an applied linguist, Mukhlis teaches in the area of grammar, linguistics, literacy, critical approaches to language and bilingualism and bilingual education. His research interests focus on bilingualism and biliteracy, a sociocultural approach to literacy learning in the home, school and faith settings, and pronunciation issues in the Malay language. His most recent book is *Rethinking Madrasah Education in a Globalized World* (Editor) (2018) published by Routledge. He can be contacted at mukhlis.abubakar@nic.edu.sg.

Priscilla Angela T. Cruz is Assistant Professor at Ateneo de Manila University, the Philippines. She has taught literature, writing and research for almost 20 years. Her current projects involve transdisciplinary approaches which apply linguistics to a variety of texts and fields, such as business process outsourcing and psychology. She is also working on projects involving Philippine languages, language variation and language contact and change. Currently, she is the chairperson of the Department of English, Ateneo de Manila. She can be contacted at ptan@ateneo.edu.

Sumathi Renganathan is Assistant Professor in the Department of Languages and Linguistics, Universiti Tunku Abdul Rahman (UTAR) Kampar Campus, Malaysia. She obtained her PhD (Education) from King's College London. Sumathi's research interests include indigenous and minority issues in education, language and literacy, culture and identity, ESL teaching and learning, ethnographic approach and qualitative research methodology. She can be contacted at sumathir@utar.edu.my.

Xiaofei Shi obtained her PhD in education from the University of Cambridge, UK. She is now lecturing and researching as Associate Professor at Soochow University, China, and a member of the Equity and Diversity Committee of the International Research Society for Children's Literature (IRSCL). Her research interests include children's literature, cognitive literary studies and the role of picture books in education. Her latest publication is "Wasted Innocence: Children and Childhood in Cao Xueqin's Dream of the Red Chamber" (International Research in Children's Literature, forthcoming). She can be contacted at shixf@suda.edu.cn.

Yi-Shan Tsai is Lecturer in the Faculty of Information Technology at Monash University in Australia. As an interdisciplinary researcher, her research interests range from learning analytics, feedback practice and digital storytelling to reading cultures and multimodal texts. She holds a PhD and an MPhil degree in Education from the University of Cambridge. She is a fellow of UK Higher Education Academy and currently an executive member at large of the Society for Learning Analytics Research (SoLAR). She can be contacted at yi-shan.tsai@monash.edu.

Acknowledgements

There is much to be grateful for.

The conception, writing and production of this book, in themselves, form a trajectory. That trajectory is shaped by my upbringing, career choice and the serendipity of the two paths coming together. This book is made possible with the full support provided by Universiti Teknologi PETRONAS (UTP), Malaysia, my academic home for 20 years. The privilege to pursue my graduate studies in University of Cambridge, UK, which I was incredibly lucky to have received from UTP, changed the course of my academic trajectory. Special acknowledgements go to Professor Mohamed Ibrahim Abdul Mutalib, Professor Mohd Shahir Liew, Professor Hilmi Mukhtar, Associate Professor Dr. Noor Amila and Associate Professor Dr. Lai Fong Woon for their encouragement and support.

This book has also benefited from the generous funding granted by Ministry of Education, Malaysia, under the Fundamental Research Grant Scheme (FRGS/1/2018/SS109/UTP/02/1) that provided the resource and access for fieldwork necessary for the conception and writing of the book.

I am greatly indebted to the following stalwarts for their invaluable and expert feedback, precious time and genuine interest in the way the book would eventually be shaped; Dr. Gabrielle Cliff Hodges, Professor Ahmad Murad Merican and Emeritus Professor Asmah Haji Omar. Their work have inspired many.

Across this book, the authors pay tribute to their familial trajectories that have shaped their own literacy education and literacy journeys. As much as this was an academic endeavour, it was also deeply personal for all of us. Through this, we understood how our literacy journeys have been so much a part of our research journeys.

Any and all inconsistencies remain my own.

Editor
Su Li Chong, PhD (Cantab)
Universiti Teknologi PETRONAS (UTP)
Malaysia

Introduction

Su Li Chong

How the book came to be

For the reading researcher, the Mecca, indeed the Holy Grail, of their life's work is to be able to provide a definitive answer for what it means to read. This is because such a definitive answer will quell the age-old question of what counts for reading, and more importantly, will provide measures for how reading should be taught. This book represents both a search for answers to this question and an effort to raise new questions moving forward.

As will be made increasingly clear, the definition of reading and writing in this book takes the posture of literacy as a sociocultural practice. This posture sets the stage for the reader to understand that conventional, narrowed notions of what it means to read and write will, in this book, be broadened. Particularly, reading and writing will be theorised to be more than skill-building. While this is not new in many parts of the Western world, this initiative when postured within the Asian context, represents a rare effort because of the way literacy has largely been about skill-building in this region.

It is fair to say that global, academic conversations in the field of literacy education that shape the teaching and advocacy of reading and writing have been and continue to be driven by Western perspectives. This is to be expected if one were to understand that the 19th and 20th centuries were shaped by industrial, intellectual and technological progress led by the Western world, buoyed largely by the advances of literacy. Because of shared historical and cultural trajectories, these perspectives about literacy education tend to be dominated by the single-system, alphabet-centric, Euro-American-linguistic narratives of what reading means. These perspectives are also grounded in countries which the world considers as economically developed.

Perhaps the most salient feature of these narratives is represented by The Great Reading Debate that began in earnest in the mid-20th century. As the West began to rebuild their nations in the aftermath of World War II, mass education became the factor tasked to eradicate illiteracy. For this reason, efforts to teach beginning reading to children up and down the country became critical. However, the reading debate divided reading educators in the Western world. In the decades after the war, groups of largely American academics, teachers, parents and politicians argued about whether their children should be taught to read via phonics or the whole language approach. In the great debate, proponents of the code-emphasis method, better known as phonics approach, maintain that children learn best when they achieve phonemic awareness (Chall, 1967, 1983; Flesch, 1981; Stahl, 2006). This means that the ability to recognise the Roman-alphabetic letter system and match the system with its corresponding sounds to be blended into words became the hallmark of a literate person. In this light, therefore, reading was defined as a decoding skill that could be taught to children in linear, chronological steps. In contrast, the whole-word approach was based on the theorisation that reading is more than a mechanical decoding skill. Using references from the field of psychology, Goodman (1968) and Smith (1985) believe that seeing reading as largely a mechanical ability to decode will mean excluding a fundamental aspect of recognising the reader as a unique individual with differing abilities to form meanings, located in unique, and more importantly, social contexts. To them, reading is first and fundamentally about meaning-making; hence a child learning to read should first be introduced to whole words and their attached meaning(s). The beginning reader is then understood to utilise selected cues to guess the meanings of the words within the context of the sentence.

Clearly, the actual exchanges between the two ideologies, especially where the fissures took hold, were more complex than alluded to here. Still, as the divide pit researchers and scholars against one another, on both sides of the divide, both methods of reading were accounted for and were included. Also, in real classroom contexts, the situation was not nearly as black or white as the debate may have implied. Even in her recommendation, Chall reiterated that "there is still much to learn about the process of learning to read" (Chall, 1967, p. 306).

So why is a debate from so long ago relevant to this book? This debate is important for how it stood for the sharp focus trained upon the relationship between a linguistic system and the assumed comprehension processes that occur within the minds of the reader. Further, this flags up what was central to the debate: a largely singular writing system and the quest to arrive at the best approach to unlock this system (Huey, 1908). However, in sharpening its focus to such a degree, the trajectory of reading is at risk of being reduced. Reading cannot, and indeed must not, merely be about this singular quest.

This book offers a perspective about literacy education as it emerges from a context that stands in stark contrast with the dominant narrative of what reading and writing means in the Western world. Located in another corner of the globe, Asia is inherently rich with narratives of lived literacy experience which tells of a different story, not least because Asia is home to some of the oldest civilisations in the world. Since the end of the 20th century, global economic trends have begun to flag up Asia's ascendency in financial and economic might. Known in some spheres as Asia literacy (Halse, 2015), this relatively new focus on understanding Asia has been the result of what some term as the emerging world order (Jacques, Abidin, Zainuddin, & Institute of Strategic and International Studies, 2012). Leading the pack, China's meteoric rise in terms of its GDP growth has caught global attention. Countries such as India, Indonesia, Singapore and most recently

Vietnam have also begun to count as important economies for human resource and trade. With more than half of the world's population being Asian now and in the foreseeable future, much has been said about the 21st century being the Asian century (Khanna, 2019). Yet despite this new-found attention, scholarly conversations in and across Asia about the ways in which Asians confront and live their literate lives are muted. Where they exist, these conversations are at best disparate, ill-fitting echoes of the Western narrative. This book is thus not only timely but also necessary.

Before venturing further, it is important to provide the backdrop for how this book came to be. A shift in authorial voice will thus be necessary.

I completed my doctoral studies in 2014 and left Cambridge, England, to return to Malaysia. I reconnected with my country and my region but felt that for all I had learnt about literacy in Cambridge, much was ill-fitting. It was ill-fitting for how a literacy strategy could work for an 8-year-old Malaysian child in one school but would be completely unimaginable for another 8-year-old Malaysian child in another school (Chong & Renganathan, 2018). Yet both children attend the same type of national schools and are, in principle, taught with the same standardised curriculum. For both these children, whose schools are separated only by 25 miles, they may as well be living in two different worlds. It became obvious to me that in Asia, in general, and Malaysia specifically, literacy experience is lived upon a very different trajectory from the one lived by those in the West. In fact, the literacy trajectory was differently lived, even and especially within the country and region. As the incongruence grew, I sought for answers, local to the land.

However, I found that concerted work about literacy education in this region is scant. Where important investigations had begun, its driving force is observed to be championed by work that is initiated by researchers whose perspectives are ontologically located outside the region's literacy education context. By this, I mean that this segment of research is undertaken by those who may not have lived the experience of being literate that is local to the land. This distinction is important to note because the biographical stance of some of those who research literacy issues in Asia may not be fully rooted within this region. Thus, their analyses may be unable to tap into complexities that are only knowable to those who have lived their trajectories in these lands. Kell and Kell (2014), for example, offer their analysis of East Asia's literacy and language education, highlighting how the phenomenon of Asia's international success in high-stakes testing for reading, science and mathematics is juxtaposed against an unhealthy self-imposed culture of competition that has resulted in the proliferation of shadow systems of cram schools and coaching centres. Although Kell and Kell are sharp in their critique of this region's obsession with teaching to the test, they do offer more holistic, Western-driven recommendations to propose for a shift away from test/exam obsession. Yet while Kell and Kell are not wrong in their analysis, their outsider position to the Asian context prohibits them from contemplating why governments and people in this region insist on experiencing literacy and education through such parameters. Only those who have themselves lived through the literacy experience can unravel the conundrum.

Recent research located within the field of literature education and literary studies in Asia and Asia Pacific have been able to forward important conversations about readers, the texts they read and the Asian contexts within which they belong (Loh, Choo, & Beavis, 2018; Wilson & Gabriel, 2020). As important as this body of work is, it is largely designed to address the experience of literary reading that necessarily assumes readership and readability. The focus of these contributions therefore amends to the notion of text appreciation and Asian-based themes surrounding power, otherness and transnationality of negotiating a range of literary genres. This perspective can be very differently viewed when problematised as being about linguistic skill, reading comprehension and assessments. Asmah Haji Omar (2016) provides important insights in this regard. As skill, comprehension and assessment, the meaning of literacy is contested especially as it is widely accepted as an indicator of economic and social progress. The difficulty in agreeing to a consensus of what literacy could mean in any one sub-region, let alone across a range of different regions, can be discouraging. These factors obscure our knowledge of Asia's literacy education, especially in the way that it is lived and experienced by the people of this region.

Intending to close this gap, I rallied together 11 other researchers (whom I had met on different occasions as a doctoral student through collegial work and literacy association contacts) to bring our valuable insights to bear on what it means to read and to advocate for literacy in Asia. Particularly, this book is the coming together of literacy researchers from Brunei, China, Hong Kong, Malaysia, the Philippines, Singapore and Taiwan. Unique to this book is our separate but collective biographical and bibliographical narratives depicting our own past literacy journeys as those journeys intersect with our current research in literacy education. The powerful connection between the "reading child" and the "remembering adult" has yielded important insights through "auto-study" (Mackey, 2016, pp. 7–9). Thus, this biographical and empirical connection between our past and our present allows us to explicitly consider how our contexts have changed. As beneficiaries of our respective literacy education systems, we now critically consider the very systems from which we hail. To this, we apply the question: What needs to be retained and what needs to be reviewed? The blending of the themes of the chapters in this book will constitute the beginning of a systematic, theoretical, autobiographically and auto-bibliographically informed Asian trajectory that can influence policy underpinning literacy education in Asia.

So what does "reading" mean to people in this part of the world?

In order to answer this question, one first has to have an understanding of Asia as a historical, geopolitical and sociocultural force. These facets are important for the way in which the many nations in Asia are inextricably intertwined in their shared past, even as the different nations go on to forge their own paths in the 21st century. Thus, what this chapter will do is unpack the tripartite perspective and lay out the challenges of these perspectives as they intersect with the definition and practice of being literate.

First, from a historical perspective, people from mainland China across to the Malay archipelago in a country like Malaysia have been making meaning and communicating through ancient semiotic systems that have been in existence for thousands of years. For example, the archaeological find of hundreds of thousands of pieces of inscribed ox scapulae and tortoise shells in Anyang, China, show that from as far back as 6,000 years ago, an ancient form of Chinese writing had been in use. Known as ji ǎ g ǔ or shell bones but referred to as *Oracle Bones* by the Western world, these archaeological remnants gesture towards an ancient society that was literate in an ideographic, pictographic semiotic system (Chou, 1979). As fundamental structures of the Chinese script have remained constant across the millennia, the ancient writings on the bones remain one of the few links that modern society has with antiquity (Hessler, 2011). It was understood that the writings tell of a society that practiced divination through their queries etched into the bones and the divine answers they received from their ancestral worship practice. In the Malay archipelago, prehistoric cave paintings also known as 'rock art' have been discovered showing once again that people in this region have been making meaning via written forms for thousands of years. Notably, newly uncovered archaeological sites in the Archipelago and more focused research work in the Asian context have begun to show tenable links between the semiotic systems of prehistoric people and those of indigenous peoples still living in 21st-century South East Asia (Tan, 2014). This is because fascinating similarities have been traced between these ancient cave markings with body-tattoo markings and parietal art of indigenous communities in current times. It can be argued that Asia's indigenous communities hold the key to unlocking the link between modern and ancient modes of literacy and meaning-making.

Second, from a geopolitical perspective, most Asian nations share a history tinged by a colonised past. Whether from European, American or Japanese influence, these Asian countries confront the highs and lows of regenerating their own cultural ways while accepting the realisation that their ways will never again be exclusively their own, without foreign influence. Importantly, where colonial power took hold, education systems were overhauled and again, semiotic systems shifted. The upshot of this is the introduction of English or Japanese as second, other and additional language in Asian schools. This meant that students were compelled to learn to read through not one and not two but many different languages, in simultaneous streams. These students contend with writing systems that are often mutually exclusive. Thus, in formal spaces, reading has broadly been regarded as a linguistically bound skill and is therefore experienced through efferent, functional and perfunctory means. Beyond writing systems, these students are also faced with the challenge of familiarising themselves with what could be cultural demands that are foreign to them. This explains why, despite high literacy rates across many of these Asian countries, the sustenance of reading particularly for pleasure may appear elusive.

Third, Asia is acknowledged as a highly complex, volatile and even contentious region buoyed largely by the dizzyingly diverse cultural, religious and ethnic landscape. Shaped by long-standing relations formed through ancient trade, cultural exchanges and even intermarriages, Asian countries' sociocultural landscape proves to be a challenge, especially for perspectives aligned with standardised, internationalised testing that are driven by mainstream narratives of literacy. This is because standardisation necessitates a fair amount of reductionist thinking, so that widely shared but narrowed notions of what it means to measure reading can be formed. Yet in the way Rosenblatt (1938) had argued for the individual transactional experience of meaning-making in reading, such standardisations may push out equally important narratives of literacy when their script, patterns or medium can find no mould in mainstream spaces. With less international traction, this region also tends to be economically challenged and often politically volatile. This means that for many of the poorest and most marginalised in Asia's developing nations, learning to read is largely a school-based initiative and is often assumed to be a ticket out of poverty. To be able to read and write is to be given a chance at surviving in this often harsh and unpredictable region.

Thus, these tripartite-factors affect literacy and educational opportunities in ways that cut deeply into Asia's historical landscape. As such, the literacy narratives of people within this region can become a profound source of knowledge that potentially tells of the success and failures of literacy policy and practice, particularly as they converge or collide with Asia's historical, geopolitical and sociocultural trajectory.

Linking transactional reading theory, reading as a sociocultural practice and Asia literacy

There may be a tendency to immediately think of reading theories as being about theoretical arguments surrounding how individual readers process visual cues and in their minds convert those cues into fixed, accepted meanings—all occurring through a presumably chronological loop. This worldview is influenced, not in any small way, by early 20th century Taylorian ideals of industrialisation that measure outcomes in terms of chronology and output yield (Taylor, 1911). In and around that period, Huey (1908) published work on what became known as the psychology and physiology of reading, which some today regard as representing the advent of reading research. Despite some questionable arguments and exaggerations on Huey's part, especially where contrasts were made upon so-called civilised (i.e. literate) society and uncivilised (i.e. illiterate) groups, Huey's detailed work in terms of measuring and understanding saccades, visual perception, inner speech and comprehension was important for how it gave chronological structure to the theorisation of the reading process and became critical points for measuring reading ability. In fact, much of Huey's endeavour was still at the heart of reading research even at the turn of the 21st century (Alvermann, 2000).

Beyond the microcosmic, chronological perspective, Huey also provided grounds for seeing reading to be located within broader contexts driven by cultural undercurrents. With respect to this broadened view, a paradigm shift was recognised that was important to capture the scope of reading, meaning-making and context. In this light, Rosenblatt's transactional theory, which is based on the notion of transaction, language and selection, became another fundamental reading theory in the 20th century (Rosenblatt, 1938). Drawn from Dewey's pragmatist epistemology, Rosenblatt borrows the term "transaction" which finds its basis in the concept that "the knower, the knowing and the known are seen as aspects of one process" (Rosenblatt, 2005, p. 3). In terms of reading, Rosenblatt refers to the triadic relationship of the knower, the knowing and the known as the "reader", the "text" and the "poem" with the poem denoting the abstract space for the fluid transaction of reading (Rosenblatt, 1978). Rosenblatt emphasises the subjective, non-entity and highly unpredictable sense of the reading transaction, thereby alluding to the "poem" being a representation of the "subjective" *what* of the reading transaction. Rosenblatt also goes on to argue that this fluidity has important implications for language use because "language is always internalized by a human being transacting with a particular environment" (Rosenblatt, 2005, p. 4). This concept of language being contextualised is important because it accounts for the social, cultural and even historical aspects of the way language is formed and used. The reader is acknowledged as being positioned within unique sociocultural contexts.

This emergence of socioculturally sensitive arguments brought about what would later be regarded as a new paradigm in understanding literacy issues across an international, multicultural, multimodal arena. Perhaps more than others, research work in *multiliteracies* and *new literacy studies* form the two major movers and sculptors of this paradigm. Recognising the immense speed in which the English language is changing, due largely to mass migrations and cross-cultural influences, The New London Group (2000) rejected more insular perspectives that located the act of reading and writing within strict, monolingual and monocultural settings. Instead, they adopted a more inclusive and multidimensional theoretical perspective to understand what reading or literacy could mean to a variety of people in a variety of settings surrounded by a variety of often invisible but present tensions and forces (Cope & Kalantzis, 2000). More importantly, work in this paradigm has brought about new ways of seeing schooling and meaningful education for the marginalised, especially in terms of how these children's sociocultural contexts may work against them (Gee, 2000, 2008; Kress, 2000; Wyse, Andrews, & Hoffman, 2010). New literacy studies have also spotlight the "multimodal" way of re-presenting semiotics that has provided new platforms of meaning-making. In this regard, collective work seen in the research of Cliff Hodges (2016), Mackey (2016) and Arizpe and Cliff Hodges (2018) captures and represents important narratives of lived experience of literacy as a sociocultural practice.

In much of the earlier discussion, it is obvious that this body of work is located in and drawn from the Western world. The Euro-American-centric perspective share inherent similarities as far as writing systems, lived experience as developed nations and sociocultural notions of language and literacy may be concerned. This is not to say that there are no differences or disparities across the countries, but by and large, much work and learning experience is comfortably shared across the borders. In contrast, and as was pointed out in the preceding section, published work on literacy education in Asia is scattered, if not scarce. As a result, there is as yet no unifying theory of literacy to emerge from this region. However, if Asia's literacy narratives have been given little attention, there has been increasing attention on understanding Asia as a region. At this point, the discussion will digress from literacy theories in Asia to touch upon emerging theories about Asia. This is important, as it will impact the way the trajectory for literacy education in Asia can begin to be charted.

Perspectives on Asia can be thought of in binary terms. The first is the narrative that is based on the Western gaze on Asia. Spoken of as a region that, while inscrutable, is controversial and often out of sync with Western ways of being and knowing, Asia is seen to be a region of largely developing nations that still struggles with reconciling the old with the new. This is important to note because the "old" is, as cautioned by Jacques, inaccurately assumed to be Asian while the "new" is referenced to mean "Western" (TED, 2013, March 1). Such a straightforward representation oversimplifies the ontological question of what it is to be Asian solely in terms of what is considered as Western and what is not. Not only is this perspective inaccurate but it also clearly undermines and marginalises the potential influence that local narratives can have over local contexts.

Chiming with this is the other perspective of Asia that is born from its own Eastern gaze that has stood its ground for far longer. This perspective galvanises its proponents to continuously speak from their local, internal locus of knowledge. Perhaps argued for most famously by Said (1978/2003), this debate is represented by the call for communities outside the circle of Western nations to be understood not through external prisms but through prisms located within the community. More than that, this call is a challenge for us to speak from our lived experience and theorise those experiences through frames relevant to our contexts, so that solutions that befit our problems can be found. Thus, the epistemological and ontological question of knowledge production must mean that we should, in Merican's (2005, p. 87) words, "[dismantle our unquestioning] habits of knowledge-seeking and epistemes" in order to derive knowledge that is located in the subjectivity of the knower. In calling for seeing Asia as method, Chen (2010, p. 223) argues for a critical perspective that allows for a theoretical positioning which:

> (o)nce recognizing the West as fragments internal to the local, we no longer consider it as an opposing entity but rather as one cultural resource among many others. Such a position avoids either a resentful or a triumphalist relation with the West because it is not bound by an obsessive antagonism.

Indeed, what this book will not do is drive a deeper wedge into the divisive "West and the Rest" narrative. At the time that this book was written, the world was undergoing major cultural, economic and global shifts brought on by the Covid-19 pandemic. New world orders are beginning to form as new allies and partnerships seem to be forged. Perhaps more than ever, the "distance" between East and West will recede into the background as priorities are reshaped. Thus, important to this conversation is the theoretical positioning that attempts to "multiply frames of references in our subjectivity" (Chen, 2010, p. 223). This means that while the knower's subjective experience must be valued for how it is historically constructed and intersected, an objectively driven analysis must provide for the overarching connection across the subjectivities.

The theoretical underpinning for this book, therefore, is premised upon Chen's (2010) idea of multiplication of frames, which brings together the subjectivity of the knower and objectivity of the known. In this book, the authors' frames of references are driven by our biographical knowledge of our lives and our lands but located within the research objectivity of our empirically bound fieldwork in literacy education. By objectivity, I do not mean it in the post-positivist sense but in the context of research conduct that requires objective considerations for research design. Arizpe and Cliff Hodges (2018), for example, have demonstrated that small-scale, qualitative research design can show up the importance of individual reading trajectories when empirical research in literacy education across continents are put together. As such, the remembering adult (Mackey, 2016) and their lived literacy experience (Rosenblatt, 1969) become important springboards from which to chart their literacy trajectories. This book's theoretical underpinning is further shaped by Chen's (2010) multiplicity of frames of reference to bring together the subjectivity (biographical stance) and objectivity (empirical research) of the authors' literacy trajectories. The subjectivity, that is, the biographical stance, is premised upon familial and personal histories. The objectivity, that is, the empirical research, is shaped by important literacy and sociocultural theory. Figure 0.1 depicts the literacy trajectory theoretical framework.

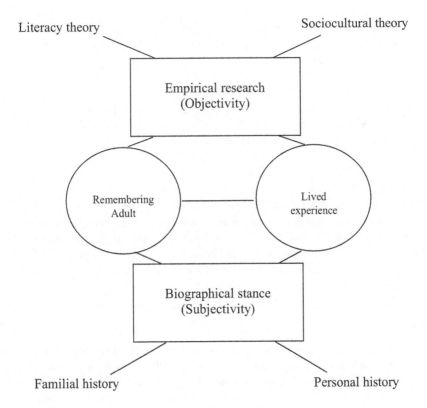

Figure 0.1 Literacy trajectory theoretical framework

Hence, key to understanding Asia's literacy narratives lies in a paradoxical move to shift our gaze from what would be skill-based literacy to focus instead on the sociocultural, historical contexts that relate with and are deemed to be the drivers for why communities adopt particular literacies. This means that in order to understand literacy education, the oblique route that unpacks the region's historical and cultural narratives will provide the means through which the communities' challenges, conundrums, motivation and compromises can be made sense of. From here, broad-based policies can be shaped to fit the ways of the land.

Asia's literacy narratives: the region's lived literacy experience

Within the scope of this book, *Asia* is taken to mean the subregion East Asia (China, Hong Kong and Taiwan) and the subregion South East Asia is taken to mean these countries (Brunei, Malaysia, Singapore, the Philippines). The historical and cultural connections in East Asia are obvious because of the way China, Hong Kong and Taiwan are politically and economically connected, even as deep dissent and divisive policies drive their societies into warring factions (Chang, 1992; Gregory, 1995). Yet despite their differences, fundamental linguistic and cultural mores are inevitably shared. In the same way, South East Asia (Brunei, Malaysia, Singapore and the Philippines) are connected by the subregion's historical and political ties in terms of the Malaysian-Singaporean-Indonesian-the Philippines group of islands. Due to their historical link in terms of trade and mission work, peoples within this subregion also share common linguistic structures, religious and cultural mores. In their shared past, these nations at one time or another had formed parts of each other's historical narratives and governance. East Asia and South East Asia are also connected in the way that China has historically valued the Maritime Silk Road, which brought and continues to bring trade to, and more importantly, through South East Asia into South Asia, the Middle East, Europe and the rest of the world. With so many connective ties, any impact in one subregion will be felt in another. In this book, Asia is deemed less as a geographical construct than a socioculturally and socio-economically connected set of people with shared histories and lived experience.

This book is divided into three sections which deal with lived literacy experience in Asia's home and school contexts; Asian readers' texts transactions and the intersections in Asia's literacy policy and practice. In the following paragraphs, the authors' first names are referred to. This is to accommodate the different ways in which Asian names are arranged.

Part 1

Part 1 of the book is focused upon the crossroads between home and school contexts. In many Asian nations, school and home cultures have been found to be cultural sites that are often clashing when notions of lived literacy are considered. Although not unlike Heath's (2012) work that drew out the cultural differences between home and school contexts in urban America, the situation in Asia can be markedly more divergent. As explained in the preceding section, postcolonial nations experience subtle forms of colonisation. For example, government-imposed policy that favours English as a medium of school instruction continue to be dominant in formalised education even as local communities struggle to reconcile home with school narratives of being literate. This struggle shows up in how multiple ways of knowing and being are not included nor accepted despite there being mounting evidence of the legitimacy of local communities' own versions of meaning-making.

Chapter 1 sees Mukhlis Abu Bakar's longitudinal research journey that revolves around the Malay community in Singapore. With the privilege of possessing ethnographic insight into the literate lives of his research participants, Mukhlis examines the role that knowledge capital, formed in middle-class Singaporean homes, plays in the cultural spaces of school and higher education. Mukhlis paints a fascinating picture of bold contrasts between the Singapore of the 1960s and 1970s with today's 21st century Singapore by highlighting how the cultural capital he grew up with differs from that of his research participants'. Ultimately, the trajectories of both the researcher and the researched in this chapter show that there is sufficient room and recourse for them to chart a workable path that makes use of home and school-based capital to not just survive but thrive in a highly literate country.

In Chapter 2, Sumathi Renganathan's contribution reveals hidden knowledge of the literacy lives of a minority population in Malaysia. In this chapter, Sumathi's longitudinal research work with the Semai people, an indigenous community in Malaysia, highlights how those living in the margins are many times removed from mainstream perspectives. Despite acknowledged as being among the oldest communities in the country, the indigenous Semai people are not recognised for their ancient experience of the land which has been handed down the generations via non-written, oral traditions. This chapter raises the critical question of how dominant narratives of literacy that are borrowed in the first place can fail the most marginalised and disenfranchised of a multi-ethnic community.

Chapter 3 brings to light the paradox of reportedly high literacy rates among youths in the Philippines, as it stands in stark contrast to Lalaine F. Yanilla Aquino's empirical data showing poor levels of reading, writing and comprehension among Filipino undergraduates. Lalaine drills down into her multipronged research design to provide a diagnosis for why even at such high levels of education, young adult learners still struggle with being effective readers. Affected largely by the twin factors of socio-economic disadvantage and the English as a Second Language (ESL) learning experience being presented in bilingual contexts, academically low-performing Filipino undergraduates find themselves negotiating literacy skills if only to survive their academic requirements.

Part 2

Part 2 of the book contrasts transactions of literature, texts and readers as these transactions are seen through how literature and literacy are connected and changed in the Asian context. The chapters in this section raise questions about how the acceptance of dominant approaches to confronting texts can pose the risk of dismantling traditional perspectives of text negotiation in this region. This has far-reaching implications, because readers in this region cannot be removed from local ways, even as globalised perspectives look set to alter the landscape.

Xiaofei Shi in Chapter 4 discusses critical changes that have occurred in China's emergent literacy education by casting the shifts on the way children's Western-based picturebooks have appeared alongside the *lianhuan hua*, China's traditional pocket-sized storybooks. Xiaofei posits that the emergence of picturebooks, while proving positive for the internationalisation of the English language in China, may have an opposite effect on Chinese emergent readers, especially as the Chinese script is pictographic in nature. This shift may have a lasting effect on the original function of the *lianhuan hua*, which has always served as a means of providing historical knowledge and even traditional wisdom contrasted against a fast-changing environment that also demands new forms of globalised knowledge.

In Chapter 5, Dahlia Janan's focus on reader, text and context is dissected through theoretical and empirical conceptions of readability. Dahlia's keen analysis nudges the debate on reading and readability towards locating the reader at the centre of the discussion, especially in the way that readers are socially and culturally placed. Dahlia performs a comparison across two culturally and socially contrasting readers in Malaysia and UK respectively to test her framework. In so doing, important transactions within the meaning-making process show how the definition of reading and readability can be broadened.

Chapter 6 sees Priscilla Angela T. Cruz exploring the interpretation of a literary text from the position of a literature teacher. Priscilla critically considers the power imbalance observed in the following perspectives: student as reader, teacher as guide and canon as historical backdrop. Priscilla argues that the literature teacher straddles the balance between openness to student responses and maintaining a certain level of "correctness". However, "correct" ways of viewing a text can discourage students from loving literature. Priscilla then explores what meanings both students and teachers offer on a literary text to determine what commonalities between the two sides can be exploited to come to an empowering literature pedagogy, one that builds on the convergences of meanings from both sides.

In Chapter 7, Jia Wei Lim scrutinises Malaysia's secondary school English literature curriculum by considering how its syllabus has changed from 1957 until the present time. Jia Wei's close analysis, which traces fundamental shifts made to the subject's reading list, assessment methods and learning goals shows that some measure has gone into localising what was originally "English, British Literature". Today, as "Literature in English", this subject bears a breadth that includes texts written by non-Western authors. This analysis goes some way to show the deep influence that British rule still had over Malaysia's literacy education. Crucially, however, Jia Wei's inclusion of the empirical voices of her research participants and her own becomes a powerful illustration of how lived experience of what she refers to as *literary literacy* is far more rooted in the way readers are socialised into the culture of literary reading and meaning-making than in the structural shifts of syllabus located outside the reader. This facet of her argument demonstrates that the length of any reader's trajectory has to be traced backwards, especially in how familial influence fundamentally shapes the cultural structure of the reading psyche.

Chapter 8 sees Yi-Shan Tsai elevate the role of comics as a vehicle for literacy while highlighting the struggle that local Taiwanese comics must confront in seeking legitimacy, especially in terms of market share, educational value and reader acceptance. This trajectory is built upon the author's own experience of growing up indulging in the forbidden pleasures of comic reading and her ensuing scholarship in literacy and texts. Yi-Shan explains through a historical tracing of the struggle how Taiwanese comics producers are locked in an uneasy yet unbreakable bind with their Japanese colonisers' cultural influence over the way the comics are conceived and created. Yet the social acceptance of Manga by readers in Taiwan and the world over has proven to exert (soft) power over even the most controlling of governmental measures. Yi-Shan offers a middle-ground suggestion for how a Taiwanese comic book can be utilised for both its didactic and entertainment value within the context of literacy education.

Part 3

Part 3 steps back and takes a broad perspective in order to examine some of Asia's literacy policy and practice. This section addresses how or whether the region's literacy policy and its prevailing practice have been altered to fit new times so that a new trajectory can be reimagined.

In Chapter 9, Chin Ee Loh adopts a historical perspective in order to understand how Singapore's language and literacy curriculum is enacted and experienced in a way that allows examination of how policy, practice and personal experiences are intertwined. In this chapter, Chin Ee examines her personal engagements with the reading curriculum in Singapore's educational context, first as a student in the 1980s to 1990s, then as a teacher in the 2000s and finally as a researcher, teacher-educator and parent in the present time. Drawing on Bourdieu's (1977) concept of field, cultural capital and habitus, she seeks to trace the changing fields of Singapore's reading landscape from the 1980s until the present time and to examine how what counts as cultural capital for language learning has shifted across the years. English continues to hold value in Singapore as a global language of education and trade but is continually being repositioned in the context of Singapore's engagement with a multilingual, global world. Using personal stories, Chin Ee makes links to her current research on reading in Singapore secondary schools and international research in order to explain why reading futures among students of different social classes depend so much on parental investment and familial practices. Finally, she highlights how policy and practice must shift to ensure equitable access to reading, particularly reading for pleasure, for all students.

In Chapter 10, Faye Dorcas Yung argues that for historical reasons similar to many of its South East Asian counterparts, Hong Kong's language environment reflects its economic and political turns. The country's current policy for language education is to educate students to become biliterate and trilingual (fluent in Chinese and English in reading and writing and fluent in Cantonese, English and Putonghua in listening and speaking). In this chapter, Faye reviews the historical development of literacy in English by charting the changes and development of the two subjects "English Language" and "Literature in English". Faye argues that the society's demand for a people proficient in English is not met without compromises. The limited formal lesson time allocated for language education, contribute to the shaping of English and Literature education in Hong Kong.

Chapter 11 sees Malai Zeiti Sheikh Abdul Hamid exploring the connection between levels of language proficiency and uptake of reading within the bilingual context of Brunei's education system. Reflecting a country's heritage as an ex-British colony, Brunei's challenge is with seeing through its policy for students to be proficient and literate in both English and the Malay language. In her analysis, Malai Zeiti argues that for Brunei, its literacy policies are ultimately governed by Brunei's deep adherence to the nation's monarchical-cultural standards and mores. The lived literacy experience, therefore, cannot be separate from the cultural laws of the land. An important contrast is made with Malai Zeiti's own background, which steered her literacy trajectory in a direction that seems compatible with international standards, thus making amenable her own literacy and language capital.

Closing the book is Chapter 12—my own chapter that offers a systematic comparison of six Malaysian-based projects which were conducted across more than one decade (2006–2020) in two different continents. The rationale for this comparison is to produce a critical review of research projects that examined the literacy lives of Malaysian students from primary to higher learning levels. The comparison is analysed across aspects of participant selection, research methodology, findings and implications of the research projects. This chapter argues that although obvious focal points relating to new literacies and new mediums need to be acknowledged and require new theorisation, it is the challenge in broadening the definition of reading to become meaning-making that is most needed in the Malaysian context. This chapter suggests a number of centripetal ways in which the challenge can be overcome, contributing therefore to a slice of the Asian perspective to being literate. From here, a Framework for Respect in Literacy Education (FRiLE) is proposed so that policy can begin to shift.

Concluding remarks

Towards the aim of charting a new trajectory for literacy education in Asia, the contributors and contributions of this book have provided individual and collective threads that will be woven together so that this fabric of a combined society can emerge.

It is our hope that our own literacy trajectories will go some way to begin discussions for charting Asia's new literacy trajectory.

References

Alvermann, D. E. (2000). New discoveries in literacy for the 21st century. *The Journal of Educational Research, 93*(3), 130–132.

Arizpe, E., & Cliff Hodges, G. (Eds.). (2018). *Young people reading: Empirical research across international contexts.* Abingdon: Routledge.

Asmah Haji Omar. (Ed.). (2016). *Languages in the Malaysian education system.* New York: Routledge.

Bourdieu, P. (1977). *Outline of a theory of practice* (R. Nice, Trans.). Cambridge: Cambridge University Press.

Chall, J. S. (1967). *Learning to read: The great debate; An inquiry into the science, art, and ideology of old and new methods of teaching children to read.* New York: McGraw-Hill.

Chall, J. S. (1983). *Stages of reading development.* New York: McGraw Hill.

Chang, P. (1992). China's relations with Hong Kong and Taiwan. *The Annals of the American Academy of Political and Social Science, 519,* 127–139.

Chen, K. H. (2010). *Asia as method.* Durham: Duke University Press.

Chong, S. L., & Renganathan, S. (2018). *Reading readiness: A comparative analysis of factors influencing 8-year-olds' literacy sustenance in rural and urban Perak.* A Report submitted to Ministry of Education, Malaysia.

Chou, H. (1979). Chinese oracle bones. *Scientific American, 240*(4), 134–149.

Cliff Hodges, G. (2016). *Researching and teaching reading: Developing pedagogy through critical inquiry.* Abingdon, Oxon: Routledge.

Cope, B., & Kalantzis, M. (Eds.). (2000). *Multiliteracies.* London: Routledge.

Flesch, R. (1981). *Why Johnny still can't read: A new look at the scandal of our schools / Rudolf Flesch; Foreword by Mary L. Burkhardt.* New York: Harper & Row.

Gee, J. P. (2000). New people in new worlds: Networks, the new capitalism and schools. In B. Cope & M. Kalantzis (Eds.), *Multiliteracies* (pp. 43–68). London: Routledge.

Gee, J. P. (2008). *Social linguistics and literacies.* Abingdon, Oxon: Routledge.

Goodman, K. S. (1968). *The psycholinguistic nature of the reading process* (K. S. Goodman, Ed.). Detroit: Wayne State University Press.

Gregory, J. (1995). China, Taiwan, Hong Kong: U.S. Challenges. *Great Decisions,* 59–68.

Halse, C. (Ed.). (2015). *Asia literacy in the Asian century.* London: Routledge.

Heath, S. B. (2012). *Words at work and play: Three decades in family and community life.* Cambridge: Cambridge University Press.

Hessler, P. (2011). *Oracle bones.* New York: Harper Collins Publishers Inc.

Huey, E. B. (1908). *The psychology and pedagogy of reading.* New York: The Macmillan Company.

Jacques, M., Abidin, M., Zainuddin, Z., & Institute of Strategic and International Studies. (2012). China and the emerging world order. *ISIS Focus Institute of Strategic and International Studies, 10,* 4–8.

Kell, M., & Kell, P. (2014). *Literacy and language in East Asia.* Singapore: Springer.

Khanna, P. (2019). *The future is Asian.* London: Simon & Schuster.

Kress, G. R. (2000). Multimodality. In B. Cope & M. Kalantzis (Eds.), *Multiliteracies: Literacy learning and designs of social futures* (pp. 182–202). London: Routledge.

Loh, C. E., Choo, S. S., & Beavis, C. (Eds.). (2018). *Literature education in the Asia-Pacific: Policies, practices and perspectives in global times.* Abingdon, Oxon: Routledge.

Mackey, M. (2016). *One child reading: My auto-bibliography*. Edmonton, Alberta, Canada: The University of Alberta Press.

Merican, A. M. (2005). Prophets, philosophers and scholars: The identity of communication and the communication of identity. *Jurnal Komunikasi: Malaysian Journal of Communication, 21*, 83–107.

The New London Group. (2000). A pedagogy of multiliteracies. In B. Cope & M. Kalantzis (Eds.), *Multiliteracies* (pp. 9–37). London: Routledge.

Rosenblatt, L. M. (1938). *Literature as exploration*. London: D. Appleton-Century Company Incorporated.

Rosenblatt, L. M. (1969). Towards a transactional theory of reading. *Journal of Literacy Research, 1*(31), 31–49.

Rosenblatt, L. M. (1978). *The reader, the text, the poem: The transactional theory of the literary work*. Carbondale: Southern Illinois University Press.

Rosenblatt, L. M. (2005). *Making meaning with texts: Selected essays*. Portsmouth, NH Heinemann Educational Books.

Said, E. W. (1978/2003). *Orientalism*. London: Penguin Books.

Smith, F. (1985). *Reading without nonsense*. New York, NY: Teachers College Press.

Stahl, K. (Ed.) (2006). *Reading research at work: Foundations of effective practice*. New York: Guilford Publications.

Tan, N. H. (2014). Rock art research in South East Asia: A synthesis. *Arts, 3*, 73–104.

Taylor, F. W. (1911). *The principles of scientific management*. New York and London: Harper & Brothers Publishers.

TED. (2013, March 1). *Martin Jacques: Understanding the rise of China*. Retrieved from www.ted.com/talks/martin_jacques_understanding_the_rise_of_china

Wilson, B., & Gabriel, S. P. (Eds.). (2020). *Asian children's literature and film in a global age*. Singapore: Palgrave Macmillan.

Wyse, D., Andrews, R., & Hoffman, J. (Eds.). (2010). *The Routledge international handbook of English, language and literacy teaching*. London: Routledge.

Part 1

Negotiating lived literacy across and within home-school contexts

1 Negotiating school literacy from preschool to adulthood

Examples from Singapore

Mukhlis Abu Bakar

I was thrown a fairly decent float to help me swim from one side of the channel to the other. Some others were not as fortunate; they were given floats with little holes in them which they patched with the loose ends of their clothing; others had to cling on to thin wooden planks; yet others had no means of support other than sheer grit and physical strength. I wondered what the scenery of the channel would be like had I sat on a canoe, if only I had one. Others on a motor boat would not only have enjoyed the scenery but delighted at the chance to ride the waves that came their way.

On reaching the shore, those with their clothes dry had time to pick coconuts from the swaying trees that lined the beach before moving on to dreamland on chauffeur-driven cars. Others who landed later had to recover from their ordeal. Enjoying the soft flesh of the coconut was furthest from their minds not that they don't need them, perhaps more so. I was fairly exhausted but still had reserved energy to pick what's left of the coconuts. I made my way to dreamland but not without much haggling over the taxi fare. Those left on the beach either decided to make that their dreamland or harboured hopes of getting to dreamland if they could hitch a ride from a passing car.

Author's post in Facebook, 3 June 2020

Introduction

Researchers have pointed out that schools may not always be the place where everyone has an equal chance to perform, because hidden inside are all kinds of ways in which in practice certain kinds of social, cultural and class positions are being privileged (Street, 2014). Literacy is one of the dominant ways in which such privileging may be enacted. By literacy, I do not mean the mental processes of decoding, comprehending and inferencing per se but how these are embedded in social practice (Gee, 2015). In other words, children do not just acquire language and literacy skills; they learn different ways of relating to texts, different ways of being a reader and writer, through participation in social practices and through the pursuit of social relations (Heath, 1983). For some children, the purposes and meanings that are attached to literacy in their family may conflict with those they experience in school. And this in turn may affect their participation in classroom language activities, their curriculum experience and their educational achievement (Gay, 2018).

Such perspectives on literacy are illustrated in this chapter using data from a research study in Singapore that started 14 years ago. It was a two-year ethnographic study on the lived literacy experience of eight Malay preschoolers moving on to primary school. The aim was to document their literacy experience in and out of school and the impact the experience has on their schooling (Mukhlis, 2006, 2007, 2016). I recently reunited with four of the children who are now young adults and had extensive interviews with two of them. I lost contact with the other four children. The aim was to surface the challenges they faced in their literacy learning throughout their school life, how they overcame them, with whose help, how the effects of those experiences accumulated over time, and whether the school field has changed in its attitudes towards their "cultural capital" (Bourdieu, 1977).

This chapter provides an account of the trajectory of two of the children as they journeyed from kindergarten to post-secondary education. It also offers an account of my own literacy trajectory, an autobiography spanning some 25 years, from kindergarten to the completion of my doctoral studies. This provides another layer of meaning to the relationship between cultural capital and school outcome, and between structure and agency. The children's literacy trajectories and mine were set during different stages of Singapore's development. Mine began in the 1960s during the nascent period of nation-building where parents were generally less involved in the schooling process and placed less academic pressure on the young, The children's took off in the 21st century, when the Singapore society has grown competitive, pushing parents to take a more active role in their children's literacy development.

Singapore is an island city-state whose population stands at 5.8 million in 2020, the majority of whom are Chinese (74.2%), with Malays (13.2%), Indians (9.2%) and others comprising the minority groups (World Population Review, 2020). Children attend English-medium schools where English is the primary medium of instruction while the mother tongue languages are taught as a second language. State-sponsored meritocracy has pushed parents to place great importance on academic achievement, and they go to great lengths to ensure that their children do well (Gopinathan, 1997). The meritocratic principle, however, offers equal opportunities, not outcomes, and is largely unconcerned with inherent inequalities (Tan, 2008). The Facebook post that opens this chapter serves to illustrate just that.

Literacy practices and cultural capital

Sociocultural conceptions of literacy suggest that children learn culturally appropriate ways of using language and constructing meaning from texts in their early years at home. Children learn the meaning of print by being surrounded by it in their immediate environment, by their explorations in play, and by understanding its role in their everyday lives. Through their interactions with more experienced members of the cultural group (e.g. parents, siblings, peers and friends) in a process of guided participation (Rogoff, 1990; Taylor, 1998), children learn that literacy functions not as isolated events but as components of the social activities in their homes and communities.

Different social and cultural groups participate in numerous and varied literacy events (Barton & Hamilton, 2000), just as perspectives and beliefs about the nature, purpose and uses of literacy are many and varied. In a study by Baker et al. (1996), middle-class families viewed literacy as a source of entertainment, while lower-income families regarded it as a skill to be cultivated. Studies of Mexican immigrant families in the United States further showed that highly educated parents were perceptive of their children's educational needs and provided them with different kinds of home literacy experiences that are related to different kinds of skills (Sénéchal, LeFevre, Thomas, & Daley, 1998).

Students with cultural capital that is valuable in helping them to progress in class (e.g. proficiency in literate school discourse) are generally thought to fare better in school than those with less valuable cultural capital. However, there are differences in how cultural capital is brought to bear in the classroom setting or "field", as Bourdieu (1977) puts it. Students may or may not choose to activate the capital, and they may also vary in the right skills to activate it. Furthermore, there are, in the realm of school, what scholars call "moments of inclusion" (e.g. placement in an academically gifted programme) and "moments of exclusion" (e.g. retention) (Lareau & Horvat, 1999) which enhances and weakens respectively a child's position of advantage in his or her life trajectory.

Much of the work reviewed here made use of ethnography in field research, which has exposed the range of meanings and functions which literacy can have in different contexts (Heath & Street, 2008). There is a suggestion behind much of the work that models of literacy which operate in schools are rather specialised in comparison with their range of uses in people's everyday lives (Barton & Hamilton, 2000).

Lived literacy of Malay Singaporean children

My ethnographic work with the eight Malay families offers a glimpse of the lived literacy experience of Malay children in Singapore (Mukhlis, 2006, 2007, 2016). All the families, regardless of their socio-economic background, had high hopes for their children. However, how literacy was transmitted to the children differed between the families, with the literacy practices of the higher socio-economic class more closely matching that of the school. This placed the children on different starting points in school. In this chapter, the focal participants, Adam and Naila (not their real names), both come from middle-class families. Still, there are differences in the way literacy is practised in their respective homes.

The first child, Adam, took meaning from texts through talk and play with his mother, a doctoral graduate. He enjoyed the interactive reading sessions, engaging in argumentation and forming opinions as he went along. At an early age, he acquired what might be considered as scientific literacy (Lucas, 1983) through the science discourse that he entered into with his mother. He was prepared well as a learner, but his engagement with the school was not always in harmony with what was expected of a student in Singapore. He moved on to the Express stream in secondary school,[1] completed his polytechnic education, and now plans to pursue a university degree.

The second child, Naila, had access to considerable supplementary educational resources. Her graduate parents had the economic capital to buy the materials they needed and the cultural capital to know what to get. In instructing Naila on literacy, her mother, an ex-teacher, focused on the meaning and purpose of written texts (storybooks and worksheets) and ventured into the explicit teaching of concepts and introduction of new information. Naila had extensive exposure to ways of learning from printed materials, including religious texts tutored by her father. She did well enough to be selected for the Integrated Programme (IP)[2] in a top school and is now at the university.

The next section details the journey the children went through, how they navigated between their home and school cultures, or in the words of Clancy, Simpson, and Howard (2001, p. 57), how they "adjusted to an extra range and layer of experiences, demands and expectations relating to cultural, language, and social skills". Despite the considerable cultural and economic capital their families had, the school and the classroom as cultural sites were still not easy and flexible places for these two children to fit in.

Making the transition to primary school and beyond

Adam the young scientist

As a young child, Adam was exposed to meaning-based approaches to literacy instruction, where his mother and other adults in the family engaged in extended discourse around text and intertextual references. They entertained his queries and his exploration beyond the immediate text, which enabled him to imagine "possible worlds, worlds beyond the mundanities of here and now" (Bruner, 1984, p. 196). Bedtime reading was a regular event, and he looked forward to this at the end of each day. The informal setting, where Adam would often lean on his mother on a cosy sofa bed in their bedroom, facilitated the mother–child interactions with a text. The collection of books that he was exposed to was not limited to storybooks but also included expository books expanding his receptive and productive vocabulary, morphology and discourse complexity. The following is an excerpt of a typical interaction between mother and child while reading a book on sea animals.

| 1 | *Mother:* | OK, now, let me read some more. "Squids are part of a family called mollusc. Molluscs have no bones, instead their bodies are protected by a shell. A squid's shell is inside its body". Hmm, next time we see a squid, in the kitchen, we go and check it out, OK? |
| 2 | *Adam:* | You ask [. . . .] (Adam's grandmother) to open. |

3	*Mother:*	Yeah, we'll slice it up and then we check what's. . .
4	*Adam:*	Don't slice it up, later we cannot see the bone. . .
5	*Mother:*	But how do you see inside the squid if you don't slice it up?
6	*Adam:*	Slice a bit.
7	*Mother:*	Yeah, a little bit. You gently cut it so you don't disturb the insides. How about that?
8	*Adam:*	Yeah, yeah, yeah, yeah, yeah, yeah, yeah, yeah.

In this free-flowing and "non-linear" manner in which the mother read with Adam, the boy was introduced to a way of approaching texts that allowed him to understand and evaluate what he was reading, clarify his doubts and offer his own thoughts which in turn aroused his curiosity. In many of the reading events at home, Adam was provided with the opportunity to relate what was being read to his own experience, such as a movie he has watched and an object that he found familiar. His mother not only read but added information not particularly evident in the original text and experimented with ideas. Such interactions made everyday reading fun for Adam and enabled him to be an active participant and to engage in real and imaginary worlds beyond his immediate environment. Adam thus grew up as a divergent learner (Runco & Acar, 2012).

Adam had benefitted from a one-to-one extended discourse with adults. On many occasions early in primary school, he tried to enact that with his teacher but was told that he was interrupting the lesson or that he was not focused. Given his divergent ways of learning, it is likely that he was fascinated by what the lesson meant to him and that he wanted to explore the ideas.

Adam the young adult

Reflecting on his childhood and school years, what stood out was the role Adam's mother played in facilitating his literacy development. His mother sent him to an English tutor when Adam appeared to struggle in putting his thoughts into writing. The dialogic conversations which she regularly made available to him since he was young continued and he enjoyed them. Adam often compared his teacher with his mother, as follows:

Of his mother:

It was easy to talk to my mum about science. I felt that anything I didn't really understand, or I wanted to discuss something with my mum, I just asked her.

Of his teacher:

Didn't really get to discuss in school that much. It was more of a one-way conversation with the teachers I felt. They were just really teaching us. They weren't really like discussing it with us. Ask questions, you answer but, it wasn't a discussion. Definitely not as interesting as the conversations with my mum.

The potential of Adam's divergent thinking was apparently overlooked in school, and he did not respond well to convergent ways of learning. As a result, he found some lessons boring, even after taking into account that he might not be as interested in some subjects as others. This continued until his secondary school years.

Most of the lessons were okay. I felt that a lot of them I got bored very, very, quickly. For Math it was the subject, I found that it was very, very, dry and it was too much work, ya. Then for literature and uh, History, I didn't like the way they kind of forced us to write in a certain way. We would do the questions and then we would copy the answers. So I didn't feel that that really helped us to learn. Yeah, but, erm, maybe it was because of the exam. The O-levels was very copy-and-paste kind of work.

Adam clearly resisted an exam-centric education, which tends to stifle a student's imagination, creativity, and sense of self, qualities crucial for a child's ultimate success in and out of the classroom (Kirkpatrick & Zang, 2011). On the other hand, when teachers go out of their way to make lessons alive and engage in extended discourse which in turn stimulates curiosity in the student, this brings about increased motivation and successful learning, as Adam himself testified:

I found that facts and the experiments were much more interesting for Geography and Biology. Biology I just felt that I could absorb the information much faster. My Biology teacher was very good. She always made lessons interesting. There were discussions [that] I felt [were] very engaging, good. It helped us remember the information much better. Very excited for her lessons. Always got to discuss different things, sometimes we discuss out of the syllabus. I didn't really need to study for Biology, I already was able to get very good grades.

Adam enjoyed being with his peers and kept himself busy with sports and outdoor pursuits through school-based co-curricular activities (CCA) as well as outside-of-school activities arranged by his mother, who saw the value of her son engaging in such activities. They not only develop a student's disposition but also enhance academic learning (Chong & Hung, 2016). According to Adam:

I enjoyed my first three years (in secondary school), definitely made a lot of friends. I did lots of co-curricular activities, even ones that were not organized by the school. My mum just sent me. So I went for robotics, I did *silat*, I did swimming. During the holidays, my mom will send me to science camps.

And he did cycling, too, his latest hobby, as I discovered during the interview. After secondary school, Adam chose the polytechnic route because he considered his GCE "O" level results not good enough to get him into the top junior colleges. He appeared happy with the more independent approach to teaching and learning at the polytechnic and is now considering continuing his education at a university once he has completed his national service.

Naila the young schooler

Like Adam, Naila was exposed to meaning-making experiences in literacy at home. However, given Naila's mother's previous experience as a teacher, Naila had more exposure to school-like ways of learning. In the following interview excerpt, Naila's mother was helping her do a worksheet on food which Naila brought back from her kindergarten. It involved cutting out the pictures of different types of food and pasting them in the boxes corresponding to "healthy" or "junk" food.

1	*Mother:*	What must we put down here?
2	*Naila:*	Healthy food.
3	*Mother:*	And here?
4	*Naila:*	Junk food.
5	*Mother:*	Junk food.
. . .	. . .	
6	*Mother:*	. . . What pictures must we put under healthy foods?
7	*Naila:*	Don't know.
8	*Mother:*	Which one? Look at the picture. Which one? Which food must we put in this box? What's that? (Pointing to a picture of apples.)
9	*Naila:*	Carrots. Apples.
. . .	. . .	
10	*Mother:*	Carrots give you what?
11	*Naila:*	Give you?
12	*Mother:*	Vitamins or carbohydrates?
13	*Naila:*	Vitamins.
14	*Mother:*	How about rice? Does it give you fats, carbohydrates or vitamins? Which one?
15	*Naila:*	Carbohydrates.
16	*Mother:*	Carbohydrates makes you strong, gives you energy. How about apples? Apples give you?
17	*Naila:*	Vitamins.
18	*Mother:*	Vitamins. OK, clever girl.

There are multiple facets to Naila's learning within this single activity: the categorisation of food, the basis for the categorisation and the metalanguage used in such discourses. Naila received extensive support from her teacher-mother not only in negotiating the demands of the curriculum but also in developing and displaying her cognitive ability, the kind of support which in the classroom would have been less accommodating and personal than what she experienced at home.

Naila's mother would sometimes introduce a related topic and talk about everyday life. Once, Naila was reading to her mother a story about a birthday party when the latter took the opportunity to start a conversation by asking Naila about her favourite birthday present. This triggered a recall from memory and the sharing of experiences not only by Naila but also her elder sister who was listening nearby. The printed text thus became a tool for eliciting discussion and memory recall. From the children's perspective, looking at books also meant getting the opportunity to talk about their life, learn new things and make meaning from them (Heath, 1983).

Naila the young scholar

The almost "school-like" manner in which Naila's mother negotiated printed texts with her had acculturated her into ways of behaving that had allowed her to use oral and written language in literacy events with ease and bring her knowledge to bear in school-acceptable ways. She went on to a top secondary school and landed in a class among gifted students. They (unlike her and four others in the class) came from a gifted education programme in primary school, a programme for the intellectually gifted. That was when self-doubt began to creep in, as follows:

> It was a culture shock for me to be put in a group of very, very elite kids. I feel like they are born with that natural intelligence and sharpness. But I have to work hard to get things. They absorb very quickly, but I take a longer time. So that made me feel like I was much more behind than they were. I guess it was the issue of loneliness and friendship also because these kids knew each other since primary school.

Naila and her schoolmates were the cream of the crop, yet a different educational and cultural experience appeared to have positioned her differently than her classmates with respect to the curriculum and pedagogy which she had to adapt to. Some cultural capital may be more valued in school and given a higher "exchange value" than others (Comber, 2004, p. 115). Naila said:

> Because everybody's good, so those who fall through the cracks tend to get forgotten in a sense. I didn't get to learn much because there was a lot of focus on those who were more outspoken, those who were very participative in class, that kind of thing. Those who were more reserved, or were like quite lost, then the teachers didn't really make an effort to reach out to them.

Coming from a different background did make Naila feel that she was different. She thought she was ignored by her teacher during the few occasions when she was brave enough to raise her hand to ask a question. She said:

> Even though I formulate all these ideas in my head, I don't say it out but these people are the ones who do. I actually do have ideas, it's just that

I don't speak out. I was always scared of that (her ideas not being good enough). I guess it's the environment of school, as in elite school and you can't help but feel (that) you are a small fish in a huge pond.

One size did not appear to fit all even among the brightest of students, and this was not left unnoticed by the school. But the alternative (a pullout programme) could run the risk of students suffering drawbacks because they miss classroom instruction or feel inadequate for being pulled out of their regular class (Meyers, Gelzheiser, Yelich, & Gallagher, 1990). In the case of Naila, however, it did not appear to affect her negatively, but it did dawn upon her that all four who were pulled out for Math were from the minority ethnic background. She said:

> So, they pull us out of the main class then put us in a different class where we were like taught in a smaller group which I felt that was better because since this teacher (in the main class) can't give me the guidance that I need, then another teacher can, in a smaller group, so that was a good thing. I work better in small class environment because I don't feel so intimidated by the majority.

As with Adam, Naila's mentor and source of comfort was her mother. It did not help that during the crucial early years in secondary school, Naila's mother was diagnosed with a brain tumour and could not attend to her as much as she would have had she been healthy. Naila said:

> My struggles also came from home because that's when my mum was diagnosed with the brain tumour. That was when the main source of support was a bit absent in a sense. So, she wasn't as present as she was in primary school. So that was a disorienting factor for me also. So, I had to learn how to be like completely independent.

Despite the odds, Naila managed to pull herself together and do well enough to move to the junior college level where the classroom size was cut to half (19 as opposed to 40), which suited her learning style and helped her to regain her confidence. It was also the time that she made a switch from the sciences to the arts, which was more in tune with her interest, as was the perceived change in how teachers there related to students. Naila said:

> I feel (that) the key difference in JC (junior college) was that the teachers were a lot more invested in our education. If they sense that you are falling behind, they would call you for consultations. Not you (who) seek them out. My tutors were mostly very dedicated so that made me feel like I had someone to fall back on, if I really didn't know.

That change in the classroom environment and her mother's recovery from a potentially fatal illness turned things around for Naila and prepared her well for the "A" level examination. All the local universities she applied to made her an offer, but she decided on one with a scholarship that was hard to refuse. I remember playing a little part in the decision when her father called me to ask for my advice. Naila is now well into her second year at the university.

Reflecting on my own literacy trajectory

The hidden curriculum

It was hard to recall my early literacy experience. There was a smattering of storybooks lying around at home, but I hardly remember my mother reading them to me, even storybooks in Malay, the language she was literate in. Neither did she sit down next to me as I did my homework. I was introduced to written texts at the kindergarten where I spent a good two years, uncommon in the 1960s. At Primary 6, my mother sent me to a neighbour who was a pre-university student, for tuition, perhaps hoping that the student's educational fortune would rub off on me. I also recall the occasional query from my father, a clerk, over dinner, asking if I had done my homework. These were indicative of the value my parents placed on education despite their not being involved directly in my literacy learning.

What contributed to my literacy development and facilitated my well-being in school was the norms and customs that I inherited at home. I came from a family background that has very strict etiquette on how one was to behave. I remember being alone with my grandparents at their home one day. I sat at the table with them for lunch, and throughout the entire time, I could not help feeling anxious that I might trip up on some set decorum and get a scolding. On another occasion, when my cousins and I played at their house, just the look on my grandmother's face was enough to rein us in from playing in the rain outside.

I was thus socialised from my youth into particular ways of behaving, which is not unlike the "hidden curriculum" in school—the unwritten, unofficial and often unintended lessons, values and perspectives that students learn (e.g. behave, sit upright, listen when talked to) (Portelli, 1993). A hidden curriculum may reinforce the lessons of the formal curriculum and contribute to a student's success. I was in Primary 5 when I was asked to pass a document to Miss Suppiah, my Primary 1 Form Teacher. I handed her the document, but before I could leave, she placed her hands on my shoulder, turned me to face her class and went on to describe how good a student I was and that they should try to emulate me.

The young apprentice

My mother was a 16-year-old student when she was married off to my father and became a housewife. I knew her to be resourceful and independent, getting paid for doing all sorts of creative work at home. I remember watching her fold and transform towels and *songket* fabric into animal shapes like peacocks and swans as gifts for brides and grooms. Among friends and relatives, she was also known for her *kek lapis*, a Malay version of the European *spekkoek*, a layered cake that took hours to bake but gave good returns. And they can be beautifully decorated for presentation as wedding gifts.

I remember helping my mother to layer the cakes. This involved scooping a small amount of batter into a baking tin, spreading it thinly on the surface, putting it into the oven and grilling it from above. While waiting for the layer to turn golden from the heat, I took a second tin and did the same, removed the first tin from the oven and replaced it with the second, and repeated the layering process to build up the remaining layers using the same two tins. The timing must be perfect to avoid getting the layers burnt. That skill was acquired not by listening to my mother's instructions (she hardly explained except the occasional cry in Malay "Don't let water get into the batter!") but by just watching her, much like how a Roadville child would learn from his mother (see Heath, 1983). Discipline, order and attention to detail was reinforced by my mother, shaping me into a convergent learner in school.

The late reader

My lack of exposure to reading was evident when I received a parcel from a grand uncle, a journalist, who had migrated to Kuala Lumpur, Malaysia. He came to know that I was first in class and gave me a gift of two books, one of which was on dinosaurs, which I could not appreciate at that time and had no one to help me understand. This memory came to the fore, years later when I observed Ikhsan (one of the children in the ethnographic study) who, at the age of 6, and in contrast to me, could recognise and name every dinosaur that appeared on his computer screen (Mukhlis, 2007).

I developed an interest in reading only in my early teens. That was after spending time with two cousins who had read the all-time favourites such as *The Hardy Boys* and *The Famous Five*, which their parents, who were teachers, bought for them. I grew interested, borrowed them and sourced for more at bookstores, never mind that these were meant for younger readers. I remember feeling inadequate academically and asked my parents to buy for me *Encyclopedia Britannica*, the craze at that time, but I did not use them well. I began visiting the library knowing that reading was good for me but had not developed the capacity to choose books beyond those early favourites. I was like the young children in Taylor's (1998) study whose literacy behaviour preceded their competence except that I was no longer a young child.

While I emerged at the top almost every year among my class of 40 students at primary school, I did not do well enough to get to the top secondary school. Instead, I went to the same secondary school that my brother, cousins and uncles attended (see Figure 1.1). I made it past the GCE "O" levels on my first attempt, a road untrodden in my family. However, like Adam, my results were not in the top range. But unlike him, junior college was my only option, as polytechnics then were not developed as another route to university. Nevertheless, at the "A"

Figure 1.1 My primary and secondary school report books and my old pencil case

levels, I earned enough points, propped up by my excellent grade in geometrical and mechanical drawing—a subject that required students to see perspectives beyond what is visible (see Figure 1.2)—to earn a place in engineering at a local university. It was a choice that my classmates also had opted for, and we, like Adam, had to serve our national service before starting university.

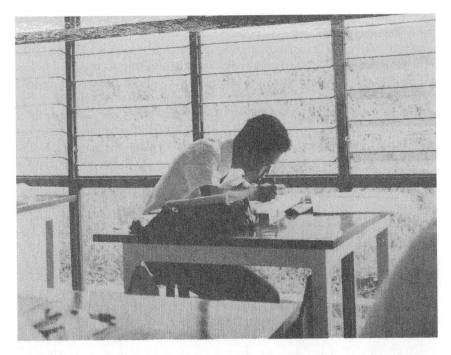

Figure 1.2 Concentrating on a task in the technical drawing room at junior college

The insecure writer

During national service, I discovered an interest in writing. I was posted to the Crime Prevention Department as a young probationary inspector, where I was tasked with preparing the "Radio Patrol". This required me to run through the previous day's list of crime reports, write a short message for the public on crime prevention, pass it to the Public Relations Department for clearance. That department then faxed the message to the broadcasting station for the radio deejays to read it out during their morning show. While I could write clearly, I thought that my limited vocabulary prevented me from churning out creative messages. There was, however, another writing task that I was better at, as it was less personal and more technical. These were project papers that outlined the processes involved in implementing department projects such as producing and marketing first-day covers that are envelopes with commemorative stamps that depict a certain topic, in this case, crime prevention.

Those writings were later to be my "data" for an assignment in "Varieties of Spoken and Written English", a course at the university, which was well received by the professor. I compared the linguistic tools used in the messages that I wrote for Radio Patrol (external consumption) and the project papers that I wrote for my superior officer (internal consumption), analysing the relationship between form and function. I should mention here that I left engineering after only two weeks in the programme upon realising that I did not want to be an engineer. I left university, worked as an editorial assistant with a magazine only to return the following year as an undergraduate majoring in the English language and mathematics. That was a life-changing decision just as it was for Naila when she switched from the sciences to the arts at the start of her junior college.

I was not a great student (my exam results were not excellent) but I enjoyed topics that caught my attention. I was in the second year when I agonised over an issue in sociolinguistics, wrote down my thoughts, which turned into an essay that I gave to the course lecturer. He embarrassed me in the lecture the next day when he critiqued my essay in front of the whole class! Apparently, striving for order, even in ideas, got me into trouble. It was also the beginning of a shift towards being a less convergent learner. In some ways, I was like Adam, who enjoyed discussion, but while he thrived in oral discourse, I was more comfortable expressing my thoughts in writing.

The academic explorer

During those times, university grades were entirely based on examination results, unlike now where examinations form 50% of total assessment, if not removed entirely. Suffice to say my grades were not stellar; I did not get into the Honours year, but I knew that I was not a failure. I enrolled in a master's programme by coursework in applied linguistics at Bangor, UK, with the support of my father who had just retired and withdrew part of his savings to finance my studies for a year. I graduated sharing the top spot with a fellow student in a class of nine. I remember the look on Sophie's face, my Greek coursemate, and her exclamation of "Jesus Christ!" after I told her that I received a distinction from Professor David Crystal for an assignment in the language pathology course. In some ways, I was like Naila, who functioned well in a small class.

I had no intention of pursuing a higher degree beyond the master's. I took up the PhD programme only at the insistence of my father, who told me to use the balance of $5000 that I still had with me for this purpose. That was not even half the tuition fee for a year, but that is another story.

I was reading up on speech perception when I stumbled upon an article about a new model of learning in artificial neural networks. For weeks I pored over the article, but there were details that I could not make sense of, and I wrote to the author, Nick Chater, of Edinburgh University. After exchanging a few emails, Nick suggested that I do my work at his University. I was taken aback, as he did not know much about me, and I did not know much about him save for that his name was on some papers I'd read. My PhD supervisor in Bangor was kind to allow me to take time off for a year to go to Edinburgh University.

I joined Nick officially as a postgraduate worker. He took me and his other PhD students on day trips to Stirling and Birmingham universities to share our work-in-progress and exchange ideas and perspectives with colleagues and graduate students there. He included me in his "connectionist" study group that met regularly to discuss language processes from a neural network perspective. Even later, after I had returned to Bangor, I was recalled to the group to participate in a workshop.

My intellectual growth took on a new trajectory and speed in Edinburgh. I presented at my first ever conference in Glasgow under Nick's watchful eye, and in Belfast on my own. We submitted papers to a prestigious conference on cognitive science in the US for two consecutive years which Nick presented. By the time I defended my thesis in 1994, my work had been published in four conference proceedings, a journal and as a chapter in a book arising from the connectionist workshop.

I had prospered in a less rigid environment than the one afforded in Singapore. When Nick invited me over to Edinburgh, he did not ask what my grades were, my religious affiliation or where I came from. He knew me only from the questions that I had for him, which were enough for him to sense that something good would come out of this young man of 29. Brijnath (2017) was right when he said that we are made by more than ourselves. We are "bits put together by others and parts assembled, an amalgamation of gifts from strangers and advice from family" (p. B10).

Summary and conclusion

Although social class is heavily tied to educational outcomes, a student's performance, as we have seen, is crucial in determining educational access. Adam and Naila grew up in middle-class homes but with different cultural capital, some more valuable than others, and this had impacted on their literacy trajectory. While Naila progressed almost seamlessly from primary school to university, save for the hiccups at secondary school, Adam's trajectory was less stable, as he had difficulty activating his cultural capital during much of his school years. Both had limited agency in shaping their trajectory, the school being the more dominant institution.

I did not have the kind of cultural capital that Naila and Adam had. Their mothers played a direct role in their literacy development, while my mother did not. Instead she instilled in me the discipline and an eye for order and detail which were critical in seeing me through school and university. The two years in kindergarten prepared me for the demands of the early primary school curriculum. From there, I was able to keep up with the upper primary curriculum and beyond. As was the case with Naila and Adam, school was the dominant agency that shaped my trajectory. It was after I left junior college that I began to have the space to "free" myself from the clutch of the system, to find myself and resume my trajectory, but this time with more agency, a risky venture nevertheless. Adam, whose strengths were hidden in school, might find this prospect appealing as he ponders his way forward.

The conceptual framework of moments of inclusion and moments of exclusion is also useful in illuminating some of the findings. While Naila's cultural capital was more valued in the classroom, at least in her primary school, Adam struggled to convert his cultural resources into an educational advantage. There were more moments of exclusion than there were moments of inclusion in the literacy trajectory of each person. Both resisted, in their own unique ways, teaching approaches that ran counter to their literacy practices and experiences. Adam resigned to being bored in the classroom but perked up when lessons were transformed in ways that enticed him. Naila felt ignored by her teacher and was separated from her "gifted" classmates, but she welcomed the pullout programme and seized the opportunity to improve her chances. I was disappointed at not making it to the Honours year but decided it was not the end of the road and took an alternative route to a higher degree.

Finally, my literacy trajectory was set in the Singapore of the 1960s and 1970s, shaped by traditional Asian values of obedience, propriety and industry. With those traits but without much of the advantages of text-based literacy learning at home, it was still possible to see my life chances improve. It is, however, probably unlikely that a family today, in the same position that my family was in, would be able to see their life chances and those of their children improve in a generation. Without the awareness of the importance of the love for books, reading, word recognition and the importance of starting these early, as well as how to work it all out, it would be hard, though not impossible, to survive in a competitive society like the one Adam, Naila and their families found themselves in. If Adam and Naila too are characters in the fictitious story in the Facebook post, I suspect they would cross the channel differently from each other and from me.

Acknowledgement

The earlier study was supported by research grants awarded by the Centre for Research in Pedagogy and Practice, National Institute of Education, Singapore (CRP 26/03 MAB and CRP 19/04 MAB). The author wishes to thank the two students and their families without whom this chapter could not have been written.

Notes

1 "Express" is a four-year course leading up to the Singapore-Cambridge GCE "O" level examination.
2 The Integrated Programme (IP) is a "through-train programme" which allows the most able secondary school students to bypass the "O" level and take the "A" level examination.

References

Baker, L., Sonnenschein, S., Serpell, R., Scher, D., Fernandez-Fein, S., Munsterman, K., & Danseco, E. (1996). Early literacy at home: Children's experiences and parents' perspectives. *The Reading Teacher, 50*(1), 70–72.
Barton, D., & Hamilton, M. (2000). Literacy practices. In D. Barton, M. Hamilton, & R. Ivanič (Eds.), *Situated literacies: Reading and writing in context* (pp. 7–15). London: Routledge.

Bourdieu, P. (1977). *Outline of a theory of practice.* Cambridge: Cambridge University Press.

Brijnath, R. (2017). Pause to say thanks to the ones who shaped you. *The Straits Times,* p. B10.

Bruner, J. (1984). Language, mind, and reading. In H. Goelman, A. Oberg, & F. Smith (Eds.), *Awakening to literacy* (pp. 193–200). Portsmouth, NH: Heinemann Educational Books.

Chong, S. K., & Hung, D. W. L. (2016). *Researching pupils' participation in school-based co-curricular activities through an ethnographic case study of learning.* London: Sage.

Clancy, S., Simpson, L., & Howard, P. (2001). Mutual trust and respect. In S. Dockett & B. Perry (Eds.), *Beginning school together: Sharing strengths* (pp. 56–61). Canberra: Australian Early Childhood Association.

Comber, B. (2004). Three little boys and their literacy trajectories. *Australian Journal of Language and Literacy, 27*(2), 114–127.

Gay, G. (2018). *Culturally responsive teaching: Theory, research, and practice.* New York: Teachers College Press.

Gee, J. P. (2015). The new literacy studies. In J. Rowsell & K. Pahl (Eds.), *The Routledge handbook of literacy studies* (pp. 35–48). London: Routledge.

Gopinathan, S. (1997). Educational development in Singapore: Connecting the national, regional and the global. *Australian Educational Researcher, 24*(1), 1.

Heath, S. B. (1983). *Ways with words: Language, life and work in communities and classrooms.* Cambridge: Cambridge University Press.

Heath, S. B., & Street, B. V. (2008). *On ethnography: Approaches to language and literacy research. Language & literacy (NCRLL).* Teachers College Press. 1234 Amsterdam Avenue, New York 10027.

Kirkpatrick, R., & Zang, Y. (2011). The negative influences of exam-oriented education on Chinese high school students: Backwash from classroom to child. *Language Testing in Asia, 1*(3), 36.

Lareau, A., & Horvat, E. M. (1999). Moments of social inclusion and exclusion: Race, class, and cultural capital in family-school relationships. *Sociology of Education, 72*(1), 37–53.

Lucas, A. M. (1983). Scientific literacy and informal learning. *Studies in Science Education, 10*(1), 1–36.

Meyers, J., Gelzheiser, L., Yelich, G., & Gallagher, M. (1990). Classroom, remedial, and resource teachers' views of pullout programs. *Elementary School Journal, 90*(5), 532–545.

Mukhlis Abu Bakar. (2006). Penggunaan Bahasa dan Amalan Literasi: Kes tiga keluarga Melayu [Language use and literacy practice: The case of three Malay families]. In Puteri Roslina Abd. Wahid (Ed.), *Persidangan Antarabangsa Pengajian Melayu* (pp. 509–520). Kuala Lumpur: Akademi Pengajian Melayu, Universiti Malaya.

Mukhlis Abu Bakar. (2007). "One size can't fit all": A story of Malay children learning literacy. In V. Vaish, S. Gopinathan, & Y.-B. Liu (Eds.), *Language, capital, culture: Critical studies of language in education in Singapore* (pp. 175–205). Rotterdam: Sense Publishers.

Mukhlis Abu Bakar. (2016). Transmission and development of literacy values and practices: An ethnographic study of a Malay family in Singapore. In R. E. Silver & W. D. Bokhorst-Heng (Eds.), *Quadrilingual education in Singapore: Pedagogical innovation in language education* (pp. 33–64). Singapore: Springer.

Portelli, J. P. (1993). Exposing the hidden curriculum. *Journal of Curriculum Studies, 25*(4), 343–358.

Rogoff, B. (1990). *Apprenticeship in thinking*. New York: Oxford University Press.

Runco, M. A., & Acar, S. (2012). Divergent thinking as an indicator of creative potential. *Creativity Research Journal, 24*(1), 66–75.

Sénéchal, M., LeFevre, J., Thomas, E., & Daley, K. (1998). Differential effects of home literacy experiences on the development of oral and written language. *Reading Research Quarterly, 33*(1), 96–116.

Street, B. V. (2014). *Social literacies: Critical approaches to literacy in development, ethnography and education*. New York: Routledge.

Tan, K. P. (2008). Meritocracy and elitism in a global city: Ideological shifts in Singapore. *International Political Science Review, 29*(1), 7–27.

Taylor, D. (1998). *Family literacy*. Exeter: Heinemann.

World Population Review. (2020). *Singapore population 2020*. Retrieved March 31, 2020, from https://worldpopulationreview.com/countries/singapore-population/

2 Where literacy practices collide

Exploring the relationship between home–school language and literacy practices of minority indigenous children from underprivileged background

Sumathi Renganathan

Introduction

This chapter sets out to explore how language and literacy are experienced and understood within and across different cultural contexts in multilingual and multicultural Malaysia. The focus is on language and literacy practices of children from a poor indigenous community in Peninsular Malaysia. These children not only come from a marginalised position but they also belong to a minority ethnic and language community. Acknowledging minority communities' social, cultural and language diversity, this chapter examines the relationship between language and literacy practices of home and at school to understand how underprivileged minority indigenous children experience school.

This chapter also provides a unique platform on which I can reflect on my own status of belonging to a minority group in Malaysia while researching with a minority community that is different from my own. It is this distinctive positioning that offers insightful reflection that helps in understanding how home and school literacy practices shape schooling experiences of different minority communities from poor socio-economic backgrounds. For any educational researcher, it is important to explore how these children can succeed academically in school. However, equally intriguing is to explore why some minority students, despite their disadvantaged background, succeed academically while others fail.

Based on my ongoing ethnographic research, which started over ten years ago, not only with indigenous children and their community but also with research in indigenous schools, I reflect on my research findings and personal experiences to discuss possible explanations for the success and failure of students from underprivileged minority background. My personal reflection is necessary because:

> Fieldwork is intensely personal; our positionality (i.e., position based on class, sex, ethnicity, race, etc.) and who we are as persons (shaped by the

socio-economic and political environment) play a fundamental role in the research process, in the field as well as in the final text.

(Palaganas, Sanchez, Molintas, & Caricativo, 2017, p. 428)

My interest in exploring and understanding literacy within and across different cultural contexts, specifically for poor minority children, stems from my own literacy experiences. I grew up in a poor neighborhood in rural Malaysia. As an Indian, I too belong to a minority ethnic and language community, where Indians only comprise about 7% of the total population of Malaysia. While it is not the intention in this chapter to compare and contrast my minority status and identity with the minority children I explore in my research, the reflection I bring into this chapter is designed to help us understand the nuances and subtleties surrounding literacy practices of minority communities from poor backgrounds.

Thus, with my biographical stance and my ethnographic research juxtaposed against a specific indigenous minority community in Malaysia, this chapter first explores issues surrounding language and literacy practices of home and school. Next, it traces the historical issues surrounding indigenous children's language and literacy practices within their communities in Malaysia. Then, the present state of home–school literacy practices and what is currently initiated to support literacy and education for these indigenous children is presented. Following this, based on the findings of my ongoing ethnographic research, I offer some insights to help us understand how some minority children, despite their disadvantaged background, do succeed in school. Finally, I discuss what lies ahead for language, literacy and schooling concerns surrounding minority indigenous children from poor socio-economic backgrounds in Malaysia.

Language and literacy practices of home and school: understanding cultural discontinuities

Literacy from a social practice perspective

In different cultural contexts, literate behavior or what it means to be literate can vary (Kress, 1997). The difficulty in using a cultural lens to view literacy practice is that the term culture itself is a phenomenon that is complex and challenging to define. Culture is ever changing, certainly not static, and can also be fluid. On one hand, in recognising cultural diversity in multicultural Malaysia, it is easy to focus on conflicting differences of these various cultures. On the other hand, in trying to arrive at a shared understanding, instead of focusing on differences, we often generalise and overlook important differences. Therefore, advocates of pluralism believe that rather than focusing on "what" a person in a specific culture represents, it is more fruitful to recognise "who" each unique individual is (Arendt, 1978; Todd, 2011). However, striving for a cultural pluralism in multicultural and multi-ethnic Malaysia remains a huge challenge.

The traditional view of literacy is often associated with the ability to read and write. In fact, in educational contexts such as schools, good reading and writing skills are important for academic success. However, the approach towards literacy from a skills-based perspective often disregards contexts where reading and writing often take place. Thus, the alternative approach of placing importance on the social contexts and cultural norms where literacy occurs views literacy as a social practice. Importance is placed on the "nature of literacy in use" (Street, 2016, p. 336). Therefore, from a social practice perspective, the acts of reading and writing vary with different social contexts, and such practices will be valued and used differently. Unfortunately, many schools adopt the narrow view of a skills-based literacy approach. Literacy education in school often emphasises surface features of language and rules of grammar rather than the larger social and ideological contexts (Street, 2016). Thus, schools are urged to place importance on the social construction of literacy, where literacy is not just "technical" skills to be taught and mastered but in fact has cultural and ideological assumptions.

The dominant view of literacy, according to Street (1984), often accepts literacy as embedded in a particular world view that excludes and marginalises other forms of literacy, while an ideological perspective of literacy acknowledges the situated nature of literacy practices within various social and cultural contexts. Therefore, viewing literacy as only happening through formal instruction in school is argued as limited. However, in many minority contexts, it is school literacy that is often used as a measure of success. For many marginalised minority children, succeeding in school implies a better life, greater opportunities and certainly a better future. In fact, in Malaysia, school literacy is so important that mere school attendance is used as a proxy for literacy (Malaysia, 2016).

Home–school literacy gap for minority children

Understanding the relationship between literacy practices at home and at school can help our understanding of school experiences among poor minority children. To explore the home–school relationship between language and literacy practices, attention to context is vital. Studies on emergent literacy also revealed the importance of children's social context that not only structures but also shapes children's early literacy practices (Mackey, 2010). Teachers and students can come from different sociocultural contexts, and thus what is taught, learned and understood as literacy can differ. Thus, members of culturally diverse societies often place different conceptions and values on their respective community or home literacy practices. However, the theory of cultural discontinuity has long hypothesised that different cultural communities experience school differently mainly because of the discontinuities between their home culture and school culture.

Home–school literacies have been explored from many perspectives. Detailed accounts of language and literacy practices of home and communities from a sociocultural perspective have been presented by New Literacy Studies (NLS) scholars such as Barton and Hamilton (1998), Heath (1983) and Street (1984). Gee (1996) showed how children's use of discourse patterns significantly differ from within and outside of school settings. In addition, specific meaning-making communicative practices at home from a multimodal perspective (Kress, 1997) have been gleaned from the ethnographic research work of Kenner (2000), Lancaster (2003) and Pahl (2002). Some studies have even shown how certain literacies in educational contexts are privileged over others, reflecting relations of power (Hope, 2011; Levy, 2011).

Studies investigating the discontinuities of home–school literacy practices seem to suggest that children would succeed in school if their home literacy practices reflect the literacy practices of school. In fact, it has also been well established that the differences between language and literacy of home and school do significantly affect success and failure of school students (Heath, 1983; Scribner & Cole, 1981). However, while knowing that these differences exist, we have yet to develop effective classroom learning approaches and methods to improve the academic success of minority disadvantaged students, especially indigenous children.

The indigenous semai orang Asli in Malaysia: a brief history on language, literacy and education

"Orang Asli", which literally translates into "Original People" in Malay, refers to different groups of indigenous people living in Peninsular Malaysia. In multicultural Malaysia, the majority ethnic group is the Malays (66%), followed by the largest minority group, the Chinese (24%), with minority Indians, indigenous peoples and other non-citizens forming the remainder. There are about 178,000 Orang Asli who can be further divided into 18 different heterogeneous sub-communities. They represent less than 0.6% of the total population of Malaysia. The Orang Asli are the earliest inhabitants in Peninsular Malaysia, and the majority live in rural or remote areas. Out of the total population of Orang Asli, the indigenous Semai constitute slightly more than 50,000 people, making them the largest indigenous Orang Asli community in Malaysia. In addition, although Malay is the national language in Malaysia, the indigenous Semai speak Semai, a Mon-Khmer language. However, the majority of Semai can easily converse in colloquial Malay.

It is important to note that Orang Asli are often ranked as the poorest and least educated in Malaysia. There are no special schools for Orang Asli children. They all attend national primary schools where the school population is predominantly Orang Asli children. These schools use Malay as the medium of instruction and English is a compulsory subject across all the years of study. Initially, Orang Asli primary schools were not taught by trained teachers. It was only after 1995, under the purview of the Ministry of Education, that trained teachers started teaching Orang Asli children. For secondary education, the Orang Asli children attend national secondary schools where for the first time they study alongside non-Asli children.

The Ministry of Education, in its effort to promote inclusive education for all, has identified Orang Asli children as a specific group that requires high-quality education relevant to their needs ("Malaysia Education Blueprint 2013–2025: Pre-school -Secondary Education," 2013). Several education-related programmes involving schools, parents and communities have been initiated by the Ministry of Education and the Department of Indigenous Development (JAKOA). These include the introduction of the Integrated Curriculum for Orang Asli and Penan Schools (KAP), Orang Asli and Penan Adult Education Class (KEDAP) and Special Comprehensive Model School, which caters for classes from Year 1 (7 years old) to Year 9 (15 years old). However, what is lacking is detailed information on the impact of such programmes on the educational progress of Orang Asli children.

Researcher–participant relationship: working in minority contexts

In the Asian context, an individual of minority standing faces different implications, in terms of status and identity. This complexity is even more pronounced with indigenous communities. Most researchers who work with indigenous communities are either indigenous scholars themselves or outsiders from dominant majority groups. Non-indigenous researchers from majority groups are often perceived as coming from a privileged status, especially when working with indigenous communities that are from poor backgrounds. Due to their immigrant ancestry, minorities like the Chinese and Indian Malaysians do not share many privileges afforded to the Malay majority community. In fact, the indigenous communities are awarded more privileges because of their native status compared to Chinese and Indian minorities. While cultural differences can never be the same, similarities can offer a close understanding of lived experiences of participants.

Personal reflection on literacy: my background and my research

I remember growing up with very few literacy resources at home. I did not grow up with storybooks and had never experienced being read bedtime stories at home. I still remember my first experience of reading *Little Red Riding Hood* and *Goldilocks and the Three Bears* when I was 9 years old in school. There were big picture books in the corner of my classroom which were made available for us to read when we finished our work early. Thus began my love for reading storybooks.

I did not receive any preschool education, as my parents could not afford it. I started school with little prior knowledge about school. Instead, I relied on my brother's schooling experiences, as he was two years older than I was. Neither of my parents completed their high school education; my father, later in life, continued his education by attending evening classes to obtain the necessary certification for employment. He went to a primary Tamil vernacular school and spoke minimal English and Malay, while my mother was English-educated and spoke a little Malay with minimal literacy skills in the Tamil language. At home we only spoke Tamil, although my siblings and I grew up speaking colloquial Malay. This is because we were the only Indian family living in a Malay village, which meant that my childhood friends were Malays. Although I hardly remember my parents reading at home, I do remember rare occasions when my father would read Tamil newspapers which he brought home from work. The books at home which I do remember are my brother's, and they were his school textbooks.

For my parents, legitimate reading and writing at home had to be related to schoolwork. Reading storybooks for pleasure meant taking time off from doing house chores. I remember hiding borrowed storybooks in between the pages of my school textbooks to be read at home so as to avoid being scolded for wasting time engaging in non-school-related literacy practices. School supplies at home such as pencils, pens and even erasers were associated with money. As such, I remember having to be mindful not to sharpen pencils too often or waste ink when using pens so that they would last longer.

I never owned any storybooks. My very own storybook came to my possession unexpectedly. When I was in Year 2 (8 years old), I was presented with a storybook for being the best student for the Malay language (Bahasa Malaysia). Ironically, the storybook was in English although in hindsight I believe there were limited storybooks in the Malay language at that time. From then on, I was strongly motivated to perform well in school so that I could have my very own storybooks. Even after more than four decades, I still have that first book that was given as a gift (see Figure 2.1), my very own literacy treasure from the past.

Home literacy practices of semai children and their schooling experiences

In many ways, based on my own literacy background, I can relate to the Semai children's struggle with school literacies. As Orang Asli communities are found in various parts of Peninsular Malaysia, the community I specifically work with are the indigenous Semai in the state of Perak, in north Malaysia. Perak has the second-largest population of Orang Asli in Malaysia. There are 26 Orang Asli schools in Perak, and 25 of them were categorised as "underperforming" schools by the Ministry of Education in 2019. The latest information in 2018 indicated that the primary school attrition rate among Orang Asli students in Perak was at 0.73% while at secondary school, it was at 51% (Mat Arif, 2018). My earlier studies have looked at the gap between everyday social practices at home and literacy practices favoured in school that affect Semai children's educational outcomes (Renganathan, 2013, 2016a, 2016b; Renganathan & Chong, 2009; Kral & Renganathan, 2018). Based on my findings, I argue that Orang Asli schools need to understand and accommodate the home–school differences to encourage academic success for these children. This is because children from poor economic backgrounds depend heavily on their schoolteachers to provide support and compensate for the lack of skill-based literacy practices and home literacy resources in order to succeed in schools (Neuman, Kaefer, & Pinkham, 2016).

Through my longitudinal case study with the Semai community and my work with Orang Asli schools, I gained many insights into the Semai children's literacy practices at home and in classrooms. My findings from actual accounts show that while positive and the much-needed intervention programmes have been initiated by the Ministry of Education, an effective implementation and monitoring process is still lacking. An example of an ongoing intervention programme is

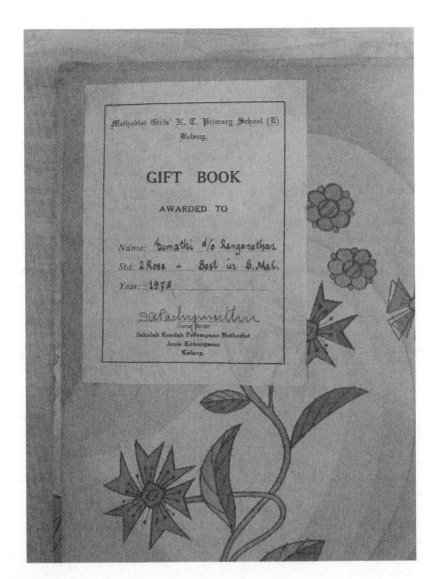

Figure 2.1 My very own literacy treasure from the past

KAP, the Primary School Curriculum for Orang Asli and Penan Students. Several factors shaped this curriculum: high dropout rate among Orang Asli children, poor literacy and numeracy skills, lack in motivation to attend schools, low value placed on education and weak academic retention skills/power (Aini, Don, & Mohd Isa, 2019). However, this intervention programme is put into place based on the premise that the children and the community come from a deficit context and thus require "fixing" based on dominant mainstream standards. Such an ethnocentric view of literacy needs to be contested (Souto-Manning, 2010). While the objectives cited for KAP were mainly to improve Orang Asli children's literacy skills and to create interest in attending school, only some schools are implementing KAP. The other programme, KEDAP, an adult literacy programme was primarily designed to address illiteracy among Orang Asli parents, while encouraging them to have positive attitudes towards lifelong learning practices (Ministry of Education, 2008). However, my findings showed that there were mixed feelings among parents regarding the objectives of this programme. While some parents cited incentives as the main motivation for their participation, others attended in order to assist their children with schoolwork at home. However, many of the parents who did complete the classes still felt inadequate in the language and literacy skills they needed to have in order to help their children with schoolwork. They still believed it was best to leave schoolwork to the teachers.

While thus far in this chapter the discussion has explored the importance of the relationship between home–school literacy practices, it does not imply that any student who does experience matching home–school literacy practices will succeed. Neither does it guarantee that any student who can successfully negotiate school literacy will be successful in school. However, research (Cairney & Ruge, 1998) has supported that "students who were most academically successful were those whose family literacy practices reproduced school literacy practices" (pg. 57). And yet what is most intriguing is that there are minority students who, despite their disadvantaged backgrounds and home–school literacy gaps, do succeed in school.

Success despite a disadvantaged background

As previously mentioned, I have worked with the indigenous Semai community for the past ten years. During my field work in the Semai village, fewer than five students managed to pursue an undergraduate degree. This corresponds with reported data that between 2008 and 2018, a total of 3,039 students had dropped out of secondary school in the state of Perak (Kaur, 2018). In addition, it was estimated that only 50% of Orang Asli children who do continue to secondary school will complete their secondary education (Kamaruddin, 2018)., I have observed that while the majority of children drop out of school without completing their education, a very small number of children go on to succeed at school and complete their education. If they come from the same village, attend the same school and experience similar home and school cultural practices, what led them to success? How do some children succeed despite their disadvantaged backgrounds while others fail? Based on my longitudinal research with the Semai children, and reflecting on my own home–school literacy experiences, I explore these questions to understand how some minority students succeed.

Longitudinal qualitative study: who finished school?

My first ethnographic research project in the primary school started in the year 2008. There were 11 students in the Year 6 class (12 years old); six girls and five boys. Since then, I have continued to record follow-up information to monitor the educational progress and changes of these children over time. While useful, just like many other longitudinal cohort studies, the challenge is in keeping track of the participants over this 12-year period. Thus, the qualitative longitudinal data presented in this chapter also suffers from being incomplete, interrupted and subject to participant attrition (Farrall, Hunter, Sharpe, & Calverley, 2015; Hunt & White, 1998; Saldana, 2003). While in my earlier publications (Rengana-than, 2016a, 2016b), I have presented the schooling experiences of some of these children, here I would like to discuss their longitudinal academic attainment.

The Orang Asli school in this village has been categorised as an underper-forming school for all these years. This is to denote that the school children's performance in the national examinations is below the average achievement at the national level. All 11 children were interviewed in 2008 to find out if they would continue their studies. Of the 11 children, only four confirmed they would continue to secondary school. Seven of them who later dropped out even then lacked interest in schooling and responded as not sure whether they would con-tinue their studies. Orang Asli parents often leave schooling decisions to their children and thus are often cited as being unaware of the importance of their children's education (Kaur, 2018). Due to their attrition, I found it a challenge to keep track of their progress. In later years, I met two of the girls who married when they were just 17 years old and were then young mothers. I also know of two boys who chose to stay in the village to support their parents, while sadly, another two boys have since passed away.

Of the four children (three girls and one boy) who continued to secondary school, the girls completed their secondary school (Year 12, 17 years old) whereas the boy, Jaley (pseudonym) dropped out of school in Year 10. Of the three girls, two of them left the village to pursue diploma level courses in another state. Both completed their diploma level studies and are currently working. As their homes were in the interior parts of the village, it was difficult to keep in touch with these two girls except to hear occasionally about them from other children in the community. The other girl, Shela (pseudonym) continued a pre-university preparatory programme and is currently pursuing her undergraduate degree in an overseas university. Shela is the first student from this 200-year-old village to have successfully furthered her studies overseas. As examples of Orang Asli students who do succeed are extremely rare, Shela's narrative, drawn from my interview data and from the many conversations I have had with her, makes for a good case that shines a light on the literacy and schooling trajectory of minority children.

Introducing Jaley and Shela

The first time I met Jaley and Shela in school their teacher identified them as being academically bright. During the interview in 2008, Jaley revealed that his ambi-tion was to become a medical doctor, while Shela wanted to become a Malay lan-guage teacher. Jaley was raised by his grandmother as his parents were separated when he was young. Jaley has a younger sister who dropped out of school and got married when she was just sixteen. I have never met Jaley's father, but his mother was one of the few members in the community who was literate in the English language. Jaley's mother and his sister moved out of the village when Jaley was in secondary school, and Jaley stayed in the village and continued schooling until he was 16. In the early years of secondary schooling, Jaley stated that he was coping well in school, but in later years he found school rather boring. He stated that he disliked some of the school subjects, particularly mathematics and English. Jaley was not serious about his studies and often played and even slept in class. Like so many before him, Jaley ended his schooling prematurely despite his family members' pleas for him to stay and complete his final school year,.

Instead, Jaley wanted to work. It is important to note that two years after dropping out of school, Jaley expressed regret for not completing his secondary education. Soon after, he took up and completed a certificate-level course. In my last conversation with him in 2019, Jaley had applied to work as a cashier in a convenience store near the village.

Shela is the third in a family of six girls. Her parents only completed primary education and are literate. Shela's two older sisters also completed high school. One of them pursued her undergraduate degree in a local university, while the other took up a certificate-level course to qualify as a teaching assistant in a preschool. As for her younger sisters, one of them chose to work and is at present working in a factory. Another younger sister who does not like school attends school "as and when she wants to". The youngest likes school because it is where she meets her friends, although she is not so keen on doing schoolwork.

Shela has consistently performed exceedingly well in school, especially in all the national examinations, throughout her schooling years. As an academically outstanding student, she was placed in the better classes (classes were streamed from Year 9 onwards) often making her the only Orang Asli student in a class of about 30 students. Whenever I meet Shela, she always assures me that she is working hard, although she finds some school subjects difficult and even dislikes some of her teachers.

Shela has recounted numerous accounts of discriminatory comments made about her by her teachers and classmates because of her indigenous heritage. This experience with teachers and classmates who looked down on her and even used derogatory names because of her Orang Asli identity, only made her work harder. She was determined to prove them wrong. In fact, now that she is studying overseas, she expressed how she values the feelings of not being judged by her Orang Asli identity and appreciates how she is treated like any other international student.

Reconciling cultural discontinuities from micro and macro perspectives: explaining schooling success

Earlier in this chapter, I drew on social practice theories that emphasise micro-ethnographies (Barton & Hamilton, 1998, 2012; Street & Street, 1991) which focused on out-of-school literacies. In addition, the cultural discontinuities highlighted the contrast between minority and mainstream culture. However, success of minority students is often measured by their accomplishments in schools. Thus, now I turn to Ogbu's cultural ecological theory (CE) of academic disengagement (Ogbu & Simons, 1998) that discusses minority students' academic achievement (Foster, 2004). The two main reasons for doing this is because firstly, Ogbu's work is focused on explaining minority groups' success and failure in school. Secondly, while Ogbu's CE theory also discusses the discontinuities of home–school culture for minority students, it explores from a macro-level perspective among various minority communities themselves. Thus, Ogbu's macro-cultural theory discusses cultural differences between groups and not individuals. An understanding of the different types of minorities is important to exploring the cultural discontinuities that lead to success or failure. Furthermore, CE theory highlights that cultural discontinuities not only happen specifically to minority students but occur for all students.

Although CE theory was mainly applied in migrant context in the US, it was developed as a global and cross-cultural theory of minority education (Foster, 2004). CE theory advocates that different kinds of minorities experience home–school cultures differently. The "primary discontinuities" are where cultural differences are apparent between students' home context with the culture and language norms of the school, whereas "secondary discontinuities" refer to minority communities seeking to preserve minority norms and values to distinguish themselves from the majority group, often to oppose discrimination. The two types of minorities that I draw on are Ogbu's classification of "involuntary" and "voluntary" minorities (Ogbu, 1983, 1985; Ogbu & Simons, 1998). CE theory discussed cultural discontinuities by exploring how society and schools treat minorities (the system) and how minorities respond to the society and to schooling (community forces).

Voluntary minorities view school as an opportunity and pathway for success in life. Even if they experience hardship or discrimination, they remain focused on gaining knowledge and skills. These minorities will learn, accept and adapt to cultural norms of the majority group (Foster, 2004; Ogbu, 1992; Ogbu & Simons, 1998). They see no threat towards their own identity and are willing to adopt new behaviours. "In Ogbu's conception voluntary minorities are steady academic achievers" (Foster, 2004, p. 327). However, involuntary minorities, because of their status in society and how they are often discriminated against or marginalised by the dominant society, want to maintain their norms and values to distinguish themselves from the majority group.

The Semai indigenous children are those who will be categorised as "involuntary" minorities because of their native status, while I will be categorised as a "voluntary" minority because of my immigrant background. Although many researchers have either disagreed or agreed with Ogbu's classifications and analyses, nonetheless they do provide a good starting point for analysing minority groups' schooling experiences in different contexts. It is important to note that local circumstances and other factors will definitely influence the application of CE theory.

While growing up, certainly many Indians in Malaysia as voluntary minorities viewed education as a pathway to success. However, at present the Indian minority students are either the third- or fourth-generation immigrants in Malaysia. Thus, it is possible that the community forces as advocated in CE theory are no longer a strong motivation to succeed among many Indian minority students. While studies of minority Indians in Malaysia are also limited (Vellymalay, 2011), a study by Santhiram (1999) indicated that Indian students' academic performance was not satisfactory. It was reported that the number of school dropouts among Indians is also disproportionately high, accounting for an estimated 13% of the total number of dropouts from primary school (Augustin, 2017). Currently, the dropout rate among Indian pupils is second only to the Orang Asli (Nair, 2019). On the other hand, Orang Asli are often regarded as indigenous people who are backward and primitive (Duncan, 2008; Gomes, 2004; Idrus, 2011). At times they were even accused of being anti-development (Idrus, 2011) and are generally framed as a failed community that is not able to embrace change and progress. Thus, they are viewed as always needing support and thus lacking in self-determination to succeed.

From a CE theory perspective, it is possible for the Orang Asli community, in wanting to preserve their language and cultural identity, to reject cultural practices in school that change or alienate them. However, the Indians who currently belong to the third or fourth generation, where once their immigrant identity would have motivated them to succeed in school, have in recent years seen a gradual decline in such motivation. I argue that while various micro and macro aspects of the theories discussed in this chapter illuminate the subtleties in cultural discontinuities that minorities experience, it is the individual agency that plays a vital role in the success of some minority students. CE theory does mention individual agency, where "individuals who follow or choose success-enhancing strategies succeed" (Ogbu, 1992, p. 292), although it was not emphasised.

When discussing the two Semai students' schooling trajectories, we find individual agency in both these students. While Shela managed to persevere and push herself to overcome the obstacles and hardships she faced during her schooling, Jaley did the same until he decided that he had had enough. When Shela cites she wanted to prove others wrong about Orang Asli, it shows the strength of individual agency that results in her success. Recalling that my late father advised me not to "grow up to be like him", I am certain that was the key factor that kept me motivated to do well in school. In later years, I learned that he was very proud of my schooling success. A recent study of six Orang Asli women who have completed tertiary education revealed similar individual agency for their schooling success (Thambiah, Man, & Idrus, 2016). Perhaps it is this individual agency factor, while often acknowledged but generally disregarded, that is missing when creating education policy for marginalised minority students like the Orang Asli.

Conclusion

This chapter has explored the discontinuities in language and literacy practices from a cultural lens between home and school for indigenous minority children. Individual students' schooling accounts presented in this chapter provided insights that invite us to question why, despite the complexity and challenges encountered in the home–school relationship, some children succeed while others fail. While the theories explored in this section helped us understand and examine the issues surrounding minority children's failure or success in schools, effective solutions to ensure positive outcomes are still difficult to establish.

The title of this chapter uses "collide" to indicate the force and magnitude of the meeting point between home–school language and literacy practices. When the indigenous students are not prepared from home to handle the language and literacy practices they encounter in school, the collision they encounter can have serious consequences for their schooling success. Schools in Malaysia mainly hold the literacy values of mainstream children who come from middle- and upper-class families. However, for marginalised minority children, their literacy level is often associated with a deficit view that frames children's home literacy practices and cultural background negatively. These children are perceived as not interested in literacy practices, cognitively weak and as having family and community members who place little value on education.

While many studies have suggested various efforts to narrow the home–school gap for better literacy outcomes, my ongoing research with the Semai show that current schooling policies and practices in Malaysia reinforce middle-class literacy values while inadvertently ignoring and devaluing indigenous children's home literacy practices. Thus, for better literacy outcomes for children from indigenous communities in Malaysia, language and literacy education in schools must favour a sociocultural reframing. Schools must be prepared to "pick up the pieces" after the collision to support the differences students encounter that can encourage school success. The few individual students who do succeed also experience this collision. However, although not prepared, they just know that their survival depends on their own strength and will to overcome the differences they continuously encounter. While there are no easy answers and explanation for an effective inclusive education for minority children like the indigenous children discussed in this chapter, education policy must acknowledge that children have individual needs and that their various school trajectories need to be supported for successful educational outcomes.

Acknowledgement

The writing of some parts of this chapter has been facilitated by activities funded generously by FRGS/1/2018/SS109/UTP/02/01.

References

Aini, Z., Don, A. G., & Mohd Isa, N. I. (2019). Education development programme to Orang Asli by the Ministry of Education Malaysia (MOE). *Jurnal Hal Ehwal Islam dan Warisan Selangor, 4*(1), 1–11.

Arendt, H. (1978). *The life of the mind.* New York: Harcourt Brace Jovanovich.

Augustin, R. (2017). *Resolving Malaysia's Indian dilemma.* Retrieved July 12, 2020, from www.freemalaysiatoday.com/category/nation/2017/09/10/resolving-malaysias-indian-dilemma/

Barton, D., & Hamilton, M. (1998). *Local literacies: Reading and writing in one community.* London: Routledge.

Barton, D., & Hamilton, M. (2012). *Local literacies: Reading and writing in one community.* London: Routledge.

Cairney, T., & Ruge, J. (1998). *Community literacy practices and schooling: Towards effective support for students.* Canberra: Department of Employment, Education, Training and Youth Affairs.

Duncan, C. R. (2008). Legislating modernity among the marginalised. In C. R. Duncan (Ed.), *Civilizing the margins: Southeast Asian government policies for the development of minorities* (pp. 1–23). New York: Cornell University Press.

Farrall, S., Hunter, B., Sharpe, G. H., & Calverley, A. (2015). What works when retracing sample members in a QLR study? Some thoughts on how to minimize attrition. *International Journal of Social Research Methodology, 19*(3), 287–300.

Foster, M. (2004). Coming to terms: A discussion of John Ogbu's cultural-ecological theory of minority academic achievement. *Intercultural Education, 15*(4), 369–384.

Gee, J. P. (1996). *Social linguistics and literacies: Ideology in discourses* (2nd ed.). London: Taylor & Francis.

Gomes, A. G. (2004). The Orang Asli of Malaysia. *International Institute of Asian Studies Newsletter, 35*(10), 10.

Heath, S. B. (1983). *Ways with words: Language, life, and work in communities and classrooms.* Cambridge: Cambridge University Press.

Hope, J. (2011). New insights into family learning for refugees: Bonding, bridging and building transcultural capital. *Literacy, 45*(2), 91–96.

Hunt, J. R., & White, E. (1998). Retaining and tracking cohort study members. *Epidemiological Reviews, 20*(1), 57–70.

Idrus, R. (2011). The discourse of protection and the Orang Asli in Malaysia. *Kajian Malaysia: Journal of Malaysian Studies, 29,* 53–74.

Kamaruddin. (2018). Orang Asli school dropout rate still serious. *Malaysiakini.* Retrieved July 12, 2020, from www.malaysiakini.com/news/441468

Kaur. (2018). Over 3000 Orang Asli school dropouts in span of 10 years. *The Star.* Retrieved July 12, 2020, from www.thestar.com.my/metro/metro-news/2018/12/06/over-3000-orang-asli-school-dropouts-in-span-of-10-years

Kenner, C. (2000). *Home pages: Literacy links for bilingual children.* Stoke-on-Trent: Trentham Books.

Kral, I., & Renganathan, S. (2018). Beyond school: Digital cultural practice as a catalyst for language and literacy. In G. Wigglesworth, J. Simpson, & J. Vaughan (Eds.), *Language practices of indigenous children and youth: The transition from home to school. Palgrave studies in minority languages and communities* (pp. 365–386). London: Palgrave Macmillan.

Kress, G. R. (1997). *Before writing: Rethinking the paths to literacy.* London: Routledge.

Lancaster, L. (2003). Beginning at the beginning: How a young child constructs time multimodally In G. R. Kress & C. Jewitt (Eds.), *Multimodal literacy* (pp. 107–122). London: Peter Lang.

Levy, R. (2011). *Young children reading at home and at school.* London: Sage.

Mackey, M. (2010, December 1). Reading from the Feet Up: The local work of literacy. *Children's Literature in Education, 41*, 323–339. https://doi.org/10.1007/s10583-010-9114-z

Malaysia. (2016). *Malaysia millennium development goals report, 2015*. U. N. Malaysia. [Record #70 is using a reference type undefined in this output style].

Mat Arif, Z. (2018). Lack of education awareness a factor in Orang Asli student dropout rate in Perak. *New Straits Times*. Retrieved from www.nst.com.my/news/nation/2018/12/436868/lack-education-awareness-factor-orang-asli-student-dropout-rate-perak

Ministry of Education. (2008, July 12). *Kelas Dewasa Ibu Bapa Orang Asli dan Penan (KEDAP). 2020*. Retrieved from www.moe.gov.my/en/bantuan-pembelajaran-menu/kelas-dewasa-ibu-bapa-orang-asli-dan-penan-kedap

Nair, M. (2019). Break the cycle of poverty among marginalised Indians. *Free Malaysia Today*. Retrieved July 12, 2020, from www.freemalaysiatoday.com/category/opinion/2019/01/17/break-the-cycle-of-poverty-among-marginalised-indians/

Neuman, S., Kaefer, T., & Pinkham, A. M. (2016). Improving low-income preschoolers' word and world knowledge: The effects of content=rich instruction. *The Elementary School Journal, 116*(4), 652–674.

Ogbu, J. U. (1983). Minority status and schooling in plural societies. *Comparative Education Review, 27*(2), 168–190.

Ogbu, J. U. (1985). Research currents: Cultural-ecological influences on minority school learning. *Language Arts, 62*(8), 860–869.

Ogbu, J. U. (1992). Understanding cultural diversity and learning. *Educational Researcher, 21*(8), 5–14.

Ogbu, J. U., & Simons, H. D. (1998). Voluntary and involuntary minorities: A cultural - ecological theory of school performance with some implications for education. *Anthropology & Education Quarterly, 29*(2), 155–188.

Pahl, K. (2002). Ephemera, mess and miscellaneous piles: Texts and practices in families. *Journal of Early Childhood Literacy, 2*(2), 145–165.

Palaganas, E., Sanchez, M., Molintas, M. V. P., & Caricativo, R. (2017, February 12). Reflexivity in qualitative research: A journey of learning. *The Qualitative Report, 22*, 426–438.

Renganathan, S. (2013). 'A Pet Rabbit, Bunny': Teaching English to Orang Asli children, an Indigenous community in Malaysia. *International Proceedings of Economics Development and Research, 68*, 145.

Renganathan, S. (2016a). Educating the Orang Asli children: Exploring indigenous children; Practices and experiences in schools. *The Journal of Educational Research, 109*(3), 275–285.

Renganathan, S. (2016b). Literacy and development for the Orang Asli in Malaysia: What matters. *Prospects: Quarterly Review of Comparative Education, 46*(3 & 4), 479–490.

Renganathan, S., & Chong, S. L. (2009). *Disparity in school's literacy practices and that of home: Understanding Orang Asli children's educational needs in Malaysia*. Singapore: International Association of Computer Science and Information Technology.

Saldana, J. (2003). *Longitudinal qualitative research: Analyzing change through time*. Walnut Creek, CA: AltaMira Press.

Santhiram, R. (1999). *Education of minorities: The case of Indians in Malaysia*. Kuala Lumpur: Child Information, Learning and Development Centre.

Scribner, S., & Cole, M. (1981). Unpacking literacy. *Writing: The Nature, Development and Teaching of Written Communication, 1,* 71–87.

Souto-Manning, M. (2010). *Freire, teaching, and learning: Culture circles across contexts.* New York: Peter Lang.

Street, B. (1984). *Literacy in theory and practice.* Cambridge: Cambridge University Press.

Street, B. (2016, October 1). Learning to read from a social practice view: Ethnography, schooling and adult learning. *PROSPECTS,* 1–10. https://doi.org/10.1007/s11125-017-9411-z

Street, B., & Street, J. (1991). The schooling of literacy. In D. Barton & R. Ivanic (Eds.), *Writing in the community* (pp. 143–166). London: Sage.

Thambiah, S., Man, Z., & Idrus, R. (2016). Orang Asli women negotiating education and identity creating a vision of the self with socially available possibilities. In K. Endicott (Ed.), *Malaysia's original people* (pp. 449–468). Singapore: NUS Press. https://doi.org/10.2307/j.ctv1qv35n.24

Todd, S. (2011). Educating beyond cultural diversity: Redrawing the boundries of a democratic plurality. *Studies in Philosophy and Education, 30*(2), 101–111.

Vellymalay, S. K. N. (2011). A study of the relationship between Indian parents' education level and their involvement in their children's education. *Kajian Malaysia: Journal of Malaysian Studies, 29*(2), 47–65.

3 The reading–writing connection

The literacy strengths and weaknesses of ESL Filipino college students based on diagnostic test results

Lalaine F. Yanilla Aquino

What I am about to share in this chapter is the result of a study I conducted on the reading and writing skills of my undergraduate students. I tried to determine their literacy strengths and weaknesses by analysing the results of their diagnostic tests. I am discussing the results of the study in the context of teaching English as a second language (ESL) and also in the light of my own literacy development growing up in a country like the Philippines.

I have always been proud of the Philippines—a country of more than 1,107 islands blessed with pristine beaches, lovely mountains with their wonderful fauna and flora, fertile plains that produce all sorts of crops and seas teeming with life and color. It was said that the Philippines is in Asia but is not quite Asia—perhaps because it is only one of two Catholic countries in Asia or perhaps because it has been under different colonisers for more than 380 years and thus its people and its ways are a curious mix of traditional and modern, conservative and liberal, Asian and Western. Still, this relatively small country in Southeast Asia (SEA) with a population of more than 109 million—people known for their warm hospitality, penchant for finding happiness even in the most dismal conditions, and resilience—has the highest literacy rate in SEA based on a United Nations (UN) report (Philstar, 2019).

My country's beauty and wonder, its interesting history, its warm and resilient people, and its high literacy rate are enough reasons to make me proud to be a Filipino. Yet the pride I feel is also due to how this country of ironies and paradoxes has somehow nurtured me into what I am now—a teacher who loves to read and write.

I have always loved reading and writing in both Filipino (my mother tongue and the Philippine national language) and English (my second language which I learned formally in school). Like most of my students, I am a product of the bilingual educational system—both Filipino and English are used as medium of instruction (MOI) in Philippine schools from the primary to the tertiary levels. English is used in teaching mathematics and science, while Filipino is used in teaching social sciences. Aside from being used as MOI, English and Filipino are also taught as subjects—the communication arts—in which the students learn reading, writing and literature in these languages. Even as I write this chapter, the MOI used in schools is still a contentious sociopolitical issue—something to be expected in a country like the Philippines, which was under different colonial powers (Spain, United States of America, Japan) in the last two centuries.

Though I am a product of the bilingual educational system, it was not the primary reason I first learned to read in English. I was reading English storybooks before I turned 6 years old, and therefore, before I went to school. When I was 4 years old, my mother bought these little books (Bible stories) being peddled in our small community. Our teenage neighbors would read those books aloud to me—I think that was how I learned to read in English. In the Philippines, there is a little yellow *ABAKADA* (*A B K D* used to be the first few letters of the Filipino alphabet) book which many parents use to teach their children how to read in Filipino. I remember reading that book with my mother, so that must be how I learned to read in Filipino. Even at the age of 5, I was already enjoying reading immensely. Reading a book felt like entering a magical world totally different from mine.

Yet it is not only reading that I have always enjoyed. I have also enjoyed writing. I wrote my first poem when I was 9 years old—again, it was in English. On Teachers' Day, I would write poetry in English or Filipino and give it to my teachers as a gift. When I was 12, I served as a news reporter in our high school paper—that was also the year I first read Antoine de Saint-Exupéry's *The Little Prince*. Two years after that, I became editor-in-chief of our high school paper and I served as such for two years—writing journalistic and literary materials in both Filipino and English. In retrospect, I have had mentors who helped me discover my talent in writing and encouraged me to write both creatively and academically. Likewise, mentors who were so passionate about teaching allowed me to enjoy my language (Filipino, English, Spanish, French, Mandarin, Russian) and literature (Philippine, Asian, Greek and Roman, Anglo-American, European) classes—from grade school to graduate school. In high school, I would read two to three short novels a week just for enjoyment. In college I would read the classics from Shakespeare to Dostoevsky to Nick Joaquin (one of the Philippine national artists for literature). I majored in creative writing and wrote fiction, poetry and drama in English and Filipino. I also served as features writer for the university newspaper, *The Philippine Collegian*, writing in both Filipino and English. I had some of my stories and poems in English published in national magazines. I won a couple of writing contests. When I was not writing academic papers or literary pieces, I was writing in my diary—constantly for more than 15 years. I reread some of my diary entries when I was preparing to write this study on literacy and I realised that I was writing more in English, my second language (L2), than in Filipino, my mother tongue (L1)—though I am comfortable in expressing myself in both languages. I guess it was because I read more English stories and poems when I was growing up. Though we only spoke Tagalog (one of the major Philippine languages spoken mostly in the island of Luzon and in Metro Manila, the national capital region) at home, most of the books that were

Figure 3.1 A picture of some of my diaries: numbered through the years for easy identification

handed down to us by some rich family friends were in English. We were poor—just a little above the poverty line—and buying books for leisure was considered a luxury; so I was happiest when we were given old books and comics. I read the Hans Christian Andersen stories in comics form—my favorite was "The Steadfast Tin Soldier."

Today, my joy is still leisurely reading—mostly young adult novels like the *Harry Potter* series and the novels of Neil Gaiman and Lois Lowry. I have had such a wonderful and amazing love affair with reading and writing that I do not see myself putting an end to this great passion of mine in the near future.

The Philippine literacy scene: ironic and paradoxical

Because I have always loved reading and writing, I thought that every Filipino student shared my passion for these literacy activities. I realised this was not the case when I started teaching English as a second language (ESL) to Filipino college students at the premier national university of the country, the University of the Philippines (UP). Some of my students do not just dislike reading and writing (particularly in English)—a few of them even detest or dread these literacy activities. Thus, to teach English in my context is not just to teach the four macro skills (reading, writing, listening, speaking) and develop in my students critical and creative thinking skills. To teach is also to invite the students into "my world" where reading and writing are wonderfully rewarding, intellectually stimulating and affectively engaging activities. It was with the view of giving my students such an invitation that I was led to construct and validate an English reading comprehension test in 2007. I thought that if I knew my students' baseline reading skills, I would be able to choose appropriate instructional materials—the kind that does not only help students become critical and creative thinkers but is also enjoyable, interesting, engaging and meaningful to read. Students need such materials if they are to become lifelong readers and learners.

The importance of helping students read with comprehension and think more critically cannot be emphasised enough. As mentioned earlier, the Philippines has the highest literacy rate (97.95%) among SEA countries, yet the high literacy rate is not an assurance that Filipinos read and think critically. At the time of writing this chapter, the Novel Coronavirus (2019-nCov) which was first reported from Wuhan, China, on 31 December 2019 has already spread to 215 countries (WHO, 2020) and so has fake news about the virus, mostly in social media. People who read articles and news about the 2019-nCov share the articles (even with ridiculous content, such as fumigating with vinegar) without checking the veracity of such reports. For instance, the Secretary of the Department of Health in the Philippines lamented that fake news hampered the cremation of the first 2019-nCov fatality in the country (Punzalan, 2020). If people are good readers and critical thinkers, fake news would not spread as fast as the virus does.

Another proof that the country's high literacy rate is neither an assurance of quality education nor learners' ability to read with comprehension is the dismal performance of Filipino students in different academic areas. When the 2018 Programme for International Student Assessment (PISA) results were released in 2019, the 15-year-old Filipino learners were at the bottom of the ranking for reading, science and mathematics among 79 countries (Paris, 2019). Moreover, the results of the National Achievement Test (NAT) show that the performance (mean = 37.44%) of Grade 6 students (10–12 years old) has been steadily declining in the last three years instead of hitting the target national average of 75% (Albano, 2019). Even more disturbing, some studies found that college freshmen (16–18 years old) had a reading level equivalent to Grade 5 (9–11 years old) (Hermosura, 2005; Navarrete, 2018). Though these figures can be so frustrating for policy makers and educators, not all hope is lost. Filipino students also win academic contests in the international arena: they won 189 medals in the 15th International Mathematics Contest in Singapore in 2019 (Rappler, 2019); they won gold at the Debate category and the silver award at the Team Writing Scholar's Cup Tournament of Champions at Yale University (*The Filipino Times*, 2019) and they also bagged gold and silver medals in the Global IT Challenge for Youth with Disabilities in Busan, South Korea (Sabillo, 2019). The poor performance of Filipino students in the PISA and the NAT juxtaposed with these academic achievements in the international arena is a glimpse into the ironic and paradoxical situation of literacy in the country.

If one were to consider the colonial past of the Philippines, it would not be hard to pinpoint where the irony and the paradox are coming from—the lack of correspondence between the country's high literacy rate and the Filipino students' poor academic performance is related to at least two issues. The first issue is that of language proficiency and MOI, which has plagued the Philippine basic education program for the longest time (see Yanilla Aquino, 2012, for a historical overview of this issue). The second issue is that of changing the basic education curriculum more often than necessary (see Yanilla Aquino, 2018 for a historical overview of this issue). These issues will be further discussed when the results of the students' reading and writing diagnostic tests in English are analysed and interpreted.

The questions I want to answer

In analysing the reading and writing diagnostic tests of my students in the past five years, I seek to answer these questions:

(1) What are the literacy strengths and weaknesses of college students as seen in the results of their diagnostic tests?
(2) What are the characteristics of good readers and good writers as exemplified in the diagnostic tests?
(3) How is reading connected to writing based on the quantitative and qualitative analyses of the diagnostic test results?

A profile of my ESL students

The undergraduate students who took the reading diagnostic test total 495. Their ages ranged from 16 to 21 years old at the time they took the test. Most of them are products of the Philippine bilingual educational system—from preschool to secondary school, they have been taught in both Filipino (the national language, which is not necessarily the first language of the students since the Philippines has more than 150 languages) and English. By the time they took the diagnostic test, most of them would have had at least ten years of formal instruction in both English and Filipino. Thus, they should not just be equipped with basic literacy skills in these languages but should have acquired a certain mastery of such skills. This assumption is also based on the fact that *most* students who enter UP have taken the UP College Admission Test (UPCAT), an entrance examination taken by more than 60,000 high school students from all over the country. It is a very competitive entrance examination, because only about 18% to 20% of the examinees qualify to be admitted to various academic programs in eight constituent universities located in 15 campuses in the Philippines. To qualify, the students have to obtain a certain percentile rank in each of the four subtests: language proficiency (Filipino and English), reading comprehension (Filipino and English), science and mathematics. Because language proficiency and reading comprehension in both Filipino and English are subtests in the UPCAT, it is assumed that the students did well in these subtests if they passed and qualified for admission to UP.

In the preceding paragraph, I use the term *most students* because other students are able to enter certain academic programs even without passing the UPCAT as long as they pass the talent determination test (e.g. for the certificate program at the UP College of Fine Arts) or get admitted through the Varsity Athletic Admission System (VAAS) program of the UP College of Human Kinetics, which aims to recruit exceptional athletes who will represent UP in national or international competitions.

Because not all students enrolled in the UP English classes are UPCAT qualifiers, it is not unlikely for an instructor to teach a class in which the learners' literacy skills range from poor to excellent. The data gathered from the diagnostic tests of 495 students from 2015 to 2019 show this disparity.

The research instruments I used

The reading diagnostic test

As mentioned earlier, I constructed and validated a reading diagnostic test in 2007. It is a 68-item multiple-choice examination that tests a hierarchy of reading comprehension abilities, including vocabulary knowledge, literal comprehension, inferential comprehension and interpretative comprehension. Since the test has also been used by other Filipino researchers in their studies, it has been named the Lalaine F. Yanilla Aquino Reading Comprehension Test (LFYA-RCT for easy identification).

The writing diagnostic test

According to Bachman and Palmer (1996, as cited in Weigle, 2002), there are two purposes in giving writing tests: (1) to make inferences about language ability, and (2) to make decisions based on those inferences: proficiency, diagnosis, achievement. The writing test given in this study is diagnostic—it is given at the beginning of the semester so that I can make inferences about the language abilities of the students and make decisions based on those inferences as to what instructional materials, teaching strategies and learning activities to use most effectively in class.

The writing test was simple enough. The students were instructed to:

(1) answer the given prompt (what does it mean to be Filipino or what does it mean to love one's country?)
(2) finish the writing task in one hour
(3) write a composition of at least three paragraphs
(4) provide the composition with a creative and interesting title

The writing prompt I chose to give (only two topics are alternately used in the span of five years--only one topic is given in a diagnostic writing activity) ensures that the students would have adequate experience or background knowledge on the topic. Giving the students a relatively easy topic also gives them the oppor-tunity to address a question which can be answered in many ways and which does not have only one correct answer. The instruction to write at least three paragraphs is to encourage the students to develop the main idea by providing at the very least, beginning, middle and concluding paragraphs. The students are not given a word limit, because they are also encouraged to make good use of the one hour given them to finish the task and show how much engagement they are willing to have with the given topic. The instruction to provide their composition with a creative and interesting title is to test how students can express the "heart" of their composition as clearly, as creatively and as succinctly as possible.

After the high scorers (HSs) and the low scorers (LSs) in the diagnostic reading test were determined, their writing samples were marked and scored using Jacob et al.'s (1981, cited in Weigle, 2002) ESL Composition Profile (ESL-CP), which made use of scores that total to 100; therefore, there was no need to compute the percentage scores. The ESL-CP makes use of analytic scoring and rates the writing samples based on these criteria: content (13 to 30 points), organisation (7 to 20 points), vocabulary (7 to 20 points), language use (5 to 25 points) and mechanics (2 to 5 points)—the highest possible score totals 100. For each crite-rion, there is a description of qualities that may be deemed very good to excel-lent, average to good, poor to fair and very poor. For example, with regard to content, very good to excellent writing is "knowledgeable, substantive, thorough development of thesis, relevant to assigned topic", while with regard to mechan-ics, a very poor sample has "no mastery of conventions; dominated by errors of spelling, punctuation, capitalization, paragraphing; handwriting illegible, or not enough to evaluate" (Jacobs et al., 1981, as cited in Weigel, 2002, p. 116).

I marked and scored each of the writing samples of the HSs and LSs based on the criteria and scoring of the ESL-CP, encoded the raw scores in Excel and com-puted and tabulated the average percentage score for each criterion.

It should be made clear at this point that one assumption of this study is that writing is a cognitive activity, and as such, the literacy strengths and weaknesses shown by the students in their writing samples can also serve as clues to the strengths and weaknesses shown by the same students in their diagnostic reading tests. In describing writing as a cognitive activity, Weigle (2002, p. 23) identified some questions addressed by models of writing:

(1) What are the cognitive processes, or mental activities, involved in writing?
(2) What sources of knowledge does the writer draw upon in writing?
(3) What other factors influence the writing process?

According to Weigle (2002), these are important issues when developing and using writing tests because they not only help define more clearly the skills being tested but also (1) point out possible areas where individual differences in skill may be found, and (2) make explicit other influences that may affect writing. Thus, in comparing and contrasting the results of the diagnostic reading test and the diagnostic writing test, I also try to infer where the differences between skilled and unskilled readers/writers are found and likewise what factors influence how effectively students express themselves in writing. Using qualitative analyses of the results of the reading and writing tests, I will try to answer the questions just presented that were enumerated by Weigle (2002).

How I gathered and analysed the data

Since the semester during which I constructed the final version of the 68-item LFYA-RCT, I have been giving the diagnostic reading test to all my undergraduate classes. But for the purpose of the present study, only the students' tests from August 2015 to August 2019 were chosen, in order to ensure that the data are more recent. Only 453 students were included in the final data set. The percentage scores of these students were arranged from highest to lowest; then the students who had percentage scores of 70% or higher were chosen as the high scorers (HSs) (n = 26), while the students with percentage scores of 40% or below were chosen as the low scorers (LSs) (n = 7)—because in the UP grading system, 70% is *fair* while a score below 50% is *fail*. The quantitative and qualitative analysis focused on these two sets of students—the HSs and the LSs (n = 33). That there are more high scorers than low scorers is something to be expected considering that most of the students have passed the UPCAT and qualified for admission to UP. That is, most of them are relatively good readers and proficient language users.

To determine the students' strengths and weaknesses in reading comprehension, an item analysis of the 68 items in the LFYA-RCT was done: for each item, the percentage of students who answered each item correctly was computed. Based on this percentage, the items were ranked from highest to lowest. The reading comprehension "strengths" were inferred from the items with the highest percentage, and the "weaknesses" were inferred from the items with the lowest percentage. The percentage difference between the highest scorers and the lowest scorers was also computed to determine the qualitative difference in their reading skills.

What I found out: good readers vs poor readers

The percentage scores of the HSs ranged from 74 to 91 (mean = 81%), while those of the LSs ranged from 24 to 40 (mean = 34%). The mean percentage scores already show the considerable difference in the average reading comprehension abilities of the HSs and the LSs.

Good readers and poor readers: similarities

The item analysis of the reading test yielded the following results: there were six items that both HSs and LSs found relatively easy, and these were mostly the ones that required literal comprehension. Eleven items were difficult for both groups, and these were the ones that required inferential or interpretative comprehension such as identifying what a given object symbolises and questions that ask how or why. Many of the items which both groups found difficult were items that test their comprehension of narratives—either a passage from a short story/novel or an expository text which makes use of narration as a rhetorical mode. Chiu (2007) noted in her study that tertiary level learners have more difficulty with literary texts in comparison to journalistic and academic texts, and the results of the reading tests support this assertion. Honestly, I found this result surprising because I have always found narrative texts easier to comprehend than expository texts.

Good readers and poor readers: differences

There were five items that most HSs, but none of the LSs, answered correctly. All of these items require inferential and interpretative comprehension (e.g. identifying the insight into human nature than can be gained from the passage or determining the purpose of the writer based on the tone of the passage).

There were 17 items that HSs found relatively easy but LSs found difficult. Of these 17 items, 9 (53%) test vocabulary knowledge, such as determining the meaning of words/expressions as they are used in the passages (e.g., *neologism, quirk, averse to flaunting, gilded, biota*). The other items test how well the students analyse, synthesise, integrate or evaluate what they read (e.g. determining the purpose of the writer, identifying what is *not* implied in a passage). These results confirm the findings of some studies (Block & Pressley, 2007; Chiu, 2007; Hermosura, 2005; Navarrete, 2018; Ogle, 2007: Olson, 2003; Tupe, 2008) that vocabulary knowledge and the ability to integrate and evaluate what is read are some of the qualities that distinguish good readers from poor readers. I can relate this to my own literacy development—growing up, I was told by adult family members and my teachers that I had a way with words.

What I found out: good writers vs poor writers

After the high scorers and the low scorers in the diagnostic reading test were identified, their writing samples were analysed using the ESL Composition Profile. The content, organisation, vocabulary, language use and mechanics of each writing sample were scored. Then the following were also tabulated: number of paragraphs, sentences, words and words per sentence. Table 3.1 shows the average percentage scores of the HSs and the LSs in the diagnostic writing test.

Table 3.1 Average percentage scores in the diagnostic writing test

	LFYA-RCT High scorers (mean = 81%)		LFYA-RCT Low scorers (mean = 34%)		Mean percentage difference
	Raw Score	Percentage Score	Raw Score	Percentage Score	
Overall rating	92	92%	53	53%	39%
Content	27	89%	17	56%	33%
Organisation	18	91%	10	49%	42%
Vocabulary	19	93%	11	54%	39%
Language Use	24	95%	13	51%	44%
Mechanics	4.8	96%	2.86	57%	39%

Table 3.1 shows the considerable difference between the mean percentage scores of the HSs and the LSs from 33% (content) to 44% (language use). Both groups were able to express their ideas about the given topic (i.e. what it means to be Filipino or what it means to love one's country) as shown in the percentage score for content, but they were definitely quite different in the way they presented these ideas in terms of clarity, coherence, organisation, vocabulary, language use and mechanics. It should be noted that the HSs have almost perfect percentage scores for language use and mechanics, while the LSs merely have a little over 50%. The LSs' group's lack of facility in the use of English has definitely also affected the clarity and coherence with which they presented their ideas. For instance, it was quite difficult to make sense of this sample writing from the LSs:

> *It is quite conscious for being a Filipino. Why? Because many people have a guts with the other westernian races, which are liberated.*

On the other hand, this sample from the HSs is much easier to understand:

> *With a government that fails to address the poverty, corruption, and fragmentation that prevails, the Filipino remains frustratingly ambivalent with regard to his citizenship.*

As shown in Table 3.2, the HSs have a higher average in all attributes. It can be inferred from these numbers how the students made good use of the one hour they were given to write a short composition. These numbers also show how much engagement the students had with the topic. Noticeably, the LSs tend to write a smaller number of paragraphs, sentences, words and words per sentence. The number of words per sentence can show the complexity of the sentence structures used by each group: the LSs tend to use simpler sentence structures and even fragments instead of complete independent clauses. For instance, here is sample from the LSs:

> *Culture is a way of life. Different countries also have different cultures, which affects the character and way of living of the people.*

(two sentences, 23 words)

Table 3.2 Average number of paragraphs, sentences and words in the sample writing

	LFYA-RCT High scorers (mean = 81%)	LFYA-RCT Low scorers (mean = 34%)
Number of Paragraphs	5	4
Number of Sentences	24	22
Number of Words	450	332
Number of Words Per Sentence	20	16

Compare and contrast it with this sample from the HSs:

> *Our people did grow together eventually, and allowed that Filipino be an all-encompassing term for residents of this country, but in some ways we are still separated by our difference of place of residence or language, and these differences sometimes make us look down on people who are Filipino.*
>
> (one sentence, 49 words).

The reading–writing connection

To establish the connection between reading comprehension and composition writing, the correlation coefficient was computed for the reading percentage scores and the writing percentage scores ($r = .94$), reading percentage scores and final grade ($r = .66$) and writing percentage scores and final grade ($r = .74$). As seen in these numbers, there is an almost perfect positive relationship between the students' scores in reading and their scores in writing, which imply that good readers tend to be good writers. There is a moderate relationship between the students' reading scores and their final grades, while there is a strong relationship between their writing scores and their final grades. This is an expected result, because a big weight of their final grades is dependent on the writing output of the students. I can relate this to my own experience as an undergraduate student—I tended to get higher grades in courses that required a lot of writing.

The connection between reading and writing is seen not only in the almost perfect positive correlation of the reading and writing scores. The connection is also factual, because *writers have to be readers*: at the basic level, they need to read what they write. It can also be inferred from the writing samples in general that the LSs engaged more in what Bereiter and Scardamalia (1987, in Weigle, 2002) calls *knowledge telling* while the HSs engage in *knowledge transforming*, as seen in how these students exerted more effort in not just addressing the writing prompt but in having a creative and logical take on the matter. Chiu (2007) found that revising and rereading are writing activities that learners will most likely skip and avoid if they are writing on their own—this may be another reason why LSs tend to write poorly: they do not read nor revise what they have already written. This is the reason why I often emphasise in my classes that writing *is* revising and as a writer, I do not mind revising my work, no matter how agonising the task can be at times.

Another thing that connects reading to writing is the fact that both are acts of composing, because both (1) require planning, drafting, aligning, revising and monitoring; (2) are essentially similar processes of meaning construction and (3) are recursive (Tierney & Pearson, 1983, in Olson, 2003). This kind of connection is evident in how HSs tend to align and revise their work (as shown in the editing they did in their samples), in how they answered correctly the more difficult reading comprehension questions that required them to infer information that is not directly found in the text and in how clearly they are able to construct meaning in their own writing.

In analysing the details of the results of the reading and writing tests, I see some parallelisms. Good readers are able to answer correctly items that test vocabulary knowledge—and these readers, who also scored high in the diagnostic writing test, tend to use a wider array of words more effectively and more appropriately. For instance, HSs effectively and appropriately used these words and expressions: *carving out an identity, form a panoramic if not united vision, a government that panders to every foreigner, jingoistic notion of patriotism,* and *like the ever-pervasive vestiges of colonial rule.* Aside from being able to determine the meaning of words as they are used in a particular context, good readers are also able to correctly identify the tone of a passage, the purpose of the author and the implied meaning of particular utterances. Again, when these good readers write, they usually have a clear thesis statement and an identifiable purpose. The good readers are also able to answer comprehension questions pertaining to the craft of writing such as why a writer would put an expression in parentheses or why a word is set in italics. In their sample writing, these readers exhibit the use of similar devices.

A look into the kind of students found among HSs yielded some interesting observations: they are the students who actually read and like to read. This observation is not only derived from the content of the reflection papers they wrote in class in which they talked about the enjoyment of reading and writing but is also based on their personal background and "academic history". Many of them are students of language enrolled in academic programs such as European Languages, English Studies, Comparative Literature, Creative Writing or Education major in English. A number of them have been taking literature classes for their electives. A number of them also belong to middle-class families and have gone abroad either for studies or for leisure. Some of them have English as their L1.

If HSs are "achievers", the LSs are not. Most of them are not UPCAT qualifiers and were able to enter UP either through passing the talent test or through the VAAS. A number of them come from the far-flung regions of the country where life is most probably difficult because of high incidences of poverty. Many of them lack self-confidence and would not actively participate in class discussions and other activities. Some of them seem to lack motivation to learn. Many of them have English as their L2.

If I were to connect my own literacy experiences with the HSs and the LSs, I would be an outlier, because though my socio-economic status and experiences were closer to those of the LSs, the enjoyment and interest I have had in anything that has to do with reading, writing, language and literature are closer to those of HSs. Perhaps I am this way because I was fortunate enough to discover the beauty and wonder of reading at an early age; perhaps because I had people around me (family and neighbors) who read to me and taught me how to read; perhaps because I had family friends who gifted me with hand-me-down books in English which allowed me to practice my reading skills or perhaps because I was encouraged by my mentors to write creatively and academically.

At this point, it would be good to interpret the results of the diagnostic tests in the context of the students being ESL learners—having a Philippine language as their L1 and English as their L2. Weigle (2002) asserts that "the differences between L1 and L2 writing are considerable, and in particular the variety of backgrounds, experience, needs, and purposes for writing is much greater for L2 writers than for L1 writers" (p. 7). In terms of cognitive processing, when students engage in writing they are expected to do more than just reproduce information. They are expected to invent and generate new ideas: to engage in writing for knowledge transformation. In addition to this cognitive processing, they need to be aware and clear about their purpose for writing: to learn, to convey emotions, to inform, to convince/persuade, to entertain/delight or to keep in touch (Weigle, 2002). Considering that they are using a language that is not their mother tongue, all these cognitive and purposive processes would be relatively difficult for them. Being able to write effectively in their L2 is no mean feat for the Filipino students who participated in this study. English, which has an opaque orthography, is quite different from Filipino (and other Philippine languages), which has a transparent orthography; moreover, the grammatical systems of the two languages are quite different. Yet as evidenced in the performance of HSs, the Filipino students are still able to effectively read and write in English, their L2.

Insights gained

When I pursued my doctorate in Reading Education, there was one important theme that cut across the different classes I took: that literacy requires three kinds of knowledge—knowledge of the world (experience), knowledge of the word (oral language) and knowledge of the printed symbol (reading/writing). These three kinds of knowledge overlap and enhance each other—the more experience an individual has of the world, the more that she or he learns new words and expressions that go with those experiences; the more words and expressions an individual has, the more she or he is able to enhance and enjoy her or his experiences; the experiences and the oral languages that an individual possesses allow her or him to better understand the printed symbols she or he reads or writes. In other words, the schemata of the learners play a crucial role in the way they learn to be literate, whether in L1 or L2.

Based on the academic and socio-economic background of the HSs and LSs in this study, the lack of relevant experiences of the LSs may be inferred from their reading and writing scores. For instance, they did poorly in the vocabulary items. Studies consistently show that students who have had multiple exposures to a word in a variety of contexts tend to develop significantly higher levels of comprehension (Block & Pressley, 2007). How can the LSs have such multiple exposures when they hardly read and when they do not have the means to travel, to attend concerts and to engage in other leisurely and intellectual activities because of their financial/socio-economic status? As I have mentioned earlier, my family was poor, but I had lots of hand-me-down books to read—such books immensely improved my "exposure" to different worlds and words. Also, my parents would take us to public parks near Manila Bay, at least once every three months, and my siblings and I (there were eight of us and I was the eldest) would enjoy running and tumbling on the grass, looking at the beautifully designed flower gardens, marvelling at the high and graceful water fountains and savouring the sights of seas and sunsets. *That* was my own *knowledge of the world* that was further enhanced by *my knowledge of the word* as I listened to the stories of my elders and mentors and as I told others of my own stories—real and imagined. Because I had both kinds of knowledge, it was not hard for me to acquire also the third one—*knowledge of the printed symbol*—as I connected what I read and wrote with what I already knew.

What follows is an enumeration of the insights gained from the analysis and evaluation of the test results:

(1) Text genre and text difficulty affect reading comprehension. Good reading materials for initial literacy instruction at the college level are characterised by familiar content with novel information, a light and straightforward style of writing, simple language structure, recognisable vocabulary and manageable concept load. Direct instruction as to the elements of a particular genre (e.g. short story) or the organisation of a passage (e.g. macro structures of expository texts) must be done even at the tertiary level, because it is counterproductive to assume that students already know these things.

(2) Most students' literacy strength—whether they are HSs or LSs—lies in already being able to understand texts at the literal level and to express themselves with adequate content in writing. Thus, instruction must focus more on enhancing the students' reading and writing abilities, so that they are able to achieve inferential and interpretative comprehension and be able to write more effectively.

(3) Vocabulary knowledge is a good predictor of good readers and good writers. Thus, all instructors, whatever course/subject or whatever level (primary, secondary, tertiary) they teach, must be *reading teachers* who ensure that instruction begins with what the students already know and builds on that prior knowledge. Schema activation must always be a part of instruction.

(4) Awareness of the craft of writing is a good indicator of good readers and good writers. Thus, language teachers must include this in the discussion of texts, whether literary or expository.

(5) Despite their ten-year instruction in English, some students still lack proficiency and facility in the use of the language, whether in reading or writing. Thus, there is definitely a need to review more thoroughly the basic education curriculum—particularly because the results of the national achievement test have continued to decline in the past three years.

I do not know exactly what made me passionate about reading and writing when my own parents were neither readers nor writers. Perhaps it was my first exposure to the wonder of the printed word when I was five years old that did the trick. If this be the case, then parents and other adult family members, as well as preschool and early grade teachers, must be made more aware of the importance of reading aloud to children and exposing them to books, stories and even poetry at an early age. Then we would have more students who share my passion for the world and the word.

References

Albano, E., Jr. (2019, September 26). Grade 6 NAT scores at 'low mastery' level. *The Manila Times*. Retrieved from www.manilatimes.net/2019/09/26/campus-press/grade-6-nat-scores-at-low-mastery-level/621772/

Block, C. C., & Pressley, M. (2007). Best practices in teaching comprehension. In L. M. Gambrell, L. M. Morrow, & M. Pressley (Eds.), *Best practices in literacy instruction* (3rd ed., pp. 220–242). New York: The Guilford Press.

Chiu, M. M. (2007). *Orchestration of reading and writing activities and response journal outputs* (Unpublished doctoral dissertation). University of the Philippines, Quezon City.

The Filipino Times. (2019, November 21). Three Pinoy students win at Yale University. *The Filipino Times*. Retrieved from https://filipinotimes.net/feature/2019/11/21/three-pinoy-students-win-yale-university/

Hermosura, J. S. (2005). *A Vygotskian-constructivist program in reading for preservice teacher education students* (Unpublished doctoral dissertation). University of the Philippines, Quezon City.

Navarrete, J. C. (2018). *An intertextual reading intervention model from improving comprehension and motivation to read* (Unpublished doctoral dissertation). University of the Philippines, Quezon City.

Ogle, D. (2007). Best practices in adolescent literacy instruction. In L. M. Gambrell, L. M. Morrow, & M. Pressley (Eds.), *Best practices in literacy instruction* (3rd ed., pp. 127–156). New York: The Guilford Press.

Olson, C. B. (2003). *The reading/writing connection: Strategies for teaching and learning in the secondary classroom*. New York: Pearson Education, Inc.

Paris, J. (2019, December 4). Philippines ranks among lowest in reading, math, and science in 2018 study. *Rappler*. Retrieved from www.rappler.com/nation/246422-philippines-ranking-reading-math-science-pisa-study-2018

Philstar. (2019, September 27). National literacy month: UN ranks Filipinos as most literate in Southeast Asia. *Philstar Global*. Retrieved from www.philstar.com/lifestyle/on-the-radar/2019/09/27/1955462/national-literacy-month-un-ranks-filipinos-most-literate-southeast-asia

Punzalan, J. (2020, February 6). 'Fake news' hampers cremation of Philippines' first novel coronavirus fatality. *ABS-CBN News*. Retrieved from https://news.abs-cbn.com/news/02/06/20/fake-news-hampers-cremation-of-philippines-first-novel-coronavirus-fatality

Rappler. (2019, August 5). Philippines captures 189 medals in Singapore math contest. *Rappler*. Retrieved from www.rappler.com/bulletin-board/237109-philippines-captures-medals-singapore-math-contest

Sabillo, K. (2019, December 4). PH youth with disabilities win big in IT competition in Korea. *ABS-CBN News*. Retrieved from https://news.abs-cbn.com/news/12/04/19/ph-youth-with-disabilities-win-big-in-it-competition-in-korea

Tupe, B. A. (2008). Metacognitive strategy instruction and bilingual readers' comprehension of expository texts (Unpublished masteral thesis). University of the Philippines, Quezon City.

Weigle, S. C. (2002). *Assessing writing*. Cambridge, UK: Cambridge University Press.

WHO. (2020, May 27). *Coronavirus disease situation report-128*. Retrieved from www.who.int/docs/default-source/coronaviruse/situation-reports/20200527-covid-19-sitrep-128.pdf?sfvrsn=11720c0a_2

Yanilla Aquino, L. F. (2012). English language as auntie: Of 'good intentions' and a pedagogy of possibilities—ELT in the Philippines and its effects on children's literacy development. In V. Rapatahana & P. Bunce (Eds.), *English language as hydra: Its impacts on non-English language cultures* (pp. 158–174. Bristol, UK: Multilingual Matters.

Yanilla Aquino, L. F. (2018). Problems and issues in teaching literature in English in Philippine secondary schools. In C. E. Loh, S. Choo, & C. Beavis (Eds.), *Literature education in the Asia-Pacific: Policies, practices, and perspectives in global times* (pp. 138–152). London and New York: Routledge.

Part 2

Contrasting transactions of literature, text and Asian readers

4 From the lianhuan hua to the picturebook

A glimpse into the evolution of literacy education and research in China[1]

Xiaofei Shi

I have spread out before me two sets of books. One set is what I read at the age of 9, while the other is what my daughter, aged two, is now reading. The books that I read in childhood are pocket-sized storybooks that include words and images (see Figure 4.1). They are called "lianhuan hua" in Chinese, which literally means linked serial pictures. The books that my daughter reads (see Figure 4.2) are termed picturebooks, and the name itself suggests that this form of book also contains both words and images. Except for this similarity, these reading materials are very different in terms of size, colour, length, and the materials on which the book is printed. The lianhuan hua is pocket-sized, while the picturebook has various sizes, from as small as the palm of one's hand to larger than a piece of A4 paper. The lianhuan hua starts with a colourful front page but is printed in black and white within, while the picturebook contains as many colours as can be imagined within and on the cover. The lianhuan hua has around 120 to 180 pages, while the picturebook is much shorter, usually 32 to 40 pages. The materials for the picturebook range from paper (soft or hardboard) to resilient plastic or cloth, while the lianhuan hua is printed only on soft paper.

Other less obvious differences between these reading materials come into plain view through a detailed comparative analysis of their plot patterns, relationships between words and images, reading experiences and possible challenges they may offer to child readers and historical contexts. Comparing the lianhuan hua that I loved and the picturebook that my daughter reads as a case study bespeaks the conception of reading as a lived experience and may provide a glimpse into how literacy education and research in China have evolved over the years. The discussions and reflections here are closely related to the context of post-socialist China. Though China has made great progress in socio-economic development since the reform and opening up in 1979, regional differences, social stratification and ethnic diversity all impact the level and quality of the educational resources that children of different backgrounds can access (Liu & Wang, 2016). In the early 1990s, it was a privilege for me to have a mother who understood the importance of literacy and ensured that I grew up being surrounded by books. Likewise, my daughter may be privileged in terms of the range of books she is provided with and the quality of our shared readings.

Figure 4.1 A photo of me reading

Therefore, the reading experiences involved in this case study may not be generalised to a majority of Chinese families, but the exposure to a wide range of texts for two generations may better position me to think about the changes in literacy education: what should be retained and what should be reviewed.

Dream of the Red Chamber vs Dear zoo

The lianhuan hua that I loved most is adapted from the novel *Dream of the Red Chamber* (henceforth *Dream*) by Xueqin Cao. Also known and translated as *The Story of the Stone*, *Dream* is a classic Chinese novel dating back to the year 1792. *Dream*, *The Romance of the Three Kingdoms*, *Heroes of the Marsh*, and *Journey to the West* are recognised as the four best-loved classic works in the history of Chinese literature. Before *Dream* was adapted into a TV series and film, its lianhuan hua version (Qian et al., 1981) had enjoyed wide popularity, especially among young people (Zhang, 2008, p. 270). My daughter takes pleasure in repeated readings of Rod Campbell's *Dear Zoo* (1982) (henceforth *Zoo*). The official website of Simon & Schuster claims that *Zoo* has been a firm favourite with toddlers since its first publication in 1982, selling over two million copies worldwide.[2] In

Figure 4.2 A photo of my daughter reading

China, parents are keen on getting their children to start learning English as early as possible. Acknowledged as a successful parent and reliable educator, Minlan Wu compiles lists of English picturebooks for children at different stages of linguistic and cognitive development. *Zoo* appears in Wu's list of the best English picturebooks for children under three (2016).

Plot patterns

The lianhuan hua is often adapted from classic novels that revolve around complex plotlines. The original novel of *Dream* presents a family saga of four generations, follows the life of some 30 main characters and over 400 minor ones, and focuses, in particular, on the romantic story of the protagonist Bao-yu and his two female cousins against the backdrop of their illustrious aristocratic family fortunes. The lianhuan hua adaptation of this complicated novel roughly falls into two categories, that is, full or partial. The former renders the entire plot into words and images, while the latter only retains some turning points or important events in the original novel. In 1981, at the age of 9, I came across the full lianhuan hua adaptation of *Dream* produced by Shanghai People's Fine Arts Publishing House. The collection comprises 16 volumes in total, with each volume named after the central plot involved therein. The 1981 adaptation remains quite loyal to Cao's original work, retaining most of the fictional events and only cutting down on the minor characters that the novel mentions in passing.

On the other hand, *Zoo* is organised around a relatively simple plot: a child writes to the zoo for a pet, and the zoo keeps sending the child the wrong animals, such as an elephant, lion, camel and so on, until the child finally gets the right one—a puppy. The recent two decades have witnessed a surge of picturebooks that employ various literary and artistic devices to deal with difficult topics, such as death, sex and violence, which results in the coinage of notions like "picturebooks for adults" (Ommundsen, 2014) and "crossover picturebooks" (Beckett, 2012), meaning those that blur the boundary line between child readership and adult readership. However, picturebooks are still mainly targeted at child readers, and the plot pattern often involves the "three-fold repetition" (Monaghan, 1974, pp. 157–160). For instance, in *Zoo*, the basic unit of the plot, that is, a child getting a gift from the zoo and then sending it back, recurs throughout the book, even more than three times. Therefore, compared to the lianhuan hua, picturebooks like *Zoo* cater to young child readers whose cognitive pattern is being formed through repetition.

The word–image relationships and related reading experiences

In the lianhuan hua *Dream*, the task of narrating the story is not equally shared between words and images but solely assigned to words, while images mainly serve to decorate or elaborate. On each page, the image is framed within a square, with the accompanying Chinese text in a rectangle to the right or left of the image. Though only one-fourth of the entire page is given to the words, the words dominate over the image in terms of conveying meaning to readers. The image may supply some details, but readers do not depend on it to understand the plotline. For instance, on page 58 of the fourth volume of *Dream*, readers can know from the words that the character Dai-yu, Bao-yu's paternal cousin and childhood sweetheart, is reading a book. She finds the book so fascinating that she soon completes quite a few chapters, and the lines ring on in her head. Bao-yu then asks her about her opinion of the book. The accompanying image portrays a slender, delicate girl with her hair done up sitting upon a rock underneath a tree and reading a book, while fallen petals cover the rim of her dress and the ground about her. A boy with a coronet on the top of his head and a court girdle at the waist stands beside the girl, slightly bending forward towards her. His gesture and tender smile imply his close relationship with the girl. The image adds some information to the words, including, for instance, the characters' style of dressing, the environment, and an inkling of their relationship. However, the image does not take the storyline forward.

Compared to *Dream*, *Zoo* possesses a much more varied and dynamic word-image relationship and foregrounds the significance of images in narrating the story. Barbara Bader suggests that the art form of picturebooks "hinges on the interdependence of pictures and words" (1976, p. 1). Various terms are coined or applied to reflect the dual narrative of picturebooks, including, for instance, "a visual-verbal entity" (Marantz, 1977, p. 150), "picture narrative" (Marcus, 1983–1984, p. 41), and "polysystemy" (Lewis, 1996, p. 109). The entire book of *Zoo* is made up of hardboard paper and plays with the device of paper engineering called "lift the flap". For instance, on the fourth spread, the verso (that is, the left half of the spread) only contains the verbal text simply in black against the entire white background. The words say, "So they sent me a . . ." (spread 4; original ellipsis). The ellipsis dots create a sense of suspension, which will not be quelled until the child reader turns to the recto (that is, the right half of the spread). The recto portrays a blue door that can be opened in two opposite directions by lifting the flaps, and the little upper left space of the door is hollowed out, which resembles a window. Only the head of an animal is revealed through the window, while the rest of it is hidden behind the door, yet the way in which the head is portrayed does not tell exactly what kind of animal it is. The notice "WITH CARE" reinforces the sense of suspension and paves the way for the climax of discovering the animal. However, the verbal text at the bottom of the recto still does not disclose what animal the zoo sends to the child: "He was too grumpy! I sent him back" (spread 4). To find out about the animal, the child reader must open the door by lifting the two flaps in opposite directions. Finally, there it is: a camel with the hump at the door. Therefore, rather than tell the story merely or mainly through words, *Zoo* relies on the interplay of words and images. Images, no longer the appendage to words, actively participate in storytelling.

The picturebook *Zoo* offers a sensory, tactile and interactive reading experience for children, as the device of lifting the flap creates a simulation of the child protagonist's unpacking the gift from the zoo, thus effectively drawing the child reader into the story. Moreover, the strategy of paper engineering drastically changes the substance of story. When child readers come to the fourth spread of *Zoo*, if they choose not to lift the flaps, the story would be to guess what animal the zoo sends through the hollowed-out space of the door that functions as a window: "Something lay there outside the door." If they open half of the door by lifting only one flap, the story would be "I opened the door slightly and carefully, something that seemed like a camel was there." If they lift the two flaps, it would be another story:

"I opened the door, and there was a camel." The creative use of paper engineering in *Zoo* embodies the fundamental materiality of picturebooks, which, according to Rebecca-Anne Do Rozario (2012), lies in the author/illustrator's full use of "page spreads", "covers", "dust jackets", "pop-ups", "embossing" and "inserts" (p. 151). The interdependence of words and images and the fundamental materiality of picturebooks challenge one fixed interpretation of the text, encourage child readers to take charge of meaning-making and turn reading into a playful experience.

Historical contexts

The format of lianhuan hua was first invented by a Shanghai publisher in the 1920s and reached the peak of its popularity in the 1980s. The lianhuan hua, with its vivid illustrations, succinct wording and intriguing storyline, appealed to child readers, especially at a time when there were not many books specifically aimed at children. According to Yushan Wei's historical overview (2020) of Chinese children's reading materials and practice (1949–1966), the number of children aged 6 to 15 amounted to 0.12 billion in the 1950s, yet only 13 million copies of children's books were published nationwide, which means that one book must be shared among ten children. Therefore, children's books were often borrowed at a low price, with the lianhuan hua as the most popular kind of book in the circulation market. In Shanghai alone, there were more than 3,000 stalls for circulating the lianhuan hua. Of course, things changed dramatically in my childhood, yet the lianhuan hua was still a popular choice for children who were on the point of moving towards chapter books and yet still needed illustrations to help them understand complicated characters. For me, it was an immeasurably pleasant experience to read *Dream*, poring over the images, savouring the poetic language, turning the characters' dialogues over the tongue and fingering the buff-coloured crispy pages.

Picturebooks have become an important part of children's reading scheme. Yiqi Shi reported on 3 May, 2018, that picturebooks made up for more than 20% of the entire children's book market. At the 55th Bologna International Book Fair, the largest and most influential display of children's books in the world, China used more than half of the display area to showcase its recent developments in the picturebook industry. For children of my daughter's generation, they are growing up surrounded by picturebooks.

The lianhuan hua adaptation of *Dream* came out only one year before *Zoo*, but the latter is still widely read these days, while the former has largely become a collector's favourite. Therefore, investigating *Zoo* and *Dream* alongside each other can offer a glimpse into the ever-evolving history and tradition of literacy education in China and can suggest some relevant research in this regard.

Looking back and around

The comparative study of *Dream* and *Zoo* reveals two trends in contemporary China's literacy education: growing emergent literacy education and the move towards multiliteracies.

Emergent literacy

The global community started attaching importance to literacy education for children under six from around 1925, when the National Committee on Reading in the United States proposed the notion of reading readiness (Li & Dong, 2004, p. 531). Reading readiness means that children should be made ready in the first few years of their lives for the formal literacy education they will receive at school. Challenging the existence of a sort of boundary line between pre-reading and real reading, as implied by the notion of reading readiness, scholars propose the concept of emergent literacy, which suggests that literacy acquisition begins at birth, and the skills of reading, writing and oral utilisation of language develop together (Teale & Sulzby, 1986). Emergent literacy education refers to the education of reading and writing skills for children under six.

Over the past 30 years, literacy education in China has been stretched to include preschool years. Among all my childhood readings, *Dream* stands out, because as I grew up, I often came back to it, moving from the lianhuan hua adaptation to the original novel. When delving deeper into what I read in preschool years, I could come up with only a few titles, including, for instance, *Calabash Brothers* (Ge, Hu, & Zhou, 1987) and *The Little Mermaid* (Andersen, 1875/1837). Mother read them to me before I could read on my own. When I inquired as to when she read these books with me, she said it should have been in kindergarten, and even Mother could not tell what she read to me before I was three years old. However, today's bookstores, online retailers and reading promoters target child readerships, including newborns, by categorising books according to different age groups, for instance, between zero and two, three and six, seven and ten, and so on, and by providing detailed instructions for adult mediators.

Compared to the commercial success of the picturebooks used for emergent literacy education, relevant academic research is disproportionately deficient in China. The Ministry of Education released *The National Guidelines for Kindergarten Education* in 2001, which included emergent literacy education as a compulsory task for any kindergarten. Correspondingly, the research on emergent literacy did not start until the beginning of the 21st century, and it is still far from a burgeoning field. A search in the database of China National Knowledge Infrastructure (CNKI), a key national information construction project supported by the Ministry of Education and the Ministry of Science, yields only around 100 related articles in the past 15 years, the majority of which work with children in kindergarten, leaving out toddlers under three.[3]

Even in Western academia, studies of emergent literacy focusing on how picturebooks impact children from zero to three are rare, with Dorothy Neal White (1954), Dorothy Butler (1980), and Maureen and Hugh Crago (1983) among a few exceptions. The majority of emergent literacy projects works with children aged four to six (Goswami, 1998; Hall, Larson, & Marsh, 2003; McCartney & Philips, 2006; Marsh & Hallet, 2008). Bettina Kümmerling-Meibauer (2011) lists three main reasons for the neglect of emergent literacy research with children under three, and these reasons are also relevant to the Chinese context.

First, picturebooks targeting very young children are "deceptively simple". Second, it is extremely difficult to work with children under the age of 3, because they have not mastered enough vocabulary and knowledge to communicate their impressions, thoughts and feelings. Third, some scholars, educationists and caretakers tend to underestimate the significance of these deceptively simple picturebooks for young children's emerging sense of literacy and literature appreciation (Kümmerling-Meibauer, 2011, pp. 1–2).

Moreover, a particular challenge for Chinese scholars researching emergent literacy education arises from the pictographic system of Chinese characters, which means that alphabetic-centric Western perspectives do not all apply. Jing Zhou and Baogen Liu (2010) use eye tracking and Chinse picturebooks to investigate how emergent literacy develops in children whose mother tongue is Chinese. They discover that the attention of preschoolers is directed first to pictures and then to Chinese characters (Zhou & Liu, 2010, p. 69). While some scholars consider phonemic awareness as the most important predictor of children's literacy acquisition in alphabetic-centric linguistic systems (Castles, Wilson, & Coltheart, 2011), visual skills seem to be more important for Chinese children, because of the inherent pictographic nature of the Chinese language (Zhou & Liu, 2010). Zhou and Liu further divide Chinese children's visual skills into four dimensions, that is, the ability to focus on images, the ability to retrieve information from images, the ability to interpret images, and the ability to communicate through images (2010, p. 70).

Multiliteracies

The move from the lianhuan hua to the picturebook also shows an increasing emphasis on multiliteracies in China's literacy education. The notion of multiliteracies emerged from the discussions of the New London group in 1994. It is a response to "the increasing multiplicity and integration of significant modes of meaning-making" and "the realities of increasing local diversity and global connectedness" (Cope & Kalantzis, 2000, pp. 5–6). Therefore, Bill Cope and Mary Kalantzis add two "multis" to the word "literacy". The first "multi" addresses significant differences in meaning making that arise out of different sociocultural and domain-specific contexts. It is no longer enough to focus solely on the national language. The second "multi" connects to multimodality, that is, how "written-linguistic modes of meaning interface with oral, visual, audio, gestural, tactile, and spatial patterns of meaning" (Cope & Kalantzis, 2015, p. 3).

Obviously, *Dream* is written in Chinese, while *Zoo* is in English, which reflects a shift from literacy education mostly in Chinese to that with an equal emphasis on English. English is among the three most important subjects of the College Entrance Examination, the method of selecting students for universities and therefore the most important examination nationwide. Of course, not every family in China can read original English picturebooks with their children. However, a search through the official websites of Taobao, Jingdong and Dangdang, the three biggest online retailers in China, reveals: advertisements for original

English picturebooks often claim that the books come together with the corresponding English audio or video, which can be freely downloaded and played to children. Wu's list of English picturebooks for young children has become a great commercial success, partially for the reason that it taps into parental eagerness and even anxiety to give their children an early start in English literacy education. In the CNKI database, as much as 80% of picturebook studies that have high citation rates revolve around the teaching and learning of English. All of these demonstrate that the use of original English picturebooks aims to cultivate literacy in the English language.

While some neurological studies show that early exposure to bilingualism may increase the plasticity of the brain (Mechelli et al., 2004), Si Chen and Zhou (2014) caution against a too optimistic view of bilingual literacy education. The quality and range of educational resources children can access significantly impact their performance in bilingual literacy. Since China has a huge population and educational resources are unevenly distributed, too much emphasis on bilingual literacy may jeopardise educational equality (Chen & Zhou, 2014, p. 83). While four centuries ago only a million or so people in the vicinity of London spoke English, the number of English speakers reached one billion at the time when the notion of multiliteracies was proposed in 2000. As Cope and Kalantzis remind us, the story of the English language includes many injustices (2000, p. 3). The dominance of English as the largest language by number of speakers raises a question: for those countries whose national language is not English, is the inclusion of English into the national curriculum showing a trend towards multiliteracies, or is it showing a trend where local ethnic minority languages and cultural differences are being overshadowed by the hegemony of English?

Regarding the second "multi-" in the notion of multiliteracies, the picturebook lends itself to a more multimodal reading experience than the lianhuan hua. While the body of a lianhuan hua is black and white, picturebooks employ various colours to convey characters' emotions and propel the development of plot. For instance, in *Zoo*, the black-and-white verso serves as a foil for the colourful recto to enhance the sense of suspension and excitement when the child unpacks the gift from the zoo. In the lianhuan hua, images often only decorate or elaborate words, while picturebooks rely on the complicated word–image interplay. Picturebooks have been regarded as an art form and an educational tool that can initiate children into visual literacy and literature appreciation since the 1980s (Colomer, Kümmerling-Meibauer, & Silva-Díaz, 2010, p. 4). Arguing against the assumption that pictures are easy to understand, Perry Nodelman shows that pictures often undercut the simplicity of words with a sophisticated view of things (2010, pp. 14–29). Maria Nikolajeva suggests that readers need to master a number of codes to interpret picturebooks, and reading picturebooks can help to develop children's visual literacy and literary competence (2010, pp. 30–46).

Moreover, picturebook reading integrates oral, audio, tactile, gestural and spatial elements. Reading picturebooks does not happen naturally. For children under two, they first need to learn the "rules of book-behaviour" (Lewis, 2001, p. 78), including, for instance, sitting still, holding the book, turning the pages, looking and pointing at the pictures instead of chewing on the book. While these rules of book-behaviour are also relevant to the reading of a lianhuan hua, picturebooks often use various devices of paper engineering to heighten the sense of reading as a tactile and spatial experience. Besides, since picturebooks are likely to be shared between adult mediators and children, reading aloud, exclamations, laughter and gesturing are bound to become part of the process of reading. As Parsons argues, picturebooks "operate as scripts and sites for performance by forming a visual and spatial backdrop, providing textual narratives, scripting dialogues, and incorporating scores for an interplay of speech, gesture and the production of abstract sounds" (2004, para. 1).

The contemporary visual turn, noted by scholars since the 1980s (Mitchell, 1994, pp. 11–12), makes increasing demands on one's ability to make meaning from and express through various communications media. In China, the Ministry of Education released the latest national curriculum for the subject of Chinese in December 2017, listing seven compulsory course units that cover the learning of language, literature and culture. One course unit focuses on cultivating students' ability to retrieve, represent and express information across different media, to understand how various media resources may be deployed and to evaluate the objectivity and ideology of the messages conveyed in mass media. The latest national curriculum distinguishes itself from the previous versions by elevating multiliteracies to an unprecedented level. The picturebook, for its creative use of images, the complicated word-image interplay and the potential for inviting children's multimodal reading experiences, constitutes a good point of departure for developing multiliteracies. This is perhaps partially the reason why *Zoo*, published only one year after the lianhuan hua version of *Dream*, is still popular nowadays, while *Dream* seems sort of outdated for children's literacy education.

Tracing the evolution of literacy education in China through a comparative case study of the lianhuan hua *Dream* and the picturebook *Zoo*, of my experience as a reader and my daughter's, reveals two positive changes: first, growing attention has been paid to children's emergent literacy; second, literacy education shows the tendency towards an emphasis on multiliteracies in response to the predominance of English and fast developments in mass media and the internet. However, two issues still need to be addressed, that is, the lack of emergent literacy research especially in terms of how young children deal with the inherently pictographic nature of Chinese characters, and the absence of ethnic minority languages and cultures in literacy education. Moreover, the rise of picturebooks prompts reflection on whether the traditional narrative form of lianhuan hua still has its value in today's and future literacy education.

Looking forward

Some researchers have already issued a death sentence for the lianhuan hua. For instance, Wenqi Sun (2016) argues that picturebooks will replace the lianhuan hua because the former caters to the dominant reading mode of contemporary society. However, Sun does not explain what the dominant reading mode is and why the lianhuan hua fails to conform to it. Yitao Tang's comparative study of the lianhun hua and Japanese manga (2017) concludes that the former serves to educate, while the latter to entertain, which accounts for the decline of the lianhuan hua. This dichotomised understanding is problematic, because the function of a particular text also depends on readers and the reading context, and there is no problem for a text to be educative.

To arrive at a more adequate understanding of the differences between the lianhuan hua and picturebooks, I propose a triangular model, as shown in Figure 4.3:

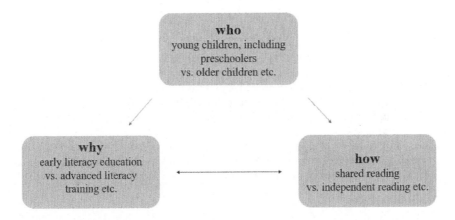

Figure 4.3 The triangular model

The model comprises three crucial elements. "Who" refers to the reader, "why" refers to the purpose, and "how" refers to the manner and strategies. The three elements are closely interrelated. The characteristics and needs of the reader determine the purpose of literacy education and how literacy education should be carried out. The purpose guides the design of literacy education, while in turn the design impacts on whether the goal can be achieved. Compared to picturebooks, the lianhuan hua may be more suitable for older children who have already started formal literacy education and mastered some vocabulary and knowledge, and who may need the aid of images to usher them into more complicated literary works. Though adult mediation may still be desirable, they can read and enjoy books on their own.

Looking again at the two piles of books before me, I am glad to see more choices emerging for children and their parents. It would be a dangerous dichotomy to say that the picturebook points to the path leading towards a bright future for literacy education, while the lianhuan hua belongs to the good old past. Rather, the lianhuan hua should be retained in today's and future literacy education. Both reading materials can be used in a mutually complementary and cross-fertilising way, depending on their target readers, purposes and strategies of education.

Notes

1 This chapter is part of the research project "Contemporary Western Picturebook Theory" (18WWC005) funded by Jiangsu Planning Office of Philosophy and Social Science and the project "Chinese Picturebooks and Their English Translations" (2017SJB1318) funded by Jiangsu Education Department.
2 The webpage can be found at www.simonandschuster.com/books/Dear-Zoo/Rod-Campbell/Dear-Zoo-Friends/9781416947370.
3 The results of the search can be found at https://kns.cnki.net/kns/brief/default_result.aspx.

References

Primary texts

Andersen, H. C. (1875/1837). The little mermaid. In *Hans Andersen's fairy tales* (H. B. Paull, Trans.). London: Frederick Warne & Co. Retrieved from http://www.surlalunefairytales.com/littlemermaid/index.html
Campbell, R. (2007/1982). *Dear zoo*. London: Little Simon.
Ge, G., Hu, J., & Zhou, K. (1987). *Calabash brothers*. Shanghai: Shanghai Animation Film Studio.
Qian, Z., Ji, X., Ji, B., Wu, Q., Wang, W., Xu, G., . . . Ding, S. (1981). *Lianhuan hua dream of the red chamber*. Shanghai: Shanghai People's Fine Arts Publishing House.

Secondary texts

Bader, B. (1976). *American picture books from Noah's ark to the beast within*. New York: Palgrave Macmillan.
Beckett, S. L. (2012). *Crossover picture books: A genre for all ages*. London: Routledge.
Butler, D. (1980). *Babies need books*. London: Penguin Books.
Castles, A., Wilson, K., & Coltheart, M. (2011). Early orthographic influences on phonemic awareness tasks: Evidence from a preschool training study. *Journal of Experimental Child Psychology, 108*(1), 203–210.
Chen, S., & Zhou, J. (2014). Shuangyu: ertong fazhan jiyu yu tiaozhan de zaijiedu [Bilingualism: Opportunities and challenges for young children]. *Quanqiu jiaoyu zhanwang [Global Education], 43*(5), 78–86.
Colomer, T., Kümmerling-Meibauer, B., & Silva-Díaz, C. (2010). Introduction. In T. Colomer, B. Kümmerling-Meibauer, & C. Silva-Díaz (Eds.), *New directions in picture book research* (pp. 4–12). New York: Routledge.
Cope, B., & Kalantzis, M. (Eds.). (2000). *Multiliteracies. Literacy learning and the design of social futures*. London: Routledge.
Cope, B., & Kalantzis, M. (Eds.). (2015). *A pedagogy of multiliteracies. Learning by design*. Basingstoke: Palgrave Macmillan.
Crago, M., & Crago, H. (1983). *Prelude to literacy: A preschool child's encounter with picture and story*. Carbondale: Southern Illinois University Press.
Do Rozario, R. (2012). Consuming books: Synergies of materiality and narrative in picturebooks. *Children's Literature, 40*, 151–166.
Goswami, U. (1998). *Cognition in children*. London: Psychology Press.

Hall, N., Larson, J., & Marsh, J. (Eds.). (2003). *Handbook of early childhood literacy*. Thousand Oaks: Sage.

Kümmerling-Meibauer, B. (2011). Emergent literacy and children's literature. In B. Kümmerling-Meibauer (Ed.), *Emergent literacy: Children's books from 0 to 3* (pp. 1–14). Amsterdam: John Benjamins.

Lewis, D. (1996). Going along with Mr. Gumpy: Polysystemy and play in the modern picturebook. *Signal, 80*, 105–119.

Lewis, D. (2001). *Reading contemporary picturebooks. picturing text*. London: Routledge Falmer.

Li, Y., & Dong, Q. (2004). Ertong zaoqi duxie nengli fazhan de huanjing yingxiang yinsu yanjiu [A research of environmental factors in preschoolers' literacy development]. *Xinli kexue [Psychological Science]*, *27*(3), 531–535.

Liu, H., & Wang, S. (2016). Zhongguo yiwu jiaoyu shishi sanshinian: chengjiu, jiazhi yu zhanwang [The thirty-year history of compulsory education in China: Achievements and the future]. *Peking University Education Review*, *14*(4), 175–184.

Marantz, K. (1977). The picture book as art object: A call for balanced reviewing. *Wilson Library Bulletin, 52*, 148–151.

Marcus, L. S. (1983–1984). Mitsumasa Anno. *The Lion and the Unicorn, 7*(8), 34–46.

Marsh, J., & Hallet, E. (Eds.). (2008). *Desirable literacies. Approaches to language and literacy in the early years*. London: Sage.

McCartney, K., & Philips, D. (Eds.). (2006). *Blackwell handbook of early childhood development*. Oxford: Blackwell.

Mechelli, A., Crinion, J. T., Noppeney, U., O Doherty, J., Ashburner, J., Frackowiak, R. S., & Price, C. J. (2004). Neurolinguistics: Structural plasticity in the bilingual brain. *Nature, 431*, 757.

The Ministry of Education of the People's Republic of China. (2001). Retrieved from http://old.moe.gov.cn/publicfiles/business/htmlfiles/moe/s3327/201001/81984.html

The Ministry of Education of the People's Republic of China. (2017, December 29). Retrieved from www.moe.gov.cn/srcsite/A26/s8001/201801/t20180115_324647.html

Mitchell, W. J. T. (1994). *Picture theory*. Chicago: University of Chicago Press.

Monaghan, D. M. (1974). The literary fairy tales: A study of Oscar Wilde's "The Happy Prince" and "The Star Child". *Canadian Review of Comparative Literature, 1*, 156–166.

Nikolajeva, M. (2010). Interpretive codes and implied readers of children's picturebooks. In T. Colomer, B. Kümmerling-Meibauer, & C. Silva-Díaz (Eds.), *New directions in picturebook research* (pp. 30–40). New York: Routledge.

Nodelman, P. (2010). Words claimed: Picture book narratives and the project of children's literature. In T. Colomer, B. Kümmerling-Meibauer, & C. Silva-Díaz (Eds.), *New directions in picture book research* (pp. 14–29). New York: Routledge.

Ommundsen, A. M. (2014). Picture books for adults. In B. Kümmerling-Meibauer (Ed.), *Picture books: Representation and narration* (pp. 17–35). New York: Routledge.

Parsons, E. (2004). Starring in the intimate space: Picture book narratives and performance semiotics. *Image & Narrative, 9*. Retrieved from www.imageandnarrative.be/inarchive/performance/parsons.htm

Shi, Y. (2018, May 3). *Zhongguo huiben jiakuai zouxiang shijie de bufa [Chinese picture books going out to the world]*. Retrieved from http://edu.people.com.cn/n1/2018/0503/c1006-29961544.html

Sun, W. (2016). *Cong lianhuan hua dao huiben de wenhua zhuanxing yanjiu [The cultural transformation from lianhuan hua to picture books]* (Unpublished Master's thesis). Zhejiang Sci-Tech University, China.

Tang, Y. (2017). *Cong lianhuan hua yu riben manhua yitu xushi jiaqiao chayi fenxi zhongguo lianhuan hua shiwei xianxiang [A comparative study of lianhuan hua and Japanese manga]* (Unpublished Master's thesis). Shanghai Normal University, China.

Teale, W. H., & Sulzby, E. (1986). *Emergent literacy: Writing and reading*. Goleta: Praeger.

Wei, Y. (2020). Xinzhongguo ertong yuedu shi [A historical overview of children's reading materials and practice in the people's republic of China]. *Chuban faxing yanjiu [Publication Studies]*, *4*, 96–106.

White, D. N. (1954). *Books before five*. Oxford: Oxford University Press.

Wu, M. (2016). *Huiben 123 [Picturebooks ABC]*. Beijing: Foreign Language Teaching and Research Press.

Zhang, H. (2008). Honglou meng de lianhuan tuhua zuopin [The lianhuan hua adaptations of *dream of the red chamber*]. *Honglou meng xuekan [Studies of Dream of the Red Chamber]*, *3*, 269–284.

Zhou, J., & Liu, B. (2010). Hanyu ertong cong tuxiang dao wenzi de zaoqi yuedu yu duxie fazhan guocheng [From image to text: Early childhood reading and literacy development of Chinese-speaking children]. *Zhongguo teshu jiaoyu [Chinese Journal of Special Education]*, *12*, 64–71.

5 A journey to matching reader and text

Dahlia Janan

The early journey as a reader

The fact that I failed to read easily in my early school days has had an effect on my interest in conducting research in the field of literacy, particularly in terms of how to match readers with texts. This area of study has always fascinated me, although the phenomenon of the relationship between readers and the difficulty of text is rarely discussed in more recent times. Although I could not read early on in Standard One (7 years old in Malaysia's primary school), I got excited every time I saw my friends read a storybook and retell a story from a book they had read. I was keen to read but always felt frustrated because I could not understand the words written in a book. My own experience as a struggling reader for whom a switch suddenly clicked when I could read at Standard Two, after falling in love with a particular book, always made me wonder how such a book could change my interest in reading. I still remember how I tried to read the book and how this interest turned me from someone who did not know how to read into a fluent reader. So my journey as a struggling reader is always fresh in my mind. This chapter discusses whether factors that affect the New Model of Readability that has been developed for an English speaker would be the same or different for readers in other languages.

Coming across *Silly Simon* along the journey

One day when I was in Standard Two, in my classroom reading corner, I found a picture book. From looking at the pictures, I found the story to be so funny that I wanted to read it very much. The title of the storybook was *Silly Simon*. Simon, the main character in the book, was so silly that it made me laugh just looking at the photos of the book. The *Silly Simon* book grabbed my attention and interest in reading so much that I had to ask my classmate who was a good reader to teach me to read *Silly Simon*. My success in reading and understanding this first book made it easier for me to read other books, and I fell in love with reading right away (see Figure 5.1).

My encounters with reading difficulty did not stop there. Years later, after I became a teacher, I realised that the ability to read and understand was

Figure 5.1 Illustration of *Silly Simon*, courtesy of my niece Nur Farah Syafaf Jamil

sometimes a problem to students. This deepened my curiosity about the connection between the reader and the text. This curiosity built my journey as an
academic to find out what makes certain texts, books, picture books or reading
materials appealing to some readers and not others. What are the elements that
make a person interested in certain reading material? And this has guided the
journey of my academic career for the past 20 years in terms of trying to find the
answer to "Matching the reader and the text".

Going back to the *Silly Simon* book, I wonder how this book triggered my
inner self to read. Was it because of the pictures or because of the funny story?
I am amazed that during those days I wanted to read *Silly Simon*, even though
the sentences are quite long for a child who does not know how to read. Studies have shown that children prefer to read picture books and books with fewer
words (Brookshire, Scharff & Moses, 2002; Strasser & Seplocha, 2007; Jalongo
et al., 2002). However, this was different for me, as I found I was fascinated by
the funny story rather than being concerned with the length of the sentences.
Studies also have shown that reading will be easier and more reasonable if it fits
the reader's experience (Ozuru, Dempsey, & McNamara, 2009). However, I was
interested in reading *Silly Simon* even though the story did not resonate with my
cultural background. For example, through reading the book, I learnt for the first
time about cheese and how it melts in hot weather. Simon's funny antics made
me want to finish reading the story. This marked the beginning of my journey as
a reader.

The journey to matching reader to text

As a result of the reading difficulty I faced in my early years, my interest in understanding how readers become engaged with certain reading material became central to my research pursuits. I am fascinated by how a certain book impacts a
reader to the extent that the reader is unable to put it down. It appears that the
reader and the reading materials are one. To date, I am still finding it interesting to investigate how readers and the reading material or text can be matched.
According to Gilliland (1972), studies of matching the reader and the text have
been called studies of readability. Wray (2004) states that text is the centre of the
literacy process. He has suggested that literacy skills are only useful when individuals apply these skills to actual literacy experiences and that the main factor in
the experience is the text.

Apart from the difficulty in reading in my early years, throughout my teaching
experience I have come to realise that the ability to read and comprehend can
sometimes be a problem. The ability to read and understand does not depend
merely on the reader, but on other factors, such as the reader's background
and environment, the teacher's and school's environment and the resources
and materials available (McKenna, Kear, & Ellsworth, 1995; Samuels, 1983;
Wu & Hu, 2007). The desire to understand ways to match reader to text deepened when I was sponsored by the Malaysian government to pursue my PhD.
I took the opportunity to conduct my research on readability. In my PhD work,

I developed a model that summarises the relationship between the three impor-tant elements that interrelate and influence a reader to comprehend a text. The three elements are the reader, the reading material and the school environment (see Figure 5.2). Based on these three main factors that influence readers as they read, I focused on examining the interaction between the reader and the reading material or the text.

The diagram in Figure 5.2 shows the interaction of three main factors that affect readability (the match between the reader and the text). The diagram also shows the factors that are related to reader and text that influence one another when reading takes place. The reader factor consists of a reader's reading ability, gender, age, social background, prior knowledge, interest, motivation, attitudes and reading goal. Text factors include the difficulty level of the text, linguistic difficulties, organisation, content structure, legibility, illustration, text's physical

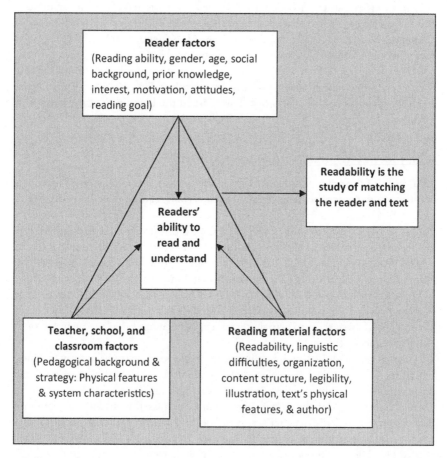

Figure 5.2 Three major factors that influence readers' ability to read and understand
Source: Janan, 2011.

features and author (Janan, 2011). Hence, the research that I have done in this area has helped to develop a new model for a renewed concept of readability, looking at the fundamental factors that affect the readability of reading material. In doing this research, I had the opportunity to look at how a reader and reading material or text interact during the reading process. In this research the focus was on developing a new model for a renewed concept of readability in the English language, where all the participants were students with English as their first language or mother tongue.

In my research I found literature that suggests that much of the previous research on readability had stemmed from the positivist paradigm and had used quantitative methods to assess the appropriateness of texts (Janan, Wray, & Pope, 2010; Janan & Wray, 2013). This approach had been widely criticised and, more recently, more qualitative methods derived from the interpretive paradigm had been used. It seems that both quantitative and qualitative methods had strengths and limitations (Janan et al., 2010; Janan & Wray, 2013). Therefore, the research that I have thus far undertaken has explored the concept of readability by combining these two research approaches.

My data collection methods included readability formulas, text feature analysis, miscue analysis, retelling and interview. The research was conducted in the United Kingdom and involved 16 boys and 16 girls between the ages of 6 and 11. In the United Kingdom, boys and girls at the age of 6 and 11 years old are equivalent to pupils in Standard One to Standard Six in the Malaysian primary school. All participants were good readers. Data were analysed using a range of tools: five online readability formulas [ATOS (Milone, 2012); Dale-Chall (Dale & Chall,1948); Flesch (1948); FOG (Gunning, 1952); SMOG (McLaughlin, 1969)]; Reading Miscue Inventory (Goodman, Watson, & Burke, 2005); Judging Richness of Retellings (Irwin & Mitchell, 1983); a text feature analysis form and a cross-interview analysis approach.

In this research 64 texts were used, and 32 of them were used in Reading Event One, where the text was selected by the participants themselves. Thirty-two others are texts which were used in Reading Event Two and selected by me to have a slightly higher readability index, in order to provide more difficult text for participants. The rationale behind this was to compare the similarities and differences of participants' interactions with the text used in Reading Event One and Reading Event Two.

The complex interactions between the participants with the texts were analysed using five approaches, including readability formulas, text feature analysis, miscue analysis, retelling and interview. The results showed that the concept of readability was influenced by both reading and textual factors. Reader factors involved complex relationships between the nine elements embedded in the reader, namely, interest, prior knowledge, attitude, reading ability, motivation, reading purpose, engagement, age and gender (Janan, 2011; Wray & Janan, 2013a, 2013b). Textual factors included eight elements, which were physical features of the text, genre, content, authors, linguistic difficulties, reading, illustration and text organisation (Janan, 2011; Janan & Wray, 2012; Wray & Janan, 2013a,

2013b). This research concluded that the concept of readability was a complex matching process involving dynamic interactions between reader and text factors and bound by specific contexts. I have summarised the research findings (see Figure 5.3) in diagrammatic form (Janan, 2011).

The developed readability model suggests that the concept of readability is influenced by both reader and textual factors and is bound by its context. This model is a dynamic model that changes as the components of the model change. Therefore, the elements in both the reader and the textual factors are not fixed. The list of elements in the reader and text factors depends on the interaction between the reader and the text and their context. Given this, readability is defined as the complex processes of dynamic interaction between the reader and the textual factors bound by a particular context.

In this chapter, I extend the discussion from the previous study to consider the notion of readability in the Asian context. Being an Asian, I wondered whether the model of readability developed for the English language would be the same for readers in Asia, since in many parts of Asia many are literate in more than two languages. Due to diverse ethnicities and cultures that intertwine with the one another, the phenomenon of codes exchanging, mixing and borrowing are constantly taking place. In trying to understand this phenomenon, I conduct a study in the Malay language regarding readability (Janan, Muhammad, & Jumadi, 2014). The research was funded by the Ministry of Education Malaysia under the scheme of the Research Acculturation Grant Scheme (RAGS).

For the research in the Malaysian setting, I replicated the research that I had done in the United Kingdom. The research approaches were the same and still

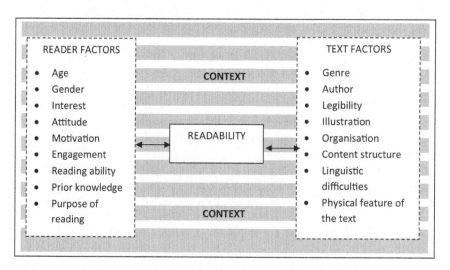

Figure 5.3 The new model of readability

Source: Janan, 2011.

combined quantitative and qualitative research paradigms. Data collection methods still included readability formulas, text feature analysis, miscue analysis, retelling and interview. The research conducted in Malaysia involved 24 teachers and 72 boys and 72 girls between the ages of 7 and 12 years old. In Malaysia, boys and girls at the age of 7 and 12 years old are pupils in Standard One to Standard Six in primary school. All participants were good readers. Data were analysed using one readability formula (Khadijah Rohani, 1982); Reading Miscue Inventory (Goodman et al., 2005); Judging Richness of Retellings (Irwin & Mitchell, 1983); text feature analysis form and a cross-interview analysis approach.

In this research, 144 texts were used and 72 of them were used in Reading Event One (RE1), where the text was selected by the participants themselves. Seventy-two different texts were used in Reading Event Two (RE2), selected by the participants' teachers. The criteria for text selection were based on text suitability for participants according to the teachers' assumptions and knowledge of their pupils' reading levels. The rationale behind these were still the same, which was to compare the similarities and differences of participants' interactions with the text used in RE1 and RE2.

The data resulting from this research were very extensive. To answer whether the model of readability developed for English literacy would be the same for use in an Asian context, I am going to present a case study comparing the phenomena of cases in the United Kingdom and in Malaysia.

Reader, text and context: factors in readability

This case study focuses on two good readers with different languages who come from different countries and cultural backgrounds and interact with texts that they chose to read. The idea of this analysis is to ascertain whether the readability model will be different if the language and cultural background of the readers were changed. The name of the cases have been changed in order to protect the confidentiality of the research participants.

Our first case is a girl whom I named Sabrina. Sabrina lives in the United Kingdom. She is 11 years old. She attends a state school in the United Kingdom and she is a free choice reader taught through the Oxford Reading Tree program (free choice readers were those who had finished their Oxford Reading Tree scheme successfully). She is a fluent reader, and her hobby is reading. Sabrina is a monolingual case, as she can only speak, read and write in English. The second case is a girl who lives in Malaysia. I name her Aina, and she is 11 years old. She attends a national school in Malaysia. Aina is categorised as a fluent reader according to the NILAM reading project. NILAM, which stands for *Nadi Ilmu Amalan Membaca* is an intensive reading program planned for all Malaysian pupils in a national school. Similar to Sabrina, Aina is a fluent reader, and her hobby is reading. Aina is a bilingual case, as she can speak, read and write in Malay and English. In this research, Aina chose to talk about the book she read in the Malay language.

As mentioned earlier, data collection involved two reading events. Sabrina and Aina were asked to read two books in two reading events called RE1 and RE2. In RE1, Sabrina and Aina were allowed to choose a book that they liked to read, and in RE2, I chose the book for Sabrina to read, and Aina's teacher chose the book for her to read. In this chapter, I will only discuss the comparison of RE1. Data collection methods involved miscue analysis, retelling and an interview. I will start this comparison by presenting data collected through the interviews. During the interviews, Sabrina and Aina were asked to talk about the book that they chose to read.

Interview

In the interview, I started my questioning by asking why they chose the book. Sabrina chose a book with the title *Eragon*, written by C. Paolini (2004). According to Sabrina, she chose to read this book because she found the story very interesting, and she further explained that it was because she liked stories that contain mysterious things. Another factor that influenced Sabrina was her cousin. According to Sabrina, her cousin gave a very impressive testimony that *Eragon* was one of the best books that he had read, and he wanted Sabrina to read it so that they could discuss it. Sabrina also mentioned she really liked the *Eragon* story because she had watched a movie that was based on it. She said:

> Well because my cousin did recommend it to me and I have watched the film and it looked good. . . . And that so when my cousin he like 14–15 read this one (*Eragon*) and said he read it load of times and he doesn't read it anymore and I can borrow it.
>
> (Janan, 2011)

Sabrina mentioned that after reading the book she preferred to read the book more than watching the movie, and this was because at some stage the movie could not show/describe the scenes that took place in the book. Nevertheless, Sabrina did mention that the movie had influenced her choice of reading. She said:

> Like mostly I like my *Twilight* books that I was talking about before cause I saw the film and everything and on the back of the DVD it say like find *Twilight* books at bookshop near you if you like it. I went ask mom can you really buy this. I bought the first two books and read on and like then I bought the other two books and finished them all now.
>
> (Janan, 2011)

Sabrina's choice of reading was also influenced by the author of a book. She mentioned she particularly liked reading story books written by Stephanie Mare.

Sabrina also believed by reading these kinds of books that she was a good reader because she had the ability to read such difficult books. Books that have suspense elements were also Sabrina's favourites, as she thought the suspense elements made the book interesting. She said:

> And I like the author Stephanie Mare. And I'm going to ask them could I buy the whole stage of books that she write. I think it is going to be a good one because she wrote *Twilight*.
>
> (Janan, 2011)

Aina read a book titled *Apabila Mama Pakai Abaya* (*When my mom wears Abaya*), by Mama Bella (2012). According to Aina, she chose to read this book because the book cover attracted her so much. She thought the cover of the book was so beautiful. Apart from that, she thought book titles that appeared with glitter or gold dust attracted her to choose the book to read. Aina also mentioned that the content of the story had influenced her to choose to read the book. She mentioned she liked it because the story was about a mom who liked to wear tight-fitting clothing and her children did not like it. She mentioned the story had moral value that attracted her. She also mentioned that because the character in the book seemed similar with what had happened in her home, it drew her to read the book until the end. She said:

> Sebab, best la cerita itu. dia menceritakan pasal mamanya yang suka pakai baju ketat-ketat, sendat-sendat, lepas tu, anaknya nak sangat melihat mamanya memakai baju yang longgar-longgar tetapi mamanya memungkiri janji mereka tu.
>
> (Janan et al., 2014).

> The reason, story best la. The story told me about mother who liked to wear tight fitted dress, snug-tight, after that the children really want to see their mother wear lose clothes but mother broke her promise.

Aina preferred books that helped to build up good personality. Most of the books she chose were on how to become a number-one person or how to be popular. Aina was concerned about the price of the books before she read them. This might be because the books she liked to read were not provided in the school library, and her parents had to buy them. Apart from that, Aina also preferred books that had less complicated language so that it was easy for her to read and understand them. She also preferred smaller-sized books, as they were easy to carry around. She said:

> Cara dia tulis tu boleh faham . . . Buku dia kecil senang dibawa ke mana-mana sahaja untuk dibaca. . . . Harga dia tak mahal sangat la.
>
> (Janan et al., 2014)

How the book is written can be understood. . . . Small books are easy to take anywhere to read. . . . The price is not very expensive.

(Janan et al., 2014)

To understand the interaction between a reader and a text more deeply, both of the cases were also asked about their reading strategies. Sabrina explained that her reading strategies when encountering difficult words in reading were that first she looked at the glossary, tried to break down words into small chunks and if that did not give her any meaning, she read the whole sentence and guessed the meaning of the word. Apart from that, she also would ask an adult like her mum. She said:

I don't know cause some of the words has announcement at the back of the book got like a glossary cause it really tells us how to pronounce and everything, and it's like really like the medieval like that. . . . I just like break it down and I think like words that might mean the same as them and if it doesn't make sense I read the rest of the sentence and eventually I get it. And if not then I just ask mom.

(Janan, 2011)

Aina, on the other hand, used the dictionary right away when encountering difficult words in reading. If she could not find the meaning from the dictionary, only then would she ask her brother or parents. According to Aina, her brother or parents did not give the answer right away but guided her to understand the meaning by going through the text together.

Tanya kepada ibu atau ayah. Pastu cari dalam kamus. Kalau tak jumpa cari jer, tanya pada abang. Mereka cakap, contohnya ini bermaksud apa . . . apa la yang dimaksudkan dalam petikan tu, pastu maksud dia selain dari maksud yang diberi itu.

(Janan et al., 2014)

Ask your mom or dad. Definitely look up in the dictionary. If you can't find it, ask your brother. They say, for example, what does this mean?

(Janan et al., 2014)

Through the interview session, it was clear that Sabrina had a positive opinion about herself. She mentioned she was a good reader, as she read really thick books compared to her friends who read only thin books. She also confirmed that her parents were told by the teacher that Sabrina was reading at the same level as 12- to 13-year-olds. She said:

Like last parents evening or something well I was in year 5 I think they spoke to my teacher. She said that I have to read like the age of 12 to 13 years old you know something like that. So I knew I was good reader then. Some kid in my class read like really thin book and I'm reading something like 700 pages.

(Janan, 2011)

Aina also thought she was a good reader. She mentioned she read all the time regardless of the place—in the classroom, at home, on the bus, while waiting for friends and even during sight-seeing. She mentioned she was a good reader because she knew how to choose a good book to read for herself. Apart from that, she said good readers also wrote the words that they understood and could find out the meaning from the dictionary. She said:

Ya. Di mana-mana sahaja saya baca buku, kat rumah, jalan-jalan pun baca buku, sambil tunggu kawan pun baca. Memahami apa yang ditulis di dalam buku itu. Faham jalan cerita dia, dia pandai memilih buku yang sesuai untuk diri dia. Sebab setiap hari mereka membaca buku, dia tulis perkataan yang tidak faham di buku lain pastu buka kamus cari perkataan yang tidak faham.

(Janan et al., 2014)

Yes. Everywhere I read books, at home reading books, while waiting for friends. Understand what is written in the book. Understands the story, good at choosing the right book for her. Because every day they read a book, they write words that they do not understand in another book and open the dictionary to find words they do not understand.

(Janan et al., 2014)

The interview session ended with questions on how Sabrina and Aina defined reading. Sabrina had a positive attitude towards reading because she could carry books everywhere. She also defined reading as words that works together to form sentences. Aina also had a positive attitude towards reading because to her, reading would prevent her from wasting time, help her to improve her speech, to be good in talking, learn new things and write poems. To Aina, reading was doing something with a book.

Miscue and retelling

To find out Sabrina's and Aina's levels of comprehension during reading, I used miscue analysis (Goodman & Burke, 1973) and retelling (Irwin & Mitchell, 1983). Miscue analysis as a research method was developed by Kenneth Goodman in 1973 with the aim of enhancing the understanding of the reading process. Miscue analysis may be a way of explaining and evaluating reader control over the reading process. Through the analysis of miscues, readers' strengths and the strategies they use to understand and build meaning can be identified (Davenport, 2002).

In these two research projects, I analysed six types of miscue: substitution, insertion, omission, repetition, correction and hesitation. *Substitution* is when the reader substitutes something else in place of the written text. An *insertion* is where the reader inserted words or phrases which were not in the text. An *omission* happens when the reader misses a word or part of a word in the text. A *repetition* miscue happens when the reader repeats a word that they have read in the text and a *correction* happens when the readers correct themselves when making a mistake reading a word or part of a word. *Hesitation* is when the reader hesitates to read a word or part of a word.

In analysing Sabrina and Aina's miscues, it was found that more than 50% of both their miscues were substitutions. Apart from that, both Sabrina and Aina made insertion miscues as well, and this suggested that they were both acting as editors to improve the text or change it to maximise their understanding. It was also detected that Sabrina made self-correction miscues when checking her reading. This analysis suggests that both Aina and Sabrina were good readers. Aina showed that she tended to make less complex miscues than Sabrina.

Sabrina's miscues were interesting, as she seemed to be making a new story out of the text she read. She seems to act as an editor to improve the text she is reading to maximise her comprehension. In Example One, Sabrina produced substitution miscues in which she substituted words for the text on the page that she was reading (see Figure 5.4). The way she substituted the text with different words was fascinating, as the substitutions still provided the text with meaning, as if she had created a different story. For instance, Sabrina changed "he whispered and she whickered back at him" in the text to "he whispered as she whispered back to him".

Sabrina's miscues were more complex in Example Two (see Figure 5.5). She not only made substitution miscues but also correction miscues as well as insertion miscues at the same time. This suggests that Sabrina was struggling to

Figure 5.4 Sabrina's miscues: Example One

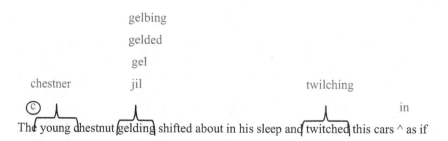

Figure 5.5 Sabrina's miscues: Example Two

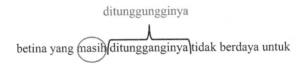

Figure 5.6 Aina's miscues: Example One

Figure 5.7 Aina's miscues: Example Two

understand the sentence, and this can be seen in how she substituted words and corrected them in her reading (e.g. reading the word "chestnut" as "chestner" and correcting it back to "chestnut". Sabrina was struggling so much with the word "gelding" that she made four corrections (i.e "jil, gel, gelded, gelbing") until finally she got the word as "gelding". In the same sentence, she substituted the word "twitched" with "twilching" and inserted the word "in".

Aina's miscues were not as complex as Sabrina's and involved only substitutions, omissions and insertions. Aina's omitted words tended to be adjectives, "masih", as seen in Example One. She also substituted the word "ditunggang-inya" with "ditunggungginya", a word which does not have any meaning, which suggests that she was having a little difficulty understanding the sentence. She also did not correct her substitution (see Figure 5.6).

Aina also inserted words into the text while reading but on a different basis to Sabrina. Sabrina's insertions were words that had meaning, whereas Aina's insertions were of words that did not have any meaning such as "*eh*" (see Figure 5.7).

Retelling

Retelling is a strategy that is used to determine how well a student has comprehended a specific story. Retelling can be used as an effective tool in improving comprehension as well as assessing it (Jennings, Caldwell, & Lerner, 2014, p. 268). In this research I have used Irwin and Mitchell's (1983) retelling scale to assess Sabrina's and Aina's comprehension of the text they read. According to this scale, Sabrina and Aina achieved different retelling levels.

As mentioned earlier, Sabrina chose to read the storybook entitled *Eragon*. Sabrina was given a 300-word passage to read and then asked to retell the passage she had read. Sabrina's retelling achieved Level 1, according to Irwin and Mitchell's (1983) retelling scale. This shows that Sabrina in her retelling related only the details of the story. She also had the tendency to include irrelevant supplementary details, and this is also shown in her miscues that included a lot of miscorrections or words in her reading aloud. Apart from that, Sabrina's retelling showed a low degree of coherence until at some point it was incomplete and incomprehensible. The reason for the low retelling level was perhaps based on the book she chose to read, which was a difficult one—in keeping with her interview data where she mentioned that she liked to read challenging books. Sabrina's choice of book provides evidence that difficult reading material does affect reader comprehension, although the readers chose the material themselves.

Aina, on the other hand, chose to read a storybook entitled *Bayi Luar Biasa*. As with Sabrina, Aina was given 300 words of a passage to read and retell. Aina's retelling shows she understood the book she chose, and she achieved Level 3, according to Irwin and Mitchell's (1983) retelling scale. This level shows that Aina's retelling relates to major ideas in the story and includes appropriate supporting and supplementary details and relevant ideas. Her retelling also shows adequate coherence, completeness and comprehension. During the interview sessions Aina mentioned she was a good reader because she knew how to choose an appropriate book for herself. In this case, Aina's choice of book was appropriate to her, as her miscues showed less mistaken corrections than those of Sabrina. Apart from that, Aina preferred to read things which were close to her daily life activities, which made the book she chose to read less unfamiliar to her compared to Sabrina's choice. Aina's retelling shows that context is a significant factor during the interaction between the reader and the text.

Discussion

The discussion section of this chapter is divided into two subsections. The first section will be discussion related to *"the new model of readability"* (Janan, 2011), and the second section is related to research on readability in Malaysia.

The new model of readability

The new model of readability (Janan, 2011), suggests that the concept of reading is influenced by the factors of the reader and the text and is tied to the context. The model is a dynamic model in that the elements in both the reader and the textual factors are not fixed but depend upon the interaction between the reader and the text and its context. The case studies of Sabrina and Aina were put forward to show the complex interactions between a reader and the text. It is clear that Sabrina and Aina interacted and transacted with their reading material in very complex ways. Their understanding of the text they read depended on many factors, some of which were internal and some external. Sabrina and Aina were also observed to use a variety of strategies to understand the text, which did not only depend on the text but also on aspects of their lives. People near or close to both of them helped or influenced them to read certain reading materials.

The case studies also suggest the need to consider factors in the reader when assessing the reading and reading comprehension process. Since text readability is closely related to reading and reading comprehension, it also seems that judgments about text readability also need to take reader factors into account. A final significant finding of these case studies of Sabrina and Aina is that different cultural backgrounds create different ways of looking at text. Thus, this study suggests that text readability involves more than just a focus on text contents and features but also lies in the reader and the context.

Sabrina and Aina's case studies suggest that *the new model of readability* (Janan, 2011) is stable as a model to explain the new view of readability. The model shows that although different languages, English and Malay, and different cultural background, British and Malay, were at play here, the factors involved during the interactions between the reader and the text remain the same. Looking back at these case studies, I can say that perhaps the similar factors in the interactions between these readers and their texts were caused by both English and Malay language texts being written in alphabetical scripts. This assumption opens up new windows for further research and discussion of readability which involve the diversity of the cultural backgrounds of Malaysians.

Research on readability in Malaysia

Now let's look at research on readability in Malaysia as it relates to the previous conclusion about *the new model of readability* (Janan, 2011). *The new model of readability* can be applied during the interaction of readers with English and the Malay language because these two languages are written in alphabetical script. This assumption opens new opportunities to conduct research on the interaction between readers and texts in other dominant languages in Malaysia such as Tamil and Chinese. This will be interesting, as the Tamil language has different forms of written text and the Chinese language has logographic written text. Sabrina's and Aina's case studies refer to the interaction between the reader and the text of their first language. Hence, as Malaysians have a diversity of races, with each individual having more than one spoken language, future research will be an opportunity to look into the interaction between readers with texts in a second language. While doing research on readability, I found out that there was only one readability formula in existence for the Malay language (Khadijah Rohani, 1982); This is another area of research which should be explored in term of research of readability, not only in Malaysia but in other Asian countries such as Singapore and Brunei, which use the Malay language. Nevertheless, readability should not be considered as the only answer to the problem of book-level assessment and determining the suitability of reading material (Janan & Wray, 2014).

Conclusion

The findings of the research show that there is little difference in the factors affecting the two cases of readers from different backgrounds when interacting with texts. In terms of the factors affecting them, more similarities were found than differences. *The New Model of Readability* (Janan, 2011) suggests that readability is determined by complex processes of dynamic interaction between the reader and the text bound by a particular context. Further research suggests that this model can be applied across different cultural backgrounds. Nevertheless, the case study findings also suggest the possibility of new research areas to be explored in term of the suitability of *the New Model of Readability* (Janan, 2011) when it comes to reading in second or foreign languages.

Acknowledgment

Some data in this chapter are based on research that has been carried out under Research Acculturation Grant Scheme (Code RAGS/2013/0019/107/72) provided by the Ministry of Education of Malaysia. The authors would like to extend their gratitude to Universiti Pendidikan Sultan Idris (UPSI), which helped manage the grants. The further development of writing this chapter has been facilitated by activities funded by FRGS/1/2018/SS109/UTP/02/01. The author would also like to acknowledge Nur Farah Syafaf Jamil for the Silly Simon illustration.

References

Brookshire, J., Scharff, L. F. V., & Moses, L. E. (2002). The influence of illustrations on children's book preferences and comprehension. *Reading Psychology, 23*, 323–339.

Dale, E., & Chall, J. S. (1948). A formula for predicting readability. *Educational Research Bulletin, 27*(1), 11–28.

Davenport, M. R. (2002). *Miscues not mistakes: Reading assessment in the classroom.* Portsmouth, NH: Heinemann.

Flesch, R. (1948). A new readability yardstick. *Journal of Applied Psychology, 32*(3), 221–233. https://doi.org/10.1037/h0057532

Gilliland, J. (1972). *Readability.* London: Hodder and Stoughton.

Goodman, K., & Burke, C. (1973). *Theoretically based studies of patterns of miscues in oral reading performance, final report.* Wayne State University, Detroit (Eric Document Reproduction Service No, ED 179 708).

Goodman, Y., Watson, D., & Burke, C. (2005). *Reading miscue inventory.* Katonah, NY: Richard C. Owen Publishers, Inc.

Gunning, R. (1952). *The technique of clear writing.* New York, NY: McGraw-Hill.

Irwin, P. A., & Mitchell, J. N. (1983). A procedure for assessing the richness of retellings. *Journal of Reading, 26*(5), 391–396.

Jalongo, M. R., Dragich, D., Conrad, N. K., et al. (2002). Using wordless picture books to support emergent literacy. *Early Childhood Education Journal, 29*, 167–177. https://doi.org/10.1023/A:1014584509011

Janan, D. (2011). *Towards a new model of readability* (PhD thesis). University of Warwick. Retrieved from http://webcat.warwick.ac.uk/record=b2585522~S1

Janan, D., Muhammad, M., & Jumadi, D. (2014). *Memadankan Pembaca Kepada Teks: Satu Tinjauan Model Baharu Kebolehbacaan Teks Bahasa Melayu/Matching reader to text: Review of a new model of readability for Malay language* (Unpublished research report). Universiti Pendidikan Sultan Idris, Tanjong Malim. Malaysia.

Janan, D., & Wray, D. (2012). *Guidance on the principles of language accessibility in national curriculum assessments: Research background.* London: OFQUAL.

Janan, D., & Wray, D. (2013). 'Research into readability: Paradigms and possibilities'. In A. Pandian, C. Liew Ching Ling, D. Tan Ai Lin, J. Muniandy, L. Bee Choo, & T. Chwee Hiang (Eds.), *New literacies: Reconstructing language and education* (pp. 296–303). Newcastle: Cambridge Scholars Publishing.

Janan, D., & Wray, D. (2014). Reassessing the accuracy and use of readability formulae. *Malaysian Journal of Learning and Instruction, 11*(1), 127–145.

Janan, D., Wray, D., & Pope, M. (2010). Paradigms in readability research. *International Journal of Arts and Sciences, 3*(17), 19–29.

Jennings, J., Caldwell, J., & Lerner, J. (2014). *Retelling story.* Cambridge: Cambridge University Press.

Khadijah Rohani Md. Yunus. (1982). *An Assessment of structural variables in Malay: A readability formula* (Disertasi Doktor Falsafah yang tidak diterbitkan). Universiti of Miami, Miami, FL.

Mama Bella. (2012). Apabila Mama Pakai Abaya. Batu Caves. PTS One Sdn.Bhd.

McKenna, M. C., Kear, D. J., & Ellsworth, R. A. (1995). Children's attitudes toward reading: A national survey. *Reading Research Quarterly, 30*(4), 934–956.

McLaughlin, G. H. (1969). SMOG grading—A new readability formula. *Journal of Reading, 22,* 639–646.

Milone, M. (2012). *The development of ATOS: The renaissance readability formula. Renaissance Learning, Inc.* Wisconsin Rapids, WI: Author. Retrieved from http://mpemc.weebly.com/uploads/5/4/0/7/5407355/development_of_atos.pdf

Ozuru, Y., Dempsey, K., & McNamara, D. S. (2009). Prior knowledge, reading skill, and text cohesion in the comprehension of science texts. *Learning and Instruction, 19*(3), 228–242.

Paolini, C. (2004). *Eragon.* London: Doubleday.

Samuels, S. J. (1983). A cognitive approach to factors influencing reading comprehension. *Journal of Educational Research, 76*(5), 261–266.

Strasser, J., & Seplocha, H. (2007) Using picture books to support young children's literacy. *Childhood Education, 83*(4), 219–224. doi:10.1080/00094056.2007.10 522916

Wray, D. (2004). *Teaching literacy: Using texts to enhance learning.* London: David Fulton.

Wray, D., & Janan, D. (2013a). Readability revisited? The implications of text complexity. *Curriculum Journal, 24*(4), 553–562.

Wray, D., & Janan, D. (2013b). Exploring the readability of assessment tasks: The influence of text and reader factors. *Multidisciplinary Journal of Educational Research, 3*(1), 69–95. doi:10.4471/remie.2013.04

Wu, H. Y., & Hu, P. (2007). Major factors influencing reading comprehension: A factor analysis approach. *Sino-US English Teaching, 4*(9), 14–19.

6 Articulating abstractions

Building teacher–student connections in the literature classroom

Priscilla Angela T. Cruz

Introduction and background

I have loved reading all my life (see Figure 6.1 of me reading at a cafe). Because I came from a family that always valued books, I had no problems finding things to read. As is common among many Filipino families, I grew up in my grandparents' compound with an extended family. My grandparents were wealthy in the decades after World War II, so my father and his sisters were allowed to buy all the books they could read during the summer months. Although family fortunes fell and we eventually became too poor to afford new books, I already had access to a legacy of reading. An aunt of mine also took up literature in college in the late sixties, so I had all her books, too. By the time I hit high school, I had already read the "classics" of Anglo-American literature. The Philippines, for decades, was under American "benevolent assimilation", so our educational curricula was largely characterised by Anglo-American texts. So as someone inheriting books from this curriculum, I had learned to love Shakespeare, Jane Austen, E.M. Forster and Louisa May Alcott by the time I was 12. This love extended to literature from Asia, Latin America, Africa, Eastern Europe and the Middle East as I encountered them in university.

However, it was hard for me to love literature as a student of literature. I studied literature for my BA and my MA, and I realise that I did not love literature then. I think it was because studying literature was about pleasing the perspective of whomever I had teaching me. Novels, short stories, poems—these were all taught in classes that had specific agendas, whether it was to analyse them from a Marxist, feminist or postcolonial perspective. There was no time to *love* a text for what I thought it meant to me. Eventually, I started teaching in the same university I studied in, and I also found that as a teacher I would have to approach my classes with an agenda, whether it was to use literature to teach close reading, critical thinking or some other position which, like all positions, are ideologically charged (Christie, 1999). I also had to be strict about examining how students engaged with literature, that is, were their interpretations of a text within certain acceptable parameters? And what kind of interpretation gets the A or the F? Because I have always known literature to be a highly personal experience, I started to wonder if there could be a better way—one that allowed teachers and

Figure 6.1 I always have a book to read, wherever I go

students, *as individuals meeting in a classroom to discuss literature*, to engage with the text, engage with each other, while at the same time produce interpretations to "examinable" standards. This interest led me to investigate what exactly a literary interpretation is and the differences between the way a teacher would handle it and the way a student might handle it.

As I eventually became an English language and literature teacher, my university career has always focused on the interface between language and literature teaching. More importantly, I moved on to focus on the close links between language as text and language as context. That led me to Systemic Functional Linguistics (hereafter SFL), which argues that language is the *realisation* (Martin & White, 2005) of context, so studying literature, or any text for that matter, could not be divorced from studying how the patterns of grammar are also patterns of culture. As such, interpretation cannot be viewed as only a skills-based activity. It is instead one that involves articulating certain patterns of meaning that are acceptable within specific contexts. It is with exploring *close reading* or what goes on when different people interpret a text, and what makes an interpretation acceptable or not, that I begin this chapter.

A word about the research context

The Philippines is a country of over 170 languages (MacFarland, 2009), but for many decades English has been the medium of instruction (MOI) of schools. A legacy from an American colonial past, it is not surprising that the "grip of English" (Lorente, 2013) remains all over the Philippines, as the language is considered valuable social capital and a ticket to varied economic and social opportunities, especially as the Philippines is a major destination for business process outsourcing firms which demand strong English skills. Furthermore, as the country exports human capital via overseas foreign workers who all need English skills to get much-coveted visas, English instruction is a valued part of education.

Literature seems to have a two-pronged role in the English curriculum in the Philippines. On one hand, it is considered part of language arts, which means that reading literary texts can be part of language teaching. However, its other role is a more regulative one (Christie, 1999). Literature has been a part of the English curriculum of the Philippines since the country's educational system was fashioned by the Americans for a colonial agenda. Martin (2009) points out that teaching Anglo-American literature to Filipinos was part of the process of creating the "brown American". As such, what literature Filipinos received at the first few decades of the 20th century were "white, Anglo-Saxon Protestant male" writing, such as texts by Longfellow, Irving, Emerson, Shakespeare and Defoe. Literature was then taught not for the sake of literature but for the sake of shaping a colonised populace. This narrow sort of reading list, consisting of the Western canon, persisted for many years and actually explains why my early experiences with literature all involved the Western classics.

Today, the Philippines is under the Department of Education (DepEd), which oversees basic education, and the Commission on Higher Education (CHED) for higher or tertiary education and university. However, the regulative use of literature still remains. I have argued elsewhere (Cruz, 2016, 2018) that although there is a lot of space now for so-called "world lit", what may still persist are texts selected for formative functions—that is, values education or shaping students to be a certain type of pedagogic subject who uphold the right perspectives toward texts. This is similar to a finding that Christie (1999) and Macken-Horarik (2003) argue. In this case, literature education is about coming to the "correct" interpretation of a text, which gets the high grade in the exam.

The problem with using literature for regulative purposes is that interpretation becomes a hierarchical zone where some meanings are more valued than others. Upholding a hierarchy of meaning may actually defeat the purpose of a literature class, which, as Paran (2010) points out, is meant to focus on internal goals, such as personal change and developing a greater understanding of one's self in society. However, standard meanings which are graded do not necessarily encourage this kind of personal growth or expression. They instead encourage the students to re-create meanings that are already available (Rothery & Stenglin, 2000; Paran, 2010), perhaps enshrined in the notion of an ideal reader (the teacher), who, as Macken-Horarik (2003) argues, upholds certain interpretations that may not, in fact, be the only ones possible. Furthermore, acceptable meanings are also ideologically charged and may be disempowering for certain groups of people (Cruz, 2017). In this chapter, I explore what goes on when people interpret a literary text outside the hierarchical structure of the classroom. In this way, the best practices of personal interpretation and classroom interpretation can be combined to design literature pedagogies that balance institutional agendas and the personal positions that students and teachers bring when they engage with literature.

The participants and data-gathering instruments

Four participants were asked to respond to interview questions which were sent by email. Two of the respondents are teachers who have taught literature classes in both secondary and tertiary education in the Philippines. The other two respondents finished a literature degree from a university in the Philippines. All participants describe themselves as readers who like to read a wide variety of material. To ensure an ethical research process, they were given consent forms to sign and were told that their participation in this study was purely voluntary. They could also stop participating anytime. All gave their consent and fully participated in the study. To protect privacy, the names *Jess, Darren, Sally* and *Cath* were assigned to each participant. As this volume has an auto/biographical stance, I also participated in the study. Where necessary, my responses will be presented using my nickname, *Prixie*.

Part of the study asked the respondents to read the poem *Mountain afternoon* and write a short interpretation. As my interest is in looking at the act of interpretation itself, no one interpretation was judged as either right or wrong. All were simply studied tactically, as "linguistic exemplars" (Martin & White, 2005) rather than as samples of "rightness" or "wrongness". It is these interpretations by the participants, and not the poem, that is the subject of the investigation conducted in this chapter.

Theorising interpretation

Central to interpreting a text is *reading comprehension*. A simple definition of this would be the ability to understand what the text is saying. However, as Harrison (2004) points out, reading comprehension is not easy to define and has to be "considered context-specific as well as text-specific" (p. 53). It is useful to unpack the notions of "context", "text", and the intersection between the two.

SFL, following the work of linguist M.A.K. Halliday, posits that context is an abstraction; that is, as mentioned earlier, *realised* through discourse, lexicogrammatical and phonological/morphological patterns (Martin & Rose, 2007). In other words, what we know as "context" is known through "text" or the "social exchange of meanings" (Halliday, 1985) that we manage through language. Halliday (2009) further relates context and language thus:

> [L]anguage evolved as part—moreover the most unconscious part—of every human culture, it functioned as the primary means whereby the deepest perception of the members, their joint construction of shared experience into social reality, were constantly reaffirmed and transmitted. Thus, in this sense the culture provided the context within which words and, more generally, grammatical systems were interpreted.
>
> (p. 68)

So knowing context is dependent on to what extent individuals know language and the social processes, or genres, that we manage through language (Martin & Rose, 2007). However, access to language is not equally given. For example, I am very comfortable with English, but I have very little access to the English used in the hard sciences. Similarly, people growing up in different English-speaking countries would have differing access to the vocabulary and grammar of other English-speaking countries, as Kachru (1986) argues in his work on world Englishes. Where interpreting is concerned, it may not be safe to assume that all readers faced with the interpreting task will access and understand the intersection between language and context in the same way. Hence, part of the fun of interpreting literature is the exchange between readers when they discuss a text (Paran, 2010). In such an exchange, there is no narrow set of meanings that need to be encouraged. There is instead a lot of play as each reader has something to say about how the text is significant to him or her. This is not at all what happens in the classroom, where students may feel that they have to guess what is on their teacher's mind to do well in the class.

Other SFL work has focused on *individuation*, which can be described as "the relationship between the reservoir of meanings in a culture and the repertoire a given individual can mobilize" (Martin, 2010, p. 23). "Cultures" are large, generalised constructs, but all cultures have their own subgroupings, whether due to age, gender or those that bond around any number of things, such as tech, "cult" TV shows and movies and even certain texts, like fan fiction. These subcultures cut across national boundaries and national cultures into groups that are held together by mutual interest. Looking at culture through individuation tells us that not all members of any one culture, or users of the same language, will have access to the same meanings the "reservoir" makes possible. So depending on what "culture" readers belong in, they may access reservoirs of potential meanings in different ways. In a poetry class I taught once, a student mentioned to me that he thought a haiku I discussed was about werewolves. This student was into the horror genre, so to him, a lot of the readings from my class took on a gothic dimension, especially when images of darkness were brought up. I was placed in the uncomfortable position of deciding whether to tell him off or to allow the exploration. Since it was a quiz, I had to tell him off, but to this day I wonder if I could have handled that situation better.

Rothery and Stenglin (2000) describe interpretation to generally involve students articulating the "culturally conventional message(s) in a literary work (novel, poem, play, thematic narrative, etc.)" (p. 225) and explain how this message is "constructed in the text" (p. 223). In her discussion on narratives, Macken-Horarik (2003) posits that these messages tend to be *axiological* (see Martin, 2008; Cruz, 2016 for further discussions on axiologies), or expressing value positions that are shared by a community. Readers are asked to feel *empathy* for characters that express these values and to *discern* or "stand over" characters, in order to evaluate them ethically (Macken-Horarik, 2003). Although her work was on narratives, Macken-Horarik's two-part reader position of empathy and discernment can be applied to all interpretation tasks, as students are asked to understand what characters or personas feel in order to evaluate them.

Another dimension of interpretation that has to be examined is writing the interpretative task itself. Harrison (2004) also describes reading comprehension as "task-related". The work of Macken-Horarick (2006) on *grammatics* is useful here. She distinguishes *grammatics* and *grammar*, where the former "refer[s] to tools for analysing language and *grammar* to refer to language choices inherent in acts of communication" (p. 106, emphasis original). This chapter will use grammatics to analyse the responses of the participants to the interpretative task. Doing so will explore interpretation as not just a content issue but a grammatical one. From the perspective of SFL, content is expressed through grammar and discourse choices (Martin, 1997), so from this angle it is possible to examine the "linguistic patterns that work together (or conspire) to produce particular fashions of meaning" (Macken-Horarick, 2006, p. 103). An analysis of the interpretation task from grammatics can also help equip teachers with the linguistic tools they can use to teach students how to do an interpretation. While teachers may not be able to easily teach the content of interpretation, which can be largely influenced by the students' experiences, using the grammatical patterns of interpreting is something that can be built in the classroom. The important question is, what are the patterns of interpretation? And how are they expressed in grammar?

Finding meaning in a poem: what goes on in an interpretation?

In her work on using narratives in school contexts, Macken-Horarick (2006) points out that the students' ability to construct a *relational reading* is important, which is the ability to relate something concrete with an abstract idea. Someone who does the interpretation task successfully is able to link this abstract idea to the text as a whole, to write an "extended analogy" (p. 119) that constantly "recodes" a literal meaning into a symbolic one (Macken-Horarick, 2006). An interpretation would articulate the symbolic meaning and link it to the concrete. This describes the process of "close reading" that teachers follow where the concrete words of the text are examined for symbolic meanings. Macken-Horarick (2006) adds that in a successful interpretation task, students see "motivated connections" (p. 103) between concrete details and abstract ideas.

For this chapter, the respondents were given a copy of the poem, *Mountain afternoon* by noted Philippine poet Danilo Francisco M. Reyes. Permission to reprint it for this chapter was granted by the author. The poem is from his collection, *Promising lights* (1999).

Mountain afternoon

> *for in this world everything is pardoned in advance*
> —Milan Kundera, *The Unbearable Lightness of Being*

In the noon
Of these mountains,
When the light is white
And does not lie,
The eyes waken without shade
To both loss and leaving:

Leaves of the bamboo
Swirling the light gold,
Nipped by the wind,
The white passing
Of clouds,
And the flight of dust
Rising to sweep through
The slopes of hills.

In this swift
Departure of things,
It is for the eyes
To imagine:

Dust collecting
On blades of tall grass,
Green and slender,
Clouds dissolving
To reveal ferns
And orchids blooming
On the hardness
Of sky shoulders,
And yellow leaves
Sailing on rain water.

If these eyes trust
That dust, clouds, and leaves
Are brought to places
Of safe keeping,

So can ears
Begin to hear the wonder
Of an angel's wings
In the blowing wind—
Dream in the haste
Of its racing—
Waiting for the angel
That will hum the heat
Of all these hills
Away.

And should those eyes
Really learn
To stare, then,
In the name
Of these mountains,
Even such madness will
Be forgiven.

Here are the respondents' interpretations of the poem. All manage the relational or symbolic reading on the whole. Responses were shortened for word count purposes.

Jess: [T]he persona seems to imply that realising nature's power on us **is** a process. It begins with the act of waking our senses, followed by a conscious effort to see the world with the lens of imagination. After which, we then trust and believe in the images that we saw through our mind's eye. The last step in the process **involves** our ability to stare and focus longingly to nature. According to the persona, the moment that we do so, this madness will be forgiven. The introduction of the word madness at this point in the poem **could probably be** a reference to one's disbelief that such occurrences **are** possible and **are** therefore permitted. . . . [T]he poem encourages us to refocus our attention to the simple patterns and processes that nature provides us. In this manner, we'd be able to see that a simple afternoon in the mountain could afford us life's greatest pleasures.

Darren: This unique way of observing nature takes the reader to the metaphysical argument for the existence of God, in terms of (1) *movement,* (2) *contingency* and (3) *order* of things. First, everything in nature moves. And since everything that moves is moved by another, there must exist an *Unmoved Mover.* Second, everything in nature **is** dependent on one another. Since all existent things depend on one another for existence, there must be at least one thing that is not dependent and so **is** a *Necessary Being.* Lastly, everything in nature moves in order. The intricate design and order of existent things and natural processes **imply** that a *Great Designer* exists.

Sally: I got the message of contrast and faith. The first stanza opens by establishing the persona waking to some state of truth ("When the light is white/And does not lie,/The eyes waken without shade," ll. 3–5). The persona sees the beginning of movement, the movement of dust; but they cannot actually see where the dust will go. . . . This **is** where faith enters the picture, specifically when the persona "trust[s]" (l. 29) what he sees and imagines. Imagination can coexist with truth because the persona *believes* that what he imagines *must* be happening. And this sort of attitude is apt for what the persona witnesses, a "[d]eparture of things" (l. 16) that, for me, **translates** as the passing from life to death (and vice versa).

Cath: I think the poem **is** about how we let life pass by because we know that in the end we will be "forgiven" or we know that there is an end to all of this anyway. The poem incorporates images of beauty and images of ugliness. The symbols of nature such as mountains and ferns are tainted with words like "dust" and "hardness." But the speaker seems to say that they don't mind the tainting of nature because they are just waiting for an "angel.". . . . I think the poem is trying to convey the idea that because of the belief that God will forgive us in the end, we let small forms of destruction in human lives take place. And because we put so much weight on this forgiveness and we will let bigger forms of madness happen. I think the speaker in the poem is waiting for his own time to be forgiven.

Prixie: The poem **is** about the small violences that occur in natural processes. It mentions all these acts of violence: dust swirling, leaves flying, clouds moving. It can be assumed that these events are observed on a mountain afternoon where the wind is violent and strong. In their flight, it's not clear where things go but it is good to think of them as 'saved' somehow. But, the poem also tells us that if we accept the violence of nature, we can understand that these changes can be considered beautiful acts of the divine. No matter how much there is hurt and loss, accepting the natural violence of our world (and this is different from artificial, man-made violence) **is** also the key to knowing that there, eventually, will be peace.

Relational readings are expressed through relational clauses (Halliday & Matthiessen, 2004; Macken-Horarick, 2006). These clauses use verbs that construe meanings of being and having to connect two pieces of information or participants. Participants in a clause are people or things who "participate" in whatever is happening. A relational connection posits that these participants are linked through class membership or identity (Halliday & Matthiessen, 2004). Interpretations are relational readings because they "relate" two things based on similarities. This connection through similarity allows for metaphoric understandings, which build on similarities between the concrete and abstract. These relationships are most commonly expressed through the verb *to be* and other verbs that express what Halliday (1994) describes as an "equative" relationship, such as "means," "indicates," "illustrates", "imply", "represents", "symbolises" and "stands for" (see Halliday, 1994, p. 123 for a discussion). Table 6.1 presents a detailed relational analysis for all responses. Only prominent relational clauses were analysed, as these are the clauses that establish the relational reading.

All responses are able to display a relational reading. Table 6.2 shows paraphrases of the abstractions the poem is connected to.

The relational reading establishes what the reader thinks is the message of the text, something all respondents were able to do. It is interesting to note that these relational clauses all occur either at the beginning or end of the interpretations, which are areas of discourse that Martin and Rose (2007) have described as "peak[s] of textual prominence" (p. 189). Locating relational meanings in prominent positions serve to indicate how they express the key meanings of the interpretations. However, although all respondents articulated a relational reading, the content of this reading is not the same. There is a similarity—all readings seem to be about something unseen—but there are differences as well.

It is not surprising that the five people involved would come up with different interpretations. Differences in people, after all, bring out differences in points of view. Darren mentions in the interview that he is a mountaineer, so the poem reminds him of the way he experiences nature as a climber. He also mentions that he once studied to be a Catholic priest, so his point of view may already have an orientation to the message of finding God in nature. Cath mentions how she is not surprised if the poem will have a religious angle, as Filipinos are very Catholic and are told that God definitely forgives. Although a link between personal experience and interpretation are difficult to establish, for my part, I know that the religious angle is probably the last that I will consider, unless a poem overtly has it, such as the poetry of Milton and Dante; hence, my interpretation is a bit more agnostic.

Table 6.1 Detailed relational analysis for all the respondents' interpretations

Respondent		Relational verb	
Jess	realising nature's power on us	is	a process.
	The last step in the process	involves	our ability to stare and focus longingly on nature.
	The introduction of the word madness at this point in the poem	could probably be	a reference to one's disbelief [[that such occurrences are possible and are therefore permitted.]] *embedded clauses are not analysed (Martin, Matthiessen, & Painter, 2010).
Darren	The intricate design and order of existent things and natural processes	imply	that a *Great Designer* exists.
Sally	[the beginning of movement]	is	where faith enters the picture.
	[what the persona imagines]	must be	happening.
	["a departure of things"]	translates	as the passing from life to death.
Cath	The poem	is	about how we let life pass by.
	The poem	incorporates	images of beauty and images of ugliness.
Prixie	The poem	is	about the small violences that occur in natural processes.
	No matter how much there is hurt and loss, accepting the natural violence of our world	is	also the key to knowing that there, eventually, will be peace.

Supporting the meaning: building the extended analogy

The second part of the interpretation task is discussing how the text expresses its purported message. Drawing from Macken-Horarik (2006), this part of the interpretation task concerns *elaboration*, where one meaning is "restated, exemplified, or further specified by another" (Martin et al., 2010, p. 235). As such, it is a grammatical resource for reformulation (Macken-Horarik, 2006). Martin and Rose (2007) further argue that elaboration allows texts to grow. In the analysis in Table 6.3, I show the relational readings identified and the elements in the response that elaborate on it.

Table 6.2 Paraphrasing the abstractions in the responses

Jess	The poem	is	about the power of paying attention to nature.
Darren	The poem	is	about the *Great Designer* or *Unmoved Mover* whose hand is visible in the movements of nature.
Sally	The poem	is	about faith in the unseen and the unseen processes of life and death.
Cath	The poem	is	about God's forgiveness.
Prixie	The poem	is	about the violence that occurs in nature but also the inevitability of peace.

Table 6.3 Elaboration in the responses

Respondents	Abstraction (in bold)	Elaborations
Jess	nature's power on us is a process	- the act of waking our senses - a conscious effort to see the world through the lens of imagination - trust and believe in the images that we saw through our mind's eye - our ability to stare and focus longingly on nature
Darren	This unique way of observing nature takes the reader to the metaphysical argument for the existence of God	- Nature moves, so there is an Unmoved Mover - Nature is dependent, so there is a Necessary Being - Nature's design is intricate, so there is a Great Designer
Sally	I got the message of contrast and faith	- the persona "trust[s]" (l. 29) what he sees and imagines - the persona *believes* that what he imagines *must* be happening
Cath	the poem is about how we let life pass by because we know that in the end we will be "forgiven" or we know that there is an end to all of this anyway	- images of beauty and images of ugliness. - the symbols of nature . . . are tainted - they don't mind the tainting of nature because they are just waiting for an "angel" - because of the belief that God will forgive us in the end, we let small forms of destruction in human lives take place - because we put so much weight on this forgiveness and we will let bigger forms of madness happen
Prixie	The poem is about the small violences that occur in natural processes	- acts of violence: dust swirling, leaves flying, clouds moving - wind is violent and strong - flight [of objects] - violence of nature . . . can be considered beautiful acts of the divine

The discursive movement from concrete to abstract is visible in the responses. Jess moves from the senses to the imagination to feelings of longing. Darren begins with God, possibly the most abstract concept, but he concretises "God" through various ways of naming: the Unmovable Mover, Necessary Being, Great Designer. These names are further concretised by if-then clauses about patterns of order visible in nature. Sally begins with the abstract—faith—and elaborates on this by talking about the contrast between what is seen through the senses and what is believed through the mind. Cath moves from the beauty and ugliness that can be seen through concrete experience and then talks of forgiveness. Finally, my own interpretation begins with concrete movements of violence—the wind blowing things away—but ends with considering these violent movements as divine acts.

Reimagining the literature class: what we can learn from the data

This chapter began with the question of what can be done to build a more equitable literature class, one that is, on one hand, mindful of the standards for interpreting that teachers have to uphold and on the other, also open to students' own interpretations, no matter how different they may be from what is expected. Paran (2010), following the work of Rosenblatt, describes this contrast as the difference between the *efferent reading*, or that which is concerned with public knowledge about literature, such as discussing plot, character, persona, and the *aesthetic reading*, or that which is more concerned with a personal experience, one that links the text with personal experiences and reactions. Based on the data, it seems that the solution is not necessarily in settling for specific parameters on the content of the interpretation, in terms of what abstraction is identified, but the ability to identify a relational reading and elaborate on it. Jess, Darren, Sally, Cath and I can all be considered to have some expertise in literature. Jess, Darren and I have taken graduate courses on literature and teach literature. Sally and Cath have AB Literature degrees, yet all of us offered different interpretations. In this section, I discuss how a literature class can be reimagined to build the skills of articulating and supporting abstract meanings.

First, the expectations for key tasks have to be made clear to the students. It is not uncommon for the literature class to work with a variety of tasks like multiple-choice assessments, role play activities, reports on character or even setting up a class play based on a text. Each activity has a different purpose. However, writing a paper on a text is probably the most valued of all tasks. This means that it has to be clear to students that they are connecting the text to an abstract idea, and it is that abstract idea that they are writing about. In my experience, most instructions for literary analysis papers would say, "Write a short essay on the theme of the poem". But the term "theme" is an abstract idea in itself. What teachers can do instead is to instruct students to think relationally. That is, to tell them that the story or poem they are reading relates to or represents an abstract concept. Students can then be told that they have to articulate that abstract concept in their work. To make it easier, teachers can offer the relational clause and ask the students to fill in the blanks: "The story/poem/film is about _____".

It seems that those with some expertise in literature can do this intuitively. To my respondents, I just gave the question, "What message did you get out of this text and why?" All four of them immediately gave a relational reading without asking for additional instructions. Perhaps instead of lecturing about theme, I can just ask my students, "What message did you get and why? Technical vocabulary can be processed later, when students are more comfortable with articulating their relational readings.

However, there is still the problem of whether the relational reading is too "far out". What to do? I think what needs to be clear to everyone is that as an abstraction, the relational reading does not offer any concrete meanings, no matter how fantastical they are, such as my student who talked about werewolves in a haiku. Rather than these specific meanings, abstractions tend to be rather general and deal with our emotional lives, so they are often about friendship, faith, love and social issues. They will not be about specifics. I have told my students in the past that what I look for is a generalisation about life that they learned from the text. For the werewolf answer, perhaps what I could have done was ask the student to think about what abstraction these werewolves could stand for—rage or hunger?—and then ask him to elaborate on that abstraction using the concrete images in the haiku. "Abstraction" or "symbolic meaning" might be a more accurate term, rather than "generalisation".

Second, after the relational reading is articulated, it is necessary now to explain how elaborations work. What teachers can do is ask students to articulate their own abstraction and then have them identify concrete details in the text. But elaborations move from the concrete to the abstract. So from concrete details, teachers can ask students to further offer abstractions based on these details. What matters here is the teacher is careful to not give the student the impression that she already has an abstraction in mind. That way, the students do not feel like they have to "guess", and they are given the power to decide on their own abstractions. Personally, I think that if students are constantly asked about their relational readings, the more likely these will be adjusted to being more accurately connected to the text. Harrison (2004) argues that "there is such a thing as a person's understanding of a text, but the more you probe it, the more the probing itself changes a person's state of understanding" (p. 53). The literature class should then not be about themes that teachers already have in mind to discuss with the students through particular texts but the other way around: students can identify the themes and teachers keep probing their understanding of these themes as elaborations are articulated. Teachers can bring in public knowledge of literature as elaborations are discussed. That way, there is a balance between the aesthetic reading and the efferent reading.

Despite the differences all five interpretations in the chapter offer, there is also a clear similarity. All seem to be about an unseen power that is transcendent of human life. Whether that power is nature's or God's is left ambiguous. Caple (2010) argues: "[M]eaning is indeed supplied by the author, but this does not necessarily restrict the meanings that the reader may get out of the text" (p. 113). To me, the similarities in the interpretation come from the fact that "expert" readers are already attuned to uncovering this meaning that has been supplied. As Reynolds and Rush (2017) point out, students are still trying to understand the language of the text, so it takes a while to get to that relational reading. In the process of building elaborations, teachers can also help students with the *grammatics* of the text so they are also guided as language users, which is the bedrock skill needed to think symbolically.

Thinking symbolically and loving literature

Apart from a text to interpret, the respondents were also asked about their relationship with literature. The interesting thing is that their responses attach a symbolic reading to literature itself. Here are parts of their responses.

Jess: It was a random classmate who instilled my love for literature. Her name is Kim and she's one of the smartest students in our block. She's very quiet but one of her striking characteristics was that she will always have a book with her. I figured that this was one of the reasons why she is so smart and why our professors really like her.

Darren: Never have I felt in my life something so special (and magical!) when I read, *Love in the Time of Cholera* and *One Hundred Years of Solitude*. I think experiencing the life of someone else—sharing their desires and fears, and confronting them—through a book is truly rewarding. Personally, I like reading these texts, because I think it makes me more human—more respectful and understanding to others.

Sally: I was also apparently weird for most people's tastes. I had quite the identity crisis, bordering cliché, with questions like "Is there something wrong with me?" But, all thoughts like that were forgotten when I was reading my books. They were a venue of escape, a safe space for my wee, troubled, tween then teenager self. I kept myself fairly happy with the warm fuzzy feelings that I got from books.

Cath: I preferred sitting on a couch or hiding in rooms and just having a book with me. I also found some sort of pride when the adults would be impressed that I was so immersed in reading at such a young age. . . . I find solace in reading more than anything else. To me, there's always a "return of investment" of sorts in reading. You always get something new from reading like a new message or a new lesson.

Building a personal symbolic relationship with literature is something teachers have to keep in mind in their classes. Jess, Darren, Sally and Cath all mention how it is important for literature classes to keep student interests in mind. For a good class, Cath suggests a wide variety of genres, so all students have many choices to read. Sally mentioned that she, like me, had a hard time loving literature when she studied it, mainly because there was too much material that she had to read in such a short amount of time. Darren pointed out the importance of knowing student desires when planning a literature program, while Jess mentioned that there should be readings that are representative of the students and their lifeworlds (Kalantzis & Cope, 2019). All these responses indicate that the way to build a good literature class is to have teachers work closely with their students so all relational readings are valued and different texts are discussed in class. The ability to think symbolically is something I think everyone can do, but talking about why texts are significant is one of the joys of reading.

As I end this chapter, I find myself asking how I would have taught *Mountain afternoon* in my classes. What if Jess, Darren, Sally and Cath were my students? How would I have handled it? My own research for this chapter tells me that what is important is that a relational reading is articulated, accepted and probed. If my students are advanced, like respondents for this study, I can just ask them to articulate that abstraction, but the excitement of the class would be in the probing. For example, I could ask Jess, "Why is a sense of imagination important in learning to love nature? Where in the poem is the power of the imagination expressed?" For Darren, I might ask, "If everything in nature moves, doesn't that mean even an Unmoved Mover or Great Designer is moved or designed by what was created? Is there something in the poem that might indicate an Unmovable Being? Or is everything movement?" For Sally, I would ask, "Truth and imagination seem to be the same, right? What parts of the poem might seem imaginative? And what makes these same imaginative parts true?" For Cath, my question would be, "What is the similarity between the violence of nature and the violence of human beings? Do both forms need forgiving? How is the poem an expression of both forms of violence?" And, looking at my own reading, I would ask myself "Why did you immediately judge the natural events of the poem to be violent?" "Violent," after all, seems to be a human category and not a natural one. My own mind considers these events to be violent, but are they? Is the poem itself considering these events to be violent?

The questions I intend to ask fall into a neat pattern: there is a question about the relational reading and then a question that elaborates on the reading by drawing the mind to the poem itself. So when discussing a literary text, the teacher should be open to all and accepting of all relational readings but should also take care to compose careful probing questions on these readings. These questions should call the students' attention to the formal elements of the text. In this way, there is no one relational reading the teacher bears in mind which the students need to guess. Rather, it is the students who articulate the reading which the teacher accepts and probes. It is through probing that a space is created for growth and transformation. Is not that the goal of engaging with literature—to let texts speak to us of growth and change?

References

Caple, H. (2010). Doubling up: Allusion and bonding in multisemiotic news stories. In M. Bednarek & J. R. Martin (Eds.), *New discourse on language: Functional perspectives on multimodality, identity and affiliation* (pp. 111–133). London and New York: Continuum.

Christie, F. (1999). The pedagogic device and the teaching of English. In F. Christie (Ed.), *Pedagogy and the shaping of consciousness: Linguistic and social processes* (pp. 156–184). London and New York: Continuum.

Cruz, P. (2016). *Construing axiology: A study of identity management in English language teaching textbooks in the Philippines* (Unpublished doctoral dissertation). Ateneo de Manila University, Manila.

Cruz, P. (2017). The 'god' of women: The voice of the divine, motherhood, and Philippine ELT. *Linguistics and the Human Sciences, 13*(3), 316–337.

Cruz, P. (2018). Teaching literature, teaching identity: Language pedagogy and building a nation through texts and textbooks. In C. E. Loh, S. Choo, & C. Beavis (Eds.), *Literature education in the Asia-Pacific: Policies, practices, and perspectives in global times* (pp. 153–166). London and New York: Routledge.

Halliday, M. A. K. (1985). *Language, context, and text: Aspects of language in a social semiotic perspective.* Oxford: Oxford University Press.

Halliday, M. A. K. (1994). *An introduction to functional grammar* (2nd ed.). London: Edward Arnold.

Halliday, M. A. K. (2009). *The essential Halliday* (J. Webster, Ed.). London and New York: Continuum.

Halliday, M. A. K., & Matthiessen, C. M. I. M. (2004). *An introduction to functional grammar* (3rd ed.). London: Hodder Arnold.

Harrison, C. (2004). *Understanding reading development.* Los Angeles: Sage.

Kachru, B. (1986). *The alchemy of English: The spread, functions, and models of nonnative Englishes.* Chicago: University of Illinois Press.

Kalantzis, M., & Cope, W. (2019, March 6). *Lifeworld diversity in meaning making.* [Video]. YouTube. Retrieved from https://youtu.be/WBoBzaMAg1s

Lorente, B. (2013). The grip of English and Philippine language policy. In L. Wee, R. Goh, & L. Lim (Eds.), *The politics of English: South Asia, Southeast Asia, and the Asia Pacific* (pp. 187–203). Amsterdam and Philadelphia: John Benjamins.

MacFarland, C. (2009). Linguistic diversity and English in the Philippines. In L. Bautista & K. Bolton (Eds.), *Philippine English: Linguistic and literary perspectives* (pp. 131–156). Manila: Anvil.

Macken-Horarik, M. (2003). Appraisal and the special instructiveness of narrative. *Text and Talk, 23*(2), 285–312.

Macken-Horarick, M. (2006). Knowledge through 'know-how:' Systemic functional grammatics and the symbolic reading. *English Teaching: Practice and Critique, 5*(1), 102–121.

Martin, I. (2009). Colonial education and the shaping of Philippine literature in English. In L. Bautista & K. Bolton (Eds.), *Philippine English: Linguistic and literary perspectives* (pp. 245–260). Manila: Anvil.

Martin, J. R. (1997). Analyzing genre: Functional parameters. In F. Christie & J. R. Martin (Eds.), *Genre and institutions: Social processes in the workplace and school* (pp. 3–39). London and New York: Continuum.

Martin, J. R. (2008). Negotiating values: Narrative and exposition. *Bioethical Inquiry, 5,* 41–55.

Martin, J. R. (2010). Semantic variation: Modelling realization, instantiation, and individuation in social semiosis. In M. Bednarek & J. R. Martin (Eds.), *New discourse on language: Functional perspectives on multimodality, identity and affiliation* (pp. 1–34). London and New York: Continuum.

Martin, J. R., Matthiessen, C. M. I. M., & Painter, C. (2010). *Deploying functional grammar*. Beijing: The Commercial Press.

Martin, J. R., & Rose, D. (2007). *Working with discourse: Meaning beyond the clause*. London and New York: Continuum.

Martin, J. R., & White, P. R. R. (2005). *The language of evaluation: Appraisal in English*. Hampshire and New York: Palgrave Macmillan.

Paran, A. (2010). Between Scylla and Charybdis: The dilemmas of testing language and literature. In A. Paran & L. Sercu (Eds.), *Testing the untestable in language education* (pp. 143–164). Bristol, Buffalo and Toronto: Multilingual Matters.

Reyes, D. F. M. (1999). *Promising lights*. Quezon City: Office of Research and Publications, Ateneo de Manila University.

Reynolds, T., & Rush, L. (2017). Experts and novices reading literature: An analysis of disciplinary literacy in English language arts. *Literacy Research and Instruction*, 56(3), 199–216. doi:10.1080/19388071.2017.1299820

Rothery, J., & Stenglin, M. (2000). Interpreting literature: The role of appraisal. In L. Unsworth (Ed.), *Researching language in schools and communities: Functional linguistic perspectives* (pp. 222–244). London and Washington: Cassell.

7   Changes for the better? A perspective based on post-secondary "Literature in English" in Malaysia

Jia Wei Lim

Before I delve into discussions about literacy in literature education, I must first describe my lived experiences as a reader, which will provide a context for my perspective of English literature, or Literature in English. This personal experience has certainly coloured my narrative of the subject, and by making my lens explicit to the reader I hope to encourage a critical and reflective reading of this chapter.

I grew up with reading as a hobby. I liked reading, and with my mother acting as my personal curator and librarian I was never short of another book to read. English, interestingly enough, is not my mother's first language. She grew up in a Hakka (a Chinese dialect) household and spoke the dialect at home. She only began learning English as a subject when she went to a local primary school in Kampung Pandan, Kuala Lumpur, but she took to it like a duck to water. Coming from a family of five girls and a small income, books were precious to her, and now that she could afford it, she made sure I had plenty of books around me. Unbeknownst to me, she carefully scaffolded my reading journey. She used *Peter and Jane* to teach me to read as I went through preschool and soon bought *Ladybird Classics* and Enid Blyton works like the *Malory Towers* and *St Claire* series to encourage me to read when I was in primary school. She would talk to me about some of the books I read. She knew all the stories, of course, as no book was handed to me without her first reading it. I was in my early teens when I first began choosing books for myself. Two choices stand out to me, even now, and they were Charlotte Bronte's *Jane Eyre* and J. R. R. Tolkien's *The Hobbit*. I was so enthralled by them that I would read them repeatedly at least once a year throughout my teenage life. Spurred by my love of those books, I began exploring more and more classics. It is with such a reader's journey that I was excited to finally be able to study "Literature in English" in my post-secondary education. I was the only student in my school to take the subject, but with support from my parents, I forged ahead and do not regret it.

That is not to say that my lived experience as a post-secondary literature student was a walk in the park. I remember enjoying some of the texts. I could read and understand them, talk about them, recall events and character details, but I was utterly perplexed as to what analysing them meant, let alone how to write a literature essay. With the guidance of a tutor, I stumbled my way through and somehow, someway, things clicked and I was able to produce what was expected

Figure 7.1 In Jane Austen's home museum parlour in Chawton, near Alton in Hampshire, UK

of me. Some texts, however, I did not like and wondered why I had to study them at all. To fulfil examination requirements, I had to read books from Indian, Caribbean, African and Malaysian writers—all of which were my first experiences with writers from different contexts and thus were unfamiliar to me. I expected to read texts like *Jane Eyre* and Shakespearean plays, and so discovered the beauty of Romantic period poets like William Wordsworth, William Blake and John Keats. Such texts I embraced. Other texts by writers like R. K. Narayan, Nguigi Wa Tiong' O and Muhammad Haji Salleh, I disliked. At the time, I thought that it was just a matter of preference that I really only preferred classic British works.

Looking back on my experiences after an exploration of the subject's development for my doctorate and further research, I now see many threads of influences that have shaped my journey as a reader.

Literacy in literature education

To begin, I first explore what literacy means in literature education. Hodgson (2019) notes that there are generally two perspectives of literacy. The first is literacy that is understood in functional terms, where the focus is on the development of language skills to a level of competence necessary for individuals to participate in daily activities such as ordering food or navigating a website. The second perspective of literacy moves beyond functionality to include personal and social awareness of meaning-making. Reading a literature text, however, does not seem to fall neatly into the perspectives of literacy that Hodgson describes. One would certainly need a certain level of functional literacy in order to read a text, but when it comes to a literature text, the form of reading required often involves interpretation or meaning-making. Yet literacy as meaning-making alone still does not encompass the various ways in which students are expected to engage with literary texts. Therefore, researchers such as Meier et al. (2017) focus on the concept of literary literacy, where the emphasis is on the skills and processes required in order to be literate in literature education.

In this chapter, I draw on the work of Freebody (2012), who proposes a Four Resources model for literacy that foregrounds various relationships between reader and text. The model neatly sums up how learners engage with literature texts.

Four Resources model for literacy

Freebody's (2012) Four Resources model of literacy contains, as the name suggests, four ways readers engage with texts. They are (1) reader as codebreaker, (2) reader as text participant, (3) reader as text user and (4) reader as text analyst.

(1) Reader as codebreaker

> We can only begin to understand a literary text if we recognise the language and writing system used in it. Take for instance, the famous line "Romeo, Romeo, wherefore art thou Romeo?" taken from Shakespeare's play *Romeo and Juliet*. To decode the line, the reader would have to first recognise the letters. They will also have to know how each letter sounds and how those sounds may be combined to produce new sounds or syllables. While "wherefore" and "thou" are not common in modern English, this lack of familiarity would not likely stop the reader from being able to at least sound the words. The reader should also be able to guess that "Romeo" is likely the name of a character based on spelling conventions, as indicated by the uppercase "R", even if the reader is not at all familiar with the play *Romeo and Juliet*.
>
> Decoding "wherefore", on the other hand, is not so straightforward. To a reader unfamiliar with early modern English spoken in Shakespeare's time, "wherefore" might seem to be a combination of "where", an adverb used for time and place, and "fore", a word that can be used as an adjective, noun or even as an exclamation used in a game of golf to warn people that a golf ball might be heading their way. Of course, not a single combination of those meanings for "wherefore" make much sense in modern English. As such, recognising letters and words alone do not help the reader to decode the word until they learn that in early modern English, "wherefore" means "why" and "art" actually means "are". Taken together then, the line "Romeo, Romeo, wherefore art thou Romeo?" can be rewritten in modern English as "Romeo, Romeo, why are you Romeo?"

(2) Reader as text participant

In this relationship, the reader participates in the construction of a text's meaning as a coherent piece. Take again "Romeo, Romeo, wherefore art thou Romeo?" (which the reader has decoded to be "Romeo, Romeo, why are you Romeo?"); the reader has to decide what the line means. Why does Juliet utter this rhetorical question? In what tone would she say the line? Taken in the context of the play, this line occurs after she first meets a young man whom she learns is Romeo from the Montague family. The Montagues are sworn enemies of the Capulets, Juliet's own family. Therefore, the reader could very well interpret the line to be a wistful lament on Juliet's part because she is not allowed to fall in love with Romeo because of their families' feud. She wishes he were of any other name, hence, from any other family in order that her affections be permitted. This meaning-making process requires the reader to consider the text as a whole and to actively participate in interpreting the text as opposed to being in a position of a passive receiver of meaning.

(3) Reader as text user

A reader as a text user not only participates in meaning-making but also takes into account the form and intention of the text. The reader also draws on their personal knowledge of the type of text to contextualise interpreted meaning. Thus, the meaning of Juliet's rhetorical question is seen as part of a play performed for an audience. On stage, Juliet is unaware that Romeo is listening, hidden from her view, but the audience can see Romeo and would likely anticipate the moment that Romeo makes his presence known. Therefore, the reader does not only understand the words used in the play or the words in the context of a story but also constructs meaning based on the text's genre. By staging the budding romance before the audience, they are encouraged to become invested in the fates of the characters, which is very much the playwright's intention. In short, the reader as a text user is aware of the text's construction and writer intention.

(4) Reader as text analyst

A reader as a text analyst takes the relationship between reader and text to a critical level. By critical, I mean that the reading of texts includes awareness and considerations of what OCR (Oxford Cambridge and RSA, 2018) terms as contexts in which texts are written and received. Thus, in reading Shakespeare's *Romeo and Juliet*, the reader should consider not only how the play reflects issues during the playwright's time as a context of production (issues such as the position of women in society, questions about independence and free will, meaning of love and family) but also how those issues or concerns have shaped the text. In the context of reception, the reader considers whether issues raised in the text are reflected in his or her world, if these issues have changed over time and whether and why different readers may respond differently to the text.

Do note that such categorisation does not imply that these ways readers engage with texts are distinct. Instead, the categories develop in an expanding fashion, where the text-participant involves the reader as a codebreaker, while the text-user involves reader as text-participant and so on. As Freebody (2012) sums it up,

> The business of "literacy" is to see through the objects meeting our eyes and ears towards seeing that they, together, constitute a message, to see through the message towards seeing that it is a coherent text, to see through the coherent text towards seeing how it forms part of a set of practical, social and/or cultural practices, and to see through these practices towards seeing how they make sense historically, morally, ideologically and philosophically.
>
> (p. 16)

As mentioned in the book's Introduction, this chapter seeks to identify the literacy practices required and promoted in literature education—asking, in other words, what is read and how should it be read as prescribed by the subject's various syllabi. Gleaned through close analysis of those documents and relevant responses of interviewed participants, those questions will frame an analysis of how "Literature in English" has changed over the years it has been offered as a subject in Malaysia. The data is mainly drawn from my doctorate research that traced the development of the subject taken in a post-secondary (or post-16) examination for students who wished to further their studies. I collected official documents such as subject syllabi and assessment papers beginning from the year 1957, which was the year Malaysia (then Malaya) gained independence. Between 1957 and 2012, the Higher School Certificate (HSC) examination was administered in Malaysia by the University of Cambridge Local Examinations Syndicate (UCLES), now known as Cambridge Assessment. During that time, "Literature in English" has undergone four phases of development. I use those phases to illustrate how literary literacy has changed through the decades and end with a commentary of the role of literature education in literacy development.

Phase One (1957–1982)

The syllabus for the subject "English" during this phase was sparse. It reads like a list of papers students can select from with corresponding lists of texts selected for study without much explanation or description. It does not contain statements of learning outcomes, aims or objectives that contemporary educators might expect.

To fulfil HSC examination requirements, students had to sit for three papers. From three papers, namely, Paper 1 "Composition and Comment", Paper 2 "Shakespeare", and Paper 3 "Chaucer, Spenser and Milton", students had to select two. The remaining paper offering would be taken from one of the options for Paper 4, each focusing on different literary periods or on a specific author. Comments will be made later regarding the choice of texts for study, as that endeavour would best be carried out through a comparison of phases of the subject's development. At this point, I wish to draw attention to a particular type of examination question used throughout this phase.

Papers 1, 2 and 3 each have two sections. Section A requires students to paraphrase selected excerpts of studied texts, while Section B provides options of general essay questions based on specific texts. Questions from the latter section are quite similar to those currently seen in post-secondary "Literature in English" papers. The form of questioning in Section A, however, was the reason why an English Subject Committee meeting was convened in 1956. The English Subject Committee was established in the mid-1940s and had its first meeting in Cambridge on 3 March 1945. The committee included HSC examiners, the Chief Examiner for English Literature and the Chief Examiner for English Language (for the School Certificate, equivalent to today's O-levels) as well as the Assistant Master and Mistress of two schools. The committee was to oversee the construction of the syllabus, question papers, text selection and examiner nominations.

In the 1957 "English" syllabus, teachers are told that in Section A, students are "required to paraphrase two of [the short passages] . . . and to relate them to their context with appropriate comment" (HSC English, 1957), while the 1957 Paper 2 Examination paper instructed students to:

(1) Rewrite each of your chosen passages in full in plain modern English. Your chief object is to make the meaning of the passage as clear as possible.
(2) Comment on what interests you most in each. (You may be able to consider dramatic effectiveness, or use of imagery, or subject matter, or diction, or more than one of these).
(3) Indicate in two or three sentences the exact context of each.
                    (HSC "English", November 1957, Paper 2, Question 1)

In the spirit of this chapter and book in general, I ask, "What are the literacy practices apparent here in attempting to answer Section A?"

As stated in the syllabus, Section A requires paraphrasing, which is an act of "restating ideas in different words" (Kissner, 2006). To do so, the student must first, to use Freebody's Four Resources model, decode the excerpts that are written in non-modern English. They must decipher words and language structures not used in their everyday lives in order to arrive at the meaning of the excerpt. Decoding in this sense is an active and conscious engagement with the written text. Notably, the demands of this task should be reduced by the fact that the student will likely have read the excerpt in class with a teacher and peers, which reduces the "strangeness" of the excerpt. Yet success in this task depends on whether or not the students are able to decode every word and line of the excerpt, after which the student must "rewrite" the excerpt in "plain modern English", likely restructuring syntax in order to make it sound more familiar to modern English speakers.

The other parts of the question instruct students to comment on what in the excerpt draws their interest. Such phrasing suggests that they need not reach for evaluation of literary significance but are free to select any aspect or element of the excerpt that they find interesting. To do so, students have to be aware of their response towards the text, which moves beyond understanding meaning required for a text-participant to being a text-user, where the reader is aware of the text as a text.

Finally, the student is required to write a few sentences to identify precisely where and when the excerpt occurs in the text. This act moves students back to being a text-participant and tests students' knowledge of the entire text. This one section in the examination involves the interplay of multiple literacy practices, where the focus is on assessing the student's understanding and knowledge of the texts.

It is documented in the English Subject Committee's 1957 meeting,[1] however, that teachers during this phase questioned "the value of paraphrase as a test of the understanding of the text". The committee secretary notes in item 2 in the minutes that

> [b]ecause of the doubts expressed by many teachers about the value of paraphrase as an examination test, and the examiners' opinion that it is the soundest practical means of testing accurate understanding of the text, it was agreed to ask the Subject Committee to consider whether a general report incorporating answers from scripts should be made by the examiners on the work in Section A only of the Shakespeare paper at the June 1957 examination.

No documents or rationale was supplied in the minutes, but what is clear is that teachers and examiners were at odds over paraphrasing as an indication of literary literacy. The differing attitudes towards paraphrasing highlight conceptualisations of what it means to be literary literate, more specifically, what it means to "understand" the text.

The use of paraphrasing in literature education, nevertheless, has persisted as teachers often spend time in classroom paraphrasing texts, or getting their students to do so, because understanding texts is an essential step towards becoming literary literate.

Phase Two (1981–1998)

This phase begins with the establishment of a Malaysian assessment body known as the Malaysian Examinations Council, abbreviated as MPM for *Majlis Peperiksaan Malaysia*, that oversaw and administered the new post-secondary examination known as the Malaysian Higher Education Certificate or *Sijil Tinggi Pelajaran Malaysia* (STPM). The syllabus during this phase very much mirrored that of Phase One except that details were provided in terms of what students were expected to achieve. Among those details, I wish to highlight the description of Paper 1: Comment and Appreciation. In Phase One, this paper was known as Paper 1: "Composition and Comment", where passages were provided for "comment and appreciation" (HSC English, 1957, p. 11) with a question requiring a summary in Section A of the paper. In the exam, students are instructed that

> [t]he arrangement of the subject-matter and the length of your summary are left to your discretion, but it should be a summary and not a paraphrase, it should be written in consecutive grammatical prose, and it should make clear the most important points in the original passage.
>
> (HSC, November 1957, Paper 1, Question 1)

In Phase Two, however, the paper was retitled Paper 1: "Comment and Appreciation". The Phase Two syllabus now states:

> The intention of the questions is to test the candidate's ability to read literature critically, he will be required to organise his response to unseen passages and to present that response as clearly and directly as possible. The question will be of a kind to allow the candidate's sensibilities full play, and will not limit themselves merely to comprehension or paraphrase.
>
> (MPM English Syllabus, 1982, p. 39)

So what has changed in terms of literary literacy in Paper 1?

The very change of the paper's title from "composition and comment" to "comment and appreciation" foregrounds different forms of literacy. To compose is an act of planning and producing a written text, hence, involving the student as text-participant where the student interprets a passage and then communicates the interpretation in the form of a summary. To appreciate, however, involves the student as text-user where the aim of reading is to evaluate the craftsmanship of a text, for example, analysing how the writer uses language or achieves certain effects. The change from compose to appreciate points towards a shift in what is emphasised in literary literacy. The former, compose, places significance on the written essay as a product of reading, while the latter foregrounds evaluation and discussion of the literary text.

Phase Two syllabus constructors also refer to different kinds of reading; reading comprehension, reading to paraphrase, and reading critically, which interestingly reflect elements of the Four Resources model for literacy. Reading comprehension and paraphrase, as discussed in Phase One, certainly involve decoding and meaning-making in order to understand a given passage. Reading critically, on the other hand, first appears in the syllabus during Phase Two and involves a student's "sensibilities". Yet what is meant by "sensibilities" and to "read literature critically" are not explained but are expanded upon in Phase Three.

During Phase Two, there are also interesting developments in what literature students were supposed to read. Among all the papers offered for examination, Paper 6 was the one that underwent many modifications. It began Phase Two as "Literature 1900–1940" in the year 1982, but interestingly enough listed a novel by Bruce Chatwin titled *On the Black Hill*, which had won the James Tait Black

Memorial Prize in that year even though it exceeded the year bracket for the paper. Such a telling addition signals that there was a desire to add to the types of modernist texts from Virginia Woolf, Thomas Hardy and James Joyce usually prescribed in this paper for students. In line with this urge, the title of Paper 6 was changed to "English Literature since 1900" in the following year. Though Chatwin's novel was removed from the list, it now contained writers from more diverse backgrounds such as Chinua Achebe and Ralph Ellison. In the year 1984, Ngugi Wa Tiong'O and V. S. Naipaul were added to the list, as was Bessie Head in 1987. However, in 1988, there was a revision of the title, removing the word "English" while bringing back the year bracket so the paper was titled "Literature 1900–1940" once again. No further documentation is available to shed light on the rationale that underlies those changes, but the rapid modifications in the syllabus document do suggest that the idea of what students should read or be exposed to was changing. There was only one more change made to Paper 6 where the year bracket was increased from 1900–1940 to 1900–1960 in the year 1991, after which only slight modifications were made to the list of texts offered for study.

On an interesting side note, Chaucer was no longer compulsory in Paper 3 from the year 1990 onwards, even though the title of the paper still bore his name.

Phase Three (1999–2012)

The beginning of Phase Three in the development of post-secondary "Literature in English" in Malaysia is marked by a pivotal moment where the title of the subject changed from "English" to "Literature in English". The texts studied for the subject were predominantly British, with an entire paper dedicated to the study of Shakespearean plays (tragedy, comedy and historical), another to Chaucer and other major authors such as Coleridge and the rest of the papers divided according to literary period. Such a structure was deemed "no longer suitable for Malaysian students since it is largely British in content and orientation" (MPM Literature in English Syllabus, 1998, Foreword).

In Phase Three, the six papers offered during Phase Two were initially streamlined into three papers, namely, "Critical Appreciation", "Shakespeare and Other British Writers", and "New Literatures in English". From the year 2002 onwards, however, "Critical Appreciation" was removed, so students only take the two remaining papers to qualify for an STPM grade in the subject.

In order to take into account literature from "all over the world, including Malaysia" (MPM, "Literature in English" syllabus, 1998, Foreword), the "New Literatures in English" paper was sectioned according to the geographical categories of Malaysia, Indian Sub-continent, West Indies and Africa. Students were to read one text from each category, while British literature, seen as the "basis of literature in English" (MPM "Literature in English" syllabus, 1998, Foreword), would include writers such as Shakespeare, Jane Austen, Thomas Hardy, John Keats and so on.

This was the subject I had experienced myself as a student. As mentioned, I gravitated towards the British writers, believing at the time that they were just better writers, with more creative use of language and enjoyable stories. Now I see that my childhood reading experiences had primed me towards such an attitude with regards to British texts, while my lack of experience reading postcolonial literature and local texts caused me to dismiss them as not being as "good". I did wonder, more than once, why I had to study those texts.

The syllabus constructors wrote:

> The basic aim of the syllabus is to develop the critical skills of candidates to enable them to engage meaningfully with texts from different literary traditions and genres, and in so doing, contribute towards the development of their aesthetic sense and moral awareness. . . . The syllabus will adopt a two-pronged approach in the study of literary works. Firstly the syllabus is intended to enhance critical appreciation of literary works, both prose and poetry, by exposing candidates to current approaches in criticism. Secondly, the syllabus is intended to sensitize students to the different social, cultural, political, and historical contexts of literary works from different regions of the world.
>
> (MPM "Literature in English" syllabus, 1998, Foreword)

In comparison to Phase Two, what it means to read critically is more specific in Phase Three, where it is described as the ability to construct meaning from different literary texts that develop the students' ability to appreciate them and increase students' awareness of their world and the world of others. Appreciation, according to the Foreword, goes beyond personal preferences and evaluations of a text. Instead, appreciation comes from the application of various approaches in literary criticism, such as feminism, postcolonial theory, structuralism and so on, that would illuminate or foreground aspects of the text's content, construction and context. Hence, even if the reader were to personally dislike or be indifferent to the text, he or she should still be critically literary literate enough to be able to discern a text's worth and significance.

The second prong mentioned in the Foreword requires readers to read and engage with not only literary works from different worlds but also their different contexts. In other words, the reader in Phase Three has to act like, as Freebody (2012) terms it, a text-analyst. The reader must be aware of how literary texts reflect as well as comment on their respective contexts of production as well as how contexts of reception may differ in responses to those texts.

Did I, as a "Literature in English" student, develop the aforementioned literacies as the syllabus intended?

I would say I partly did. I learned how to identify, analyse and evaluate literary elements and aspects, analysing, for instance, why a writer uses a particular metaphor or specific word to describe a character. However, I was not introduced to the critical approaches that the syllabus specifically mentioned would help develop critical appreciation. Shadows of those approaches were present through the discussion of themes such as freedom, position of women, and identity but never to the extent that would fulfil the aims of the syllabus. Neither was there much emphasis on the importance of understanding regional contexts. I learned quite a bit about Shakespearean England but not near as much about Ngugi Wa Tiong'O's background or context. Thus, I became a text-user rather than a text-analyst who, at the end of my one-and-a-half years of study, was still inclined to praise writers like Wordsworth or Keats and thought that other writers just did not seem to measure up.

Could I decode and participate in meaning-making of those texts? Yes, I could. Was I able to comment on writer intention and text construction? Yes, I was. But did I appreciate or value the texts as a means to explore different historical, moral, ideological or philosophical perspectives? No, I did not.

My attitude towards the texts I studied seems to correspond with that of other students who had taken the subject during Phase Three. Susan Bugis (a pseudonym), one of the former Phase Three STPM students I interviewed, took the STPM examination in the year 2010. In the interview, she says:

Susan: I don't see the relevancy of studying Malay lit. I cannot appreciate it.
Author: Relevant to whom?
Susan: To myself, to society, to future, when you work? I don't know how you can apply it to your daily life.
Author: What's the difference though? Like Malaysian lit and English lit? Why do you say that Malaysian lit is irrelevant?
Susan: It's so boring. It's rubbish.
Author: What kind of rubbish? How do you decide it's rubbish?
Susan: The way they write. There's no flow, no body . . . I'm like, what am I reading? What did I just read? It was really boring and rubbish.

I have looked back at this exchange time and time again and each time, I try to understand her perceptions of Malaysian literature in English from different angles. Her sentiments, I must confess, echoed my own when I was a STPM student. She calls *Spirit of the Keris*, an anthology of poems and short stories written in English by Malaysian writers, 'Malay Lit' and first brings up the issue of relevance. The irony contained in that issue must be pointed out. *Spirit of the Keris* was selected as a text because the MPM "Literature in English" syllabus committee believed that Malaysian texts would be more relevant to Malaysian students. Because the texts portrayed familiar individuals, traditions, values and concerns of fellow Malaysians, MPM believed that students could use that familiarity as stepping stones towards understanding and analysing the texts. Yet, Susan dismisses *Spirit of the Keris*, claiming that it is irrelevant to her and her world. This response is made more surprising when she goes on to talk about applying literature to daily life. It is very hard to see why and how texts written by Malaysian writers can be irrelevant while texts by British writers are deemed otherwise.

When asked to provide reasons why she thinks the Malaysian text is irrelevant, she pronounces it as "rubbish" due to a lack of craftsmanship or "flow" in their style of writing. To Susan, the Malaysian text lacked the sophistication and enjoyment that other texts had. Among her favourites were Shakespeare's play *Hamlet* and Thomas Hardy's war poetry, both of which she could still recite at the time of the interview four years after she had taken her examination. Her evaluation of texts places her as a text-user because she does critique the style of writing, which demonstrates an engagement with the text as a constructed text. Yet she, too, did not achieve the aforementioned goals of the STPM "Literature in English" syllabus with regards to the importance of context as would a text-analyst.

I cannot speak for Susan, but I believe what hindered me was my lack of awareness that my eyes as a reader were primed through my previous reading experiences and expectations of what constitutes literature. I had read predominantly British writers and grew up hearing of Shakespeare and other names like Dickens and Brontë. Unconsciously, those experiences defined my conceptualisation of "literature", because it was difficult to gain access to a perspective that would say otherwise in my lifeworld. Even the "literature" section of bookshops I frequented mostly stocked works by British or American writers, signified by recognisable black or beige spines, each by established publishers of classic literary texts. I now realise that I grew to rely on their evaluations of what literature is and what it is not to the point that if a text was not listed in the series, I did not think of it as literature. With such baggage, it is not surprising that I found it difficult to accept works by writers from different regions.

What was missing was guidance on how to read works from different regions. In my case, my tutor mostly focused on reading Shakespearean and Austen texts, along with poets from the Romantic period. He read through the passages and spent time discussing the meaning, essentially decoding them, to ensure that we understood the texts. As for the other texts, we sped through them because the assumption was that if we could handle the difficult texts, reading the other texts written in modern and contemporary English would not be a problem—but it was.

In her interview, Susan mentions that when it came time for her class to read the Malaysian text, her teacher told them explicitly that she personally did not like it and that they had to read the text because the syllabus says so. Such a statement from her teacher would likely have closed off any opportunity for Susan to engage with and appreciate the text. My tutor did not go to that extent, but the lack of importance with which the texts were handled did lead to similar circumstances—both Susan and I did not appreciate those texts.

Phase Four (2013 until the present)

Phase Four is very similar to Phase Three in terms of the subjects' aims and objectives. If anything, the syllabus states even more concisely that students should "give equal consideration to texts and contexts, local and international perspectives, as well as personal relevance and universal concerns" (MPM "Literature in English", 2012, Foreword). Therefore, not much has changed in terms of what it means to be literary literate in Phase Four.

What has changed is the assessment structure of the subject. Previously, students would sit for the respective papers at the end of one-and-a-half years, or three school semesters, of study. Now, the assessment structure is modular, where one paper is taken at the end of every semester. The students begin with Paper 1: "Poetry and Short Stories" and then in the next semester, focus on Paper 2: "Plays", and finally Paper 3: "Novels". Each paper contains two sections. In the first section, students are given a passage from a text they have studied in class and are asked to comment on it, often with a focus on a particular literary element like context or characterisation. The second section contains essay questions on specific texts as prescribed in the syllabus.

What has not changed, however, is STPM student response towards the types of texts studied. I interviewed seven first-semester STPM students. Among them was Mei Ling. Mei Ling became interested in literature because of her older brother, who had taken STPM "Literature in English" himself and kept files of notes and essays at home. Mei Ling stumbled across them and became intrigued by names and texts she did not recognise—chief among these in her recollection were *Hamlet* and *Jane Eyre*. Such texts attracted her because the stories were different from what she had been used to reading. In contrast, she explained that Malaysian literary text, an anthology of short stories, was not interesting because they were too familiar. While novelty might be a factor in determining whether or not Mei Ling liked a text, I believe there are other influences at play as well. In my first interview with her, I asked her to select a text from the STPM syllabus that she liked and to provide reasons for her choice. She chose "My Last Duchess" by Robert Browning. Part of the exchange is as follows:

Mei Ling: The first time usually I don't understand but it's like, what? At first you see a long poem, you like so stress. If you want to finish it and you don't understand, you have to start again somewhere. . . . Sometimes I do not understand the poems, the language. That's why I'm constantly learning. There is the struggle there but I don't mind this part of learning. It's a challenge.

Author: What do you like about 'My Last Duchess'?

Mei Ling: Because I don't know, the idea, that the man love the woman but he kill the woman. It's like love kill, like you can see there's a poem, love here. Ei, you can tell he really love her but why did he kill her? Is there such thing like you love someone then you kill them? It's very interesting ah like you get a lot to talk about with them.

I have explored Mei Ling's reading experience of the text based on her conceptualisations of literature elsewhere (Lim, 2019), but I would like to expand on the same interview excerpt again to discuss literary literacy. At first read, she seems to experience some difficulty in decoding and understanding the poem. She talks about the stress she feels when she is unable to grasp the text's meaning, which is a great contrast to her experiences reading the Malaysian text. She had no trouble understanding the Malaysian text at all, but perhaps, because of that, she was more inclined to value texts that she had to exert effort to understand. As she says in her interview, the "struggle" is perceived as a challenge to learn, to essentially develop her literary literacy. She is also clearly intrigued by the subject matter of the poem, bemused at the idea of love that kills. This interest sustains her engagement with the text which encourages her to enact different forms of Freebody's resource model categorisations in her reading experience. Though she first struggles as a decoder and text-participant, she is able to move beyond those roles when she asks questions about love. In evaluating love as depicted by Browning, she engages with her own perceptions about love which can then act as a gateway through which she could explore manifestations of love in her own culture as opposed to others as well as how definitions of love have changed through time. She is well on her way towards becoming a text-user and text-analyst.

Summing up and moving onwards

It has been an interesting personal exercise to reflect on the development of STPM "Literature in English" in relation to literary literacy. What it means to be literary literate has certainly changed throughout the years—so too has our understanding of how and why students engage with literary texts.

A point to highlight in the subject's development is a shift in the types of literary texts students are required to read. While literary works from canonical writers like Shakespeare and Austen have been consistently present in post-secondary literature, the selection is now balanced with the works of contemporary writers from different regions of the world. Thus, in response to the title of this chapter, I believe STPM "Literature in English" has changed for the better in terms of not only how literature is conceptualised but also how literary literacy is practised. Of most value is the recognition that reading a literature text, or any text for that matter, is not a passive activity, as it requires much interaction between the text, the reader and their respective worlds. "Literature in English" as a school subject certainly serves as a vital platform through which such literacy practices may be honed. Nevertheless, those very changes present new challenges, particularly in how texts are received and read in light of previous reading experiences and conceptualisations. Going forward, much more work must be done to understand reading experiences in order to uncover, challenge and work through unconscious assumptions and prejudice that readers might have concerning different texts.

I believe that teaching and learning STPM "Literature in English" can be further enhanced to help develop considered, empathetic and critical members of society. Summarising from personal experience as well as that of my research participants, I propose that literature education must not function in a one-size-fits-all manner. We cannot overgeneralise the ways in which we perceive and apply critical appreciation to texts. Instead, we have to be more intentional in the use of critical approaches in reading and be more willing to unearth, explore and if need be, challenge assumptions about reading and one's lifeworld.

Acknowledgements

I wish to thank the Tunku Abdul Rahman Fund for awarding me a research grant in the year 2014 from which the data included in this chapter was collected. The development of ideas and discourse since then have been facilitated by activities funded by the Fundamental Research Grant Scheme (FRGS/1/2018/SS109/UTP/02/1).

Note

1 The minutes are filed under the call number S/E 2/1, 2 & 3 in the Cambridge Assessment Archive at 1, Hills Road, Cambridge, UK.

References

Cambridge assessment archive

Acc 3010   Malaya Advisory Committee for Oversea Examinations Meeting Minutes, 1955–1972.
C/MAC 2/1   Malaya Advisory Committee, Feb 1946–1957.
S/E 2/1, 2 & 3 English Subject Committee meeting minutes, 1945–1979.

UCLES publications

UCLES, HSC English syllabus 1957.
UCLES, HSC English, November 1957, Question Paper I, Question 1.
UCLES, HSC English, November 1957, Question Paper II, Question 1.

MPM publications

MPM, STPM English syllabus 1982.
MPM, STPM Literature in English syllabus 1998.
MPM, STPM Literature in English syllabus 2012.
Freebody, P. (2012). Knowledge about language, literacy and literature in the teaching and learning of English. In A. Simpson (Ed.), *Language, literacy and literature* (pp. 3–25). Victoria, Australia: Oxford University Press.
Hodgson, J. (2019) Literary literacy? *English in Education, 53*(2), 113–115. doi:10.1080/04250494.2019.1613093
Kissner, E. (2006). *Summarizing, paraphrasing, and retelling: Skills for better reading, writing, and test taking.* Portsmouth, NH: Heinemann.
Lim, J. W. (2019). What might readers want? Unexpected responses from Malaysian *Literature in English* students and suggestions of potentiality in text selection. *Literacy.* https://doi.org/10.1111/lit.12206
Meier, C., Roick, T., Henschel, S., Brüggemann, J., Frederking, V., Rieder, A., . . . Stanat, P. (2017). An extended model of literary literacy. In D. Leutner et al. (Eds.),

Competence assessment in education: Methodology of educational measurement and assessment. doi:10.1007/978-3-319-50030-0_5

Oxford, Cambridge and RSA. (2018). *A-level specification: English literature H472.* Retrieved from www.ocr.org.uk/Images/171200-specification-accredited-a-level-gce-english-literature-h472.pdf

8 The role of comic books in literacy education in Taiwan

Yi-Shan Tsai

Books that teach and children that rebel

An English proverb says, "All work and no play makes Jack a dull boy", while a counter proverb in Chinese says "No study for three days makes one's face ugly and words vapid" (三日不讀書，語言無味，面目可憎). The contrast in values is clear here, where one approves of occasional playtime, while the other highlights the value of studying. The latter is a value that not only drives a culture of prioritising textbooks over extracurricular titles in reading choices at home, but is also pervasive in my childhood texts, which were dominated by didactic messages that teach children appropriate behaviour and morality. Before I could read, I was taught to recite *San Zi Jing* (三字經) which is written in triplets of characters to teach children Confucian thoughts and basic knowledge about the world, including history, geography, astronomy, number, time and colour. The oral tradition of reciting *San Zi Jing* is meant to promote literacy in children before formal schooling, even though the classical Chinese used in the text can be difficult for children to understand. When I was old enough to read on my own, I was given storybooks about filial piety, which is considered the root of basic virtues in the doctrine of Confucianism. The anthology *The Twenty-four Filial Exemplars* (二十四孝) was particularly popular among parents and educators in my time. These short stories recounted the feats of filial people (mostly children) and each story was followed by a poem praising the protagonist's love, respect and self-sacrificial deeds shown in their care of parents.

In addition to filial piety stories, I was given *Tang Shi* (唐詩) (poems composed in the Tang dynasty, a golden age of poetry in China) in school and at home to read and recite. It is believed that *Tang Shi* cultivates a child's appreciation of Chinese history, literature and culture, even though the old form of the language often requires additional commentary to understand. *Tang Shi* is widely used as chanting material to educate children and is often promoted at schools through reciting competitions. However, neither the language nor the content relates to the experience of children. The topics of *Tang* poems cover a broad set of areas, ranging from the unhappiness of an adult's life in the court to the happiness of seclusive life, from the yearning for home to the concern for country, from the beauty of nature to the transience of time. *Tang* poets wrote poems to express their emotions as well as for worldly fame. The narrator is adult; so is the intended reader. However, my early exposure to reading was not entirely dominated by high Chinese literature. In the 1980s, the publishing market in Taiwan was already full of translated works of foreign literature. I remember enjoying reading *Aesop's Fables* and fairy tales by the Brothers Grimm and Hans Christian Andersen that my parents purchased for me. Despite the embedded didacticism in these stories, the talking animals and magic fairies set my imagination free. Looking back at the texts that were approved by my parents and teachers, it is clear that childhood in my generation was predominantly conceived as a period of time when children are "apprentices" to be educated and prepared for society (Mills, 2000).

What about reading for pleasure? Playfulness is an essential quality of childhood activities, and the enjoyment of play is believed to contribute strongly to childhood learning and development (McInnes, 2019). Even when made to recite *Tang Shi*, we naughty children would wittily replace a few words in a poem with funny rhyming words to amuse ourselves. At play time, we also exchanged books that were not approved of by teachers and parents. These were usually comic books obtained cheaply with our pocket money from rental bookstores. The rebellion was partly a way to exert our agency as children and partly to seek fun. For both historical and geographical reasons, Japanese culture has had significant influence on everyday life in Taiwan, including over child and youth popular culture. I started reading manga (comic books originating in Japan) at the age of 7 when my brother started to bring copies of *Doraemon* (ドラえもん) home. Doraemon, under the pen of Fujiko Fujio, is a robot cat that travels back in time from the 22nd century to the 20th century to aid the underdog primary schoolboy, Nobita. I used to daydream about having a robot like Doraemon who could use magic gadgets to make my life easy and fun. I often spent consecutive evenings or weekends diving into a pile of manga and blocked out everything happening outside the world of the book. My mother used to frown at me when she realised that the silence in the house was not a result of my diligent work on school tasks or preparation for exams. Her view of manga as a distraction from my study and house chores induced a sense of guilt when I was caught reading manga. Sometimes, I would hide manga in my school bag or under my coat to smuggle them home, and read them secretly in my room. At school, my friends and I would swap manga and introduce each other to new titles. We collected and exchanged spin-off products of manga, such as stickers, playing cards, key chains, models and stationery. Some of us also practised drawing manga. This hobby lasted for some time until the stress of the high-stakes college entry exam took priority in my life, and I had to cut off all the possible "distractions".

The Japanese-influenced childhood reading

The long-lasting influence of the Japanese culture in Taiwan can be traced back to the 50 years of colonisation during 1895 and 1945. Scholars have marked 1912 as the beginning of children's literature in Taiwan, when a children's

Figure 8.1 Manga reading was disapproved of at home, so there is no photographic evidence of this guilty pleasure. By contrast, studying schoolwork and winning competitions were well documented. The photo is the 10-year-old me showing off the certificates displayed above the desk, which has clearly just been tidied up.

book《むかしばなし 第二埔里社鏡》describing local life was published and co-edited by a Taiwanese editor (Lin & Chiou, 2018). Following World War II, the continuous cultural influence of Japan mixed with the influx of American culture led to a number of publications that aimed to improve Chinese literacy and develop an appreciation of Chinese cultures and national identity under the governance of the Republic of China (ROC). The most notable event in the history of children's literature in Taiwan is the launch of an educational newspaper, the *Mandarin Daily News*, in 1948. This newspaper included a children's section, and a youth section in the following year, to educate child readers in the Chinese language and literature using Zhuyin (Mandarin Phonetic Symbols). Due to the tension with the Communist Party of China, martial law was enforced from 1949 to 1987. During this period, publications were strictly controlled and censored by the government, resulting in the domination of the market by the *Mandarin Daily News*. After the martial law was lifted, four children's newspapers sprouted in a year. The first was the *Mandarin Times*, which emphasised the use of comic strips to attract children and provide a "quick" and engaging pathway to Chinese education. This is the main and perhaps the only record of comics in the discussion of children's literature in Taiwan (ibid.). The separation of the historical development of comics in Taiwan and children's literature in research gives a clue to the societal view towards comics, even though they have traditionally targeted children as a main readership.

Comics as a general term for comic strips, comic books and cartoon is written in traditional Chinese as 漫畫. Both its pronunciation (manhua) and writing are similar to the equivalent term in Japanese—漫画 (also rendered in two other written systems in Japanese as まんが (hiragana) and マンガ (katakana)), pronounced as "manga" (hereafter referring to comics originating in Japan), meaning "picture unbound"(Rousmaniere, 2019). Although there is a lack of consensus, most scholars believed that the Chinese term was introduced by the artist Zikai Feng in 1925 after his return from studies in Japan (Chen, 2014). During the 50 years of Japanese colonisation, Taiwanese artists received Japanese education that included the art of making comics. As a result, Japanese elements continued to exist and to some extent became indigenised in the development of local comics after World War II. Although there were times when the market of comics produced by local artists thrived, a regulation of comics publication issued by the government in 1966 to ensure that the content of comics provides the "right" teaching to children instead of "poisoning" them was believed to have a detrimental effect on the development of local comics (Hong, 2003). The policy details regulations specifying acceptable themes, content, the choice of words and phrases, the narrative style and structure and the composition of images (including the use of lines, patterns, space, icons, shadow and facial expressions). The censorship resulted in several comics artists abandoning their pens for a different profession. It was at this time when pirate manga rose. Due to the lack of clear regulations on translated works and intellectual property at the time, publishers survived on publishing unauthorised manga until the enforcement of copyright law in 1992. However, the dominance of manga in the local market continued in a legal way. According to a local study, manga represented 90.7% of comics publications in Taiwan between 1992 and 1997 (Chen, 2014). Despite the rising awareness of the need to support local artists (Ding, 2002), various attempts by the government have failed to build up the local market. In 2012, a global habit survey of consumers' lifestyles and media preferences in 36 major cities around the world found that 65.4% of comics and animation consumed in Taipei were from Japan (Hakuhodo, 2013). More recently, the Ministry of Culture in Taiwan published a report on an investigation of the 2017 publishing industry (Lu, 2019). The report indicates that among the publications of comic books, 74.4% were translated, and the copyright obtained from overseas predominantly came from Japan. The report also points out that Taiwanese readers' familiarity with manga and hence a preference of this over local comic books has affected the marketing strategy of publishers, resulting in a bleak environment for local artists. Another national report based on the checkout records among all the public libraries in the same year indicates that 19 out of the 20 most popular titles of comic books are manga (Chen & Hong, 2019). It is fair to say that generations of Taiwanese people grew up with manga and this phenomenon appears to continue. However, despite the popularity, manga have received polarised views and the negative ones mainly concern the "unsuitable" content for children.

Manga and its controversial status

Like other forms of sequential art, such as Western comic strips, comic books and graphic novels, manga tell stories in sequential panels where words, images, speech/thought balloons and sound effects all take part in constructing the narrative. Manga are generally known to the West by its "reverse" page flipping and the visual features of characters (e.g. big eyes, small mouths, slim figures and striking hairstyles). Graphically, manga are monochromatic and visually symbolic. Manga are drawn and published in black and white, except for book covers and some colourful pages that may be inserted as a bonus for readers. As a result, manga artists focus on the use of lines, shades, and visual symbols to depict the subtleness of emotions and mood. For example, a character's momentum may be emphasised by dissolving the setting to a streaked background, and an overwhelming emotion may be depicted by turning a character into a child-like or animal-like figure as a form of visual slapstick. The symbolic drawing of manga is well described by the "God of Manga"(Ito, 2008), Osamu Tezuka, when discussing his own comics: "I don't consider them pictures—I think of them as a type of hieroglyphics. . . . In reality I'm not drawing. I'm writing a story with a unique type of symbol" (Schodt, 1983, p. 25). This emphasis on visual storytelling is evident in the ratio between words and pictures as well as the lavish uses of panels and pages to capture characters' movements and facial expressions through varying angles, distance and perspectives (Tsai, 2018). Although manga are meant to be scanned, readers are required to actively seek out clues contained in pictures and coordinate these with the verbal narrative (Schodt, 1983).

In order to serve the interests of readers of different gender and age, the manga industry has been divided into several demographic categories, such as *kodomo* (manga for children), *shōnen* (manga for teenage boys), *shōjo* (manga for teenage girls), *seinen* (manga for mature male readers), *josei* (manga for mature female readers), *yuri* (girls' love) and *yaoi* (boys' love). Whilst manga generally deal with a broad range of themes, including adventure, science fiction, historical drama, sports stories, fantasy adventures, romance, everyday drama (school life, office work and family life) and detective investigation, manga in different demographic categories have distinct styles of artwork and narrative structure. Without an understanding of the demographic divides, unselective introduction of manga to children can lead to an outcry and the increase in the stigma that holds that manga are filled with violence and sex. For example, the introduction of manga to UK schools in 2004 by the Reading Agency to promote reading for leisure was hit with criticism in a news article titled, "Child murder, incest and rape . . . is this really how our schools should be encouraging boys to read?" (Curzon, 2004). A similar outcry was seen in Taiwan when pirate manga dominated the local markets, resulting in a so-called "Sanitisation Movement of Manga" initiated by the local comics artists (Chen, 2014). In fact, manga were once also criticised as "evil books" for children in Japan (Chen & Chen, 2009). The debate over the "appropriateness" of manga for children, however, can be highly dependent on contexts due to different social standards and concepts of childhood (Lo et al., 2019).

Despite the controversy over manga, its global popularity has had some positive impact on its social status. In its country of origin, manga have been recognised as a form of national treasure and a cultural ambassador (Suter, 2016). Outside Japan, manga are not only a form of soft power but have also been used frequently to cultivate appreciation of reading, especially among reluctant readers and are used also in the development of social and gender identities (Bitz, 2009; Gibson, 2007; Lo et al., 2019; Madeley, 2010; Martin, 2012; Rousmaniere, 2019; Tsai, 2016). More broadly speaking, studies have pointed out the value of comic books in developing visual literacy among children and the need to broaden our definitions of texts by engaging readers in the conversation (Chen, 2014; Schwartz & Rubinstein-Avila, 2006; Tsai, 2018; Versaci, 2001). In the next sections, I discuss a government-initiated effort to promote reading by including comic books as a category of recommended books for school children in Taiwan. I revisit some of the topics discussed earlier, including the societal views of comic books as a reading option for children, the challenge of local comics in competing against manga and how we can use comic books in literacy education.

Comic books as extracurricular material in Taiwan

In order to promote reading and enhance the quality of children's publications in Taiwan, the Government Information Office started an annual campaign in 1982 (Lin, 2011) to identify quality extracurricular reading materials for primary and middle school students (aged between 7 and 15). The titles submitted by publishers were roughly categorised into two groups—books and magazines. In 1995, the categories increased to seven, and in 1996 the "education" and "other" categories were replaced by "social sciences" and "comics". In the same year, the Little Sun Award was established to recognise outstanding local publishers and individuals. Currently, there are eight categories in total, including social sciences, reference books, illustrated books, translated literature, literature, comics, general science and magazines. The campaign was held biannually between 2004 and 2007. Since 2013, the campaign was taken over by the Ministry of Culture, and senior high school students (ages between 16 and 18) were included as one of the targeted age groups.

From the historic reports of this reading campaign (accessible at http://book.moc.gov.tw/book/), two prominent struggles of local comics are visible: (1) the threat of foreign comics in market share and (2) the legitimacy of comics' status as educational material. Although the addition of comics as one of the categories for recommendation in 1996 shows the authorities' recognition of comics' value in cultivating reading appreciation among children, the 1998 report (the 16th campaign) mentions the poor quality of local comics and hence the absence of winners of the Little Sun Award. The judges observed that existing works were either created by senior comic artists or full of "Japanese-ness". They concluded,

"After six years of struggle, we must admit that our comics cannot compete with foreign works." Later reports continue to mention the same problem of foreign works overtaking local publications. In the 2004 report (the 22th campaign), it was indicated that only 28.6% of submissions were local works, and as a result the selection criteria were more lenient to the local works. However, the report of the 24th campaign in the following year suggests that the selection criteria for local comics have been tightened due to the reason that "over protection causes damage". The cycle of tightening and lowering standards continued over the years for the same purpose of promoting and increasing the quality of local comics. In 2016, the campaign report indicated prioritising recommendations of all local works "as long as there is no excessive violence or contentious images".

In general, the submitted comic books were evaluated across elements of entertainment, education, aesthetics and ideology. The theme needs to be "correct" (considered as suitable for children), the story needs to be inspirational, the drawing needs to be skillful and the font needs to be clear. Importantly, the selection focuses on educational values so as to change the "negative stigma" about comics, as indicated in the 2004 report. Interestingly, in the 2017 report, the judges argued that book recommendations need to engage children with social issues to develop critical skills from reading rather than avoiding certain issues for the sake of "protecting" children or appeasing parents and teachers. In the following year, the translations of Scott McCloud's two seminal pieces of work, *Understanding Comics: The Invisible Art* (McCloud, 2001) and *Making Comics: Storytelling Secrets of Comics, Manga and Graphic Novels* (McCloud, 2006), were recommended for primary and secondary school (including junior and senior high schools) pupils to develop critical appreciation of comics and to address the concerns of parents worried about "vulgar" content in comic books, according to the 2018 report. Although the struggle of comics for a legitimate status in children's reading material is visible in the reports over the past decades, the importance of the "relatability" between a text and the child reader (readers are able to make personal meanings of texts based on their socio-cultural experiences) (Fiske, 2010; Iser, 1974) has been highlighted twice by judges in the pursuit of educational messages from recommended comic books.

These reports reveal a recurring issue of the struggle for social recognition among local comics: recognition by publishers (in terms of returns on investment), recognition by the authorities (in terms of educational values) and recognition by children (in terms of entertainment values). Local artists are expected to explore new ways to present comics that are not only aesthetic, interesting and educational but also different from manga. The tension is visible between legitimising comics as appropriate reading material by the enhancement of didactic messages and retaining an essential quality of a popular text; that is, reflecting the intended reader's social experience and providing a platform for the negotiation of social power (Fiske, 1989). The desire to remove Japanese influence on local comics is also hard to meet given the fact that manga define the reading habits and creation experience of comics in Taiwan so much. The traces of manga elements are visible in *Blossom* (D.S., 2019), a comic book recommended in the government reading campaign in 2019. However, the relevance of the topic to society has made it deem it as "educational", though arguably lacking humour. In the next section, I discuss the social ideology embedded in the text, the interplay between words and pictures and potential uses in reading education.

Blossom (百花百色)

Blossom (百花百色) (D.S., 2019) deals with topics of gender identity and equality. The story builds on tensions between the protagonist, Yu-Fan, and the social expectations of how girls should behave—wearing skirts, pink clothing and accessories, learning music, hanging out with girls and marrying the opposite sex. Yu-Fan was born intersexual with immature development of the male reproductive organ. Following medical advice, a surgery was performed and Yu-Fan was brought up as a girl, despite the fact that both her parents and paternal grandmother had desperately wished for a boy. The story centres on Yu-Fan's internal struggle with her gender identity, the suppression of her emotions and lasting tension with her mother. After Yu-Fan's cousin, who exemplifies all the ladylike qualities in the eyes of Yu-Fan's mother, introduces her same-sex partner to the family and receives support from parents, both Yu-Fan and her mother gradually find a way to face her sexual inclination and resolve the family conflicts. The story ends with Yu-Fan's mother expressing her support of same-sex marriage in the 2019 referendum in Taiwan.

Blossom (D.S., 2019), along with a manga series, *Brother's Husband* (弟の夫) (Tagame, 2016), were recommended by the judges because they explore important social issues around same-sex relationships and "may inspire readers to reflect on their own attitudes towards these issues and concerns for others". The latter was recommended for senior high school students (aged 16–18), and the former was recommended for students above grade 5 (aged 11–12) in the primary school and up to high school. The influence of manga on the artistic style of this book is visible—from the depiction of characters to the techniques adopted to present panels. As discussed previously, Taiwanese comics artists learnt to draw comics as apprentices of manga artists during the Japanese colonisation, and manga has dominated the local comics industry since the 1970s (Chen, 2014). Both manga and anime are ubiquitous for people growing up in Taiwan. While the ideologies expressed in stories might be particular to a society, the artistic techniques have been indigenised to an extent that distinguishing between manga and Taiwanese comic books by the drawing styles can be hard.

Comics comprise a deliberate sequence of panels that contain both verbal and visual information. The relationship between words and pictures are interdependent and the boundaries between the two modes are not always clear. Readers are expected to bridge the gaps between the two modes in accordance with the different roles these gaps play in the narrative. While the artist makes the choice of what instants to capture and present within frames, the reader completes what is left out using their imagination to fill in the gutter between panels (Wallner, 2019). According to the content of each panel, the reader identifies the

Figure 8.2 Yu-Fan's refusal of her school uniform (read from right to left). The speech bubbles on the right-hand page are as follows: "The semester has started a while ago and you still rush every morning. Your sister has left long ago" (Mother). "The uniform skirt is pretty. It's a good decision to let Ah-Fan [nickname of Yu-Fan] study in the same school as her sister" (Father). "Have you packed tissues? How about a water bottle? Don't forget your lucky charm. Come back home right after school. Don't fool around." (Mother/Father).

Source: Blossom © 2019 D.S. /GAEABOOKS.CO.LTD.

relationships between panels, which enables them to piece multiple panels into a meaningful picture or a continuous event in their mind. Figure 8.2 shows a double spread of a morning scene where Yu-Fan hurried to the school. Her mother showed disapproval of her disorganised manner by making a comparison to her older sister, whereas her father praised her for the girly school uniform. However, once leaving the house, Yu-Fan started to take off feminine items—lucky charm, bow, female waistcoat and skirt. In this double spread, Yu-Fan has not spoken a word. The speech bubbles from the parents are meant to respond to Yu-Fan's action (the beginning of the right-hand page) and explain her facial expression (the end of the left-hand page), which however is left for the reader to interpret. This is a style commonly seen in manga where "less is more" and facial expressions assume a key role in conveying a character's feelings (Ryōko, 2019).

Panel transition is essential to the narrative structure of comics. The close-ups in the beginning of the recto (the right-hand page of a two-page spread) and throughout the verso (the left-hand page of a two-page spread) combine two types of techniques used for panel-to-panel transitions: action-to-action and aspect-to-aspect (McCloud, 2001). The former features the progress of a character's actions, and the latter frames different angles of a place, idea or mood and is not restricted to time. The first two panels in the recto zoom in to Yu-Fan's arms and feet as she put on the uniform in a hurry. Rather than focusing on moving from one action to another, the transition between panels here emphasises a hasty moment when multiple actions take place almost at the same time. However, the meaning needs to be inferred together with the annotations in the background which say "urgent-urgent" (急急) and "busy-busy" (忙忙). The annotations are integrated into the background like onomatopoeia and picturised in such a way that the fluid font style enhances the mood. Moreover, the second panel depicts the instant where the character moved from wearing slippers to putting on socks. Instead of using two panels to contain separate action and time, the artist uses one panel to heighten the haste depicted with streaked lines and smoke. The verso uses multiple angles and distance to depict key actions in consecutive panels each focusing on one: taking off the waistcoat, taking off a lucky charm, putting both items into the school bag and taking off the skirt. The silence in this page brings the reader's attention to the individual action framed using a technique similar to slow cinematic movements to set a mood. This is another feature commonly observed in manga—a consecutive series of extreme close-ups to prolong and heighten a moment (Clarke, 2004).

The relevance of the topics to society and the complex techniques applied to construct the multimodal narrative make this comic book ideal material for dialogue with young readers. Table 8.1 shows some example questions that may be used to prompt critical reflections on the book and allow adults to get a better understanding of children's cognitive, affective and critical engagement with the text.

Table 8.1 Example questions for using *Blossom* in literacy education

Example questions	Rationale
(1) What is this book about?	Reading appreciation
(2) Did you enjoy reading this book? What did you enjoy about it? What did you not enjoy?	
(1) How have societal views of genders changed from the depiction of the three generations in this book?	Social development
(2) Are these views particular to the Taiwanese context or universal?	
(3) What are the conflicts that Yu-Fan has with her family, friends and herself? What might have contributed to these conflicts?	
(4) Do you agree or disagree with any views held by the characters?	
(1) How might Yu-Fan's mother feel when her mother-in-law teased her for not being able to produce a son?	Empathy development
(2) How might Yu-Fan feel when her male friends refused to play dodgeball with her?	
(3) Why did Yu-Fan get into a fight with her classmates after being teased about wearing a skirt?	
(4) Do you have similar experiences to what happened to any of the characters? How did it make you feel?	
(1) What does the arrangement of the panels tell us about time and space? What has been left out of the panels?	Visual literacy
(2) What information do you get from the words, the images and both of them together?	
(3) Why do you think the artist presented the panels/ speech bubbles/background/ambient sounds this way?	
(4) What is the artist's purpose for this particular use of lines/shade/symbols?	
(5) How are cinematic editing techniques adopted here? What are the purposes of this?	

The role of comic books in literacy education in Taiwan

Compared to the time when I had to smuggle comic books home from rental bookstores, societal impressions of comic books are substantially more positive now, and manga have also made their way to public and school libraries. However, from the censorship in the 1960s to the government reading campaign, it is clear that there is persistent fear of comic books leading children astray (e.g. by imitating the violence therein and losing interest in studies). Although comics have received increasing recognition in terms of their cultural values all over the world (Rousmaniere, 2019), for these to gain a place in the Taiwanese educational contexts, it appears to be essential to communicate educational messages explicitly. While comic books can be both informative and entertaining, as seen in several classic manga (Chen & Chen, 2009), the priority of didacticism in comics competitions held by authorities can compromise the entertainment value that is one of the main attractions to child readers. Take *Blossom* (D.S., 2019) for an example. While the text provides rich material for discussion about social values and narrative structure, it lacks many of the light-hearted moments that are crucial to the release of tensions in comic book stories and which often make manga so engaging.

This emphasis on learning over playing also reflects a perception that has not changed from the time when I was taught to recite *San Zi Jing;* that is, children are vulnerable and need the guidance of adults to prepare them for society. Despite growing acceptance of comic books as material to motivate reading, the introduction of these to school libraries is often met with resistance by teachers. This phenomenon is particularly notable among societies that build upon a Confucian education model, which is strongly exam-oriented (Lo et al., 2019). A librarian in Taiwan observed the low interest among children in pursuing extra-curricular texts for entertainment or knowledge of the wider world and attributed this to the prevailing view in Taiwanese society that reading serves the function of achieving academic success (Chang, 2009). Another study has also shown a strong support from Taiwanese parents on textbook-related recommendations of storybooks (Jhang, 2017). On the other hand, the perception of comic books as a "bait" to lure students to enter the school library (Lo et al., 2019) or as a springboard for struggling readers to find interest in books that require a higher level of verbal literacy arguably positions comic books as secondary literature that only plays an assisting role in terms of shaping children's reading lives and skills. However, like all literary works, comic book stories express the author's reflections on society, human relationships and desires. The narrative is carefully constructed to invite readers into a dialogue around the issues that characters face and the emotions that they experience. More importantly, comics allow readers to laugh off issues that they may find difficult in real life and empower themselves in an imagined realm. Unfortunately, the perception of children being immature and vulnerable has led to a fear of comics and lasting debates about what children's comics should be like without directly consulting children regarding what they have enjoyed about reading comics and what they have learnt from the experience (Chen, 2014).

Reading is a dynamic process of recreation and negotiation of meanings (Iser, 1978; Rosenblatt, 1978; Selden, Widdowson, & Brooker, 2005). Scholars have argued the importance of talking to children about the texts that they choose for themselves (Meek, 1988; Styles, 1994; Tsai, 2016) so as to understand the personal meanings of these texts to the readers and their development of literacy skills when reading these texts. Comic books, as demonstrated in the previous section, provide a platform where adults (authors/artists, educators and parents) and children meet to exchange their views of the world in which they live and share their emotional experiences (Chen & Chen, 2009; Hogan, 2011; Lewkowich, 2019). Research has also found that the visual narrative of comics provides stimuli that draw readers to the psychological development of characters and help them recall the memories of personal experience and increasing self-awareness of personal skills, values and personality (Piróg & Rachwał, 2019). The same study also supported the value of reading and drawing comics in the development of storytelling competency among children. Moreover, by talking about comics with children, adults can scaffold and assess the development of visual literacy. For example, Wallner (2019) demonstrates that comics can be used in the classroom to develop children's narrative competence by guiding them to use panels and the gutter space to create the temporal and spatial logic of stories. Cook and Kirchoff (2017) point out that comic books require that readers make meaning of a variety of modes of communication, including text, image and panelling. This meaning-making process helps children develop a better sense of audience (knowing that visual design and arrangement communicate particular messages) as well as the skills to utilise a variety of ways to communicate. When using comic books in the classroom, educators may evaluate children's competency of visual literacy by observing their engagement at affective (enjoyment of reading), compositional (the use of metalanguage to interpret artistic decisions) and critical (critiques of choices made in the creation) levels (Callow, 2008).

Despite the research evidence that comic books support the development of sophisticated social, cultural and literacy skills, comics have mostly been introduced as optional reading in the library rather than being introduced to the classroom (Lo et al., 2019). This points out a need to include comic books in the development of literacy pedagogies as part of the professional development for teachers to raise the awareness and appreciation of comics as a unique narrative from (Marlatt & Dallacqua, 2019). Importantly, comics should not be treated as merely a medium to convey educational messages. They should be seen as a valuable social product that communicates human cultures, feelings, thoughts and imagination. The inclusion of Scott McCloud's works as recommended reference books in the 2019 government reading campaign in Taiwan shows an awareness of the importance of providing students with opportunities to read comic books critically. However, without recognising the social, cultural, aesthetic, literary and entertainment value of comics, the emphasis on didacticism not only confines creativity but also overlooks the most enjoyable and valuable reading experience—when readers can read themselves in the text and the text in them.

References

Bitz, M. (2009). *Manga high: Literacy, identity, and coming of age in an urban high school*. Cambridge, MA: Harvard Education Press.

Callow, J. (2008). Show me: Principles for assessing students' visual literacy. *The Reading Teacher*, 61(8), 616–626.

Chang, L.-H. (2009). The observations and reflections on reading promotion in Taiwan [臺灣推動閱讀之觀察與省思]. *National Taiwan Library Journal*, 5(4), 82–98.

Chen, C.-H., & Chen, C.-W. (2009). 漫畫在兒童教育上的另一種觀點：漫畫感受論初探 [An alternative manga perspective for children's' education: Exploring the manga feeling theory]. *Journal for Studies of Everyday Life, 1*, P37–P67.

Chen, C.-W. (2014). 台灣漫畫記 *[The historical records of manga in Taiwan]*. Taipei: Duwei.

Chen, L.-J., & Hong, W.-X. (2019). *An overview of the reading behaviour in Taiwan in 2018 [107年臺灣閱讀風貌及全民閱讀力]*. National Central Library. Retrieved from https://nclfile.ncl.edu.tw/files/201904/c67ea82a-e708-4259-8f55-79413cba70e6.pdf

Clarke, J. (2004). *Animated films*. London: Virgin Books Ltd.

Cook, M. P., & Kirchoff, J. S. J. (2017). Teaching multimodal literacy through reading and writing graphic novels. *Language and Literacy, 19*(4), 76–95. https://doi.org/10.20360/G2P38R

Curzon, J. (2004, November 21). Mail on Sunday portray manga in a bad light. *Otaku News*. Retrieved from www.otakunews.com/Article/186/mail-on-sunday-portray-manga-in-a-bad-light

Ding, W.-L. (2002). 漫畫，有學問喔！ [There is wisdom in comics!] *China Times*.

D.S. (2019). *Blossom [百花百色]*. Taipei: Gaeabooks.

Fiske, J. (1989). *Reading the popular*. Boston: Unwin Hyman.

Fiske, J. (2010). *Understanding popular culture*. London: Routledge.

Gibson, M. (2007). Manga and younger readers in Britain. Some initial observations. In *IBBYLink: British section newsletter*. London: IBBY.

Hakuhodo. (2013). *Content acceptance in Asian markets driving economic growth* (Global Habit Survey). Hakuhodo. Retrieved from www.hakuhodo.jp/pdf/2013/20131213.pdf

Hogan, P. C. (2011). *What literature teaches us about emotion*. Cambridge, MA: Cambridge University Press.

Hong, D.-L. (2003). 台灣漫畫閱覽 *[Reading Taiwanese comics]*. Taipei: Taiwan Interminds.

Iser, W. (1974). *The implied reader: Patterns of communication in prose fiction from Bunyan to Beckett*. Baltimore, MD: Johns Hopkins University Press.

Iser, W. (1978). *The act of reading: A theory of aesthetic response*. London: Routledge and Kegan Paul.

Ito, K. (2008). Manga in Japanese history. In M. W. Macwilliams (Ed.), *Japanese visual culture: Explorations in the world of manga and anime* (pp. 26–47). London: Routledge.

Jhang, F. H. (2017). The effect of a national reading policy on fourth graders' reading achievement in Taiwan. *KEDI Journal of Educational Policy, 14*(1), 79–98.

Lewkowich, D. (2019). Readers of comics and the recursive nature of adolescent emotion: Exploring the productive relation of visual response and memory in teacher education. *Literacy Research and Instruction, 58*(4), 295–316. https://doi.org/10.1080/19388071.2019.1655610

Lin, W.-B. (2011). 兒童文學與書目 *[Children's literature and titles]*. Taipei: Wanjuan.

Lin, W.-B., & Chiou, K.-R. (2018). 臺灣兒童文學史 *[The history of children's literature in Taiwan]*. Taipei: Wanjuan.

Lo, P., Allard, B., Ho, K. K. W., Chen, J. C., Okada, D., Stark, A., . . . Lai, C. (2019). Librarians' perceptions of educational values of comic books: A comparative study between Hong Kong, Taiwan, Japan, Australia and New Zealand. *Journal of Librarianship and Information Science, 51*(4), 1103–1119. https://doi.org/10.1177/0961000618763979

Lu, J.-W. (2019). *2017 Taiwanese publishing industry investigation and 2018 reading and book consumption behaviour [106 年臺灣出版產業調查暨 107 年閱讀及消費趨勢分析]*. Ministry of Culture. Retrieved from www.moc.gov.tw/download filelist_341_266_1.html

Madeley, J. M. (2010). Girly girls and pretty boys: Gender and audience reception of English-translated manga. *Queen City Comics: Astonishing Tales in Academia.* Retrieved from http://ourspace.uregina.ca/bitstream/handle/10294/3092/QueenCityComics-4-June_Madeley.pdf

Marlatt, R., & Dallacqua, A. K. (2019). Loud and clear: Using the graphic novel to challenge the status quo in content area literacy. *Journal of Language and Literacy Education, 15*(1). https://eric.ed.gov/?id=EJ1212447

Martin, F. (2012). Girls who love boys' love: Japanese homoerotic manga as transnational Taiwan culture. *Inter-Asia Cultural Studies, 13*(3), 365–383.

McCloud, S. (2001). *Understanding comics: The invisible art* (1st HarperPerennial Ed.). New York: HarperCollins Publishers Inc.

McCloud, S. (2006). *Making comics: Storytelling secrets of comics, manga and graphic novels.* New York: HarperCollins Publishers Inc.

McInnes, K. (2019). Playful learning in the early years—through the eyes of children. *Education 3–13, 47*(7), 796–805. https://doi.org/10.1080/03004279.2019.1622495

Meek, M. (1988). *How texts teach what readers learn.* Stroud: The Thimble Press.

Mills, R. (2000). Perspectives of childhood. In J. Mills & R. Mills (Eds.), *Childhood studies: A reader in perspectives of childhood* (pp. 7–38). London: Routledge.

Piróg, D., & Rachwał, T. (2019). Comics as a tool for a narrative approach in early career counselling: Theory versus empirical evidence. *British Journal of Guidance & Counselling, 47*(4), 498–511. https://doi.org/10.1080/03069885.2018.1538494

Rosenblatt, L. M. (1978). *The reader, the text, the poem: The transactional theory of the literary work* (p. 1008150). Carbondale, IL: Southern Illinois University Press.

Rousmaniere, N. C. (2019). A manga for everyone. In N. C. Rousmaniere & M. Ryōko (Eds.), *The Citi exhibition manga マンガ* (pp. 20–33). London: Thames & Hudson.

Ryōko, M. (2019). Did Hokusai create manga? In N. C. Rousmaniere & M. Ryōko (Eds.), *The Citi exhibition manga マンガ* (pp. 277–286). London: Thames & Hudson.

Schodt, F. L. (1983). *Manga! Manga! The world of Japanese comics* (p. 1021207). New York: Kodansha International.

Schwartz, A., & Rubinstein-Avila, E. (2006). Understanding the manga hype: Uncovering the multimodality of comic-book literacies. *Journal of Adolescent & Adult Literacy, 50*(1), 40–49. https://doi.org/10.1598/Jaal.50.1.5

Selden, R., Widdowson, P., & Brooker, P. (2005). *A reader's guide to contemporary literary theory* (5th ed.). London: Pearson Education.

Styles, M. (1994). 'Am I that geezer, Hermia?' Children and 'great' literature. In M. Styles, E. Bearne, & V. Watson (Eds.), *The prose and the passion: Children and their reading* (pp. 36–54). London: Cassell.

Suter, R. (2016). Reassessing manga history, resituating manga in history. In N. Otmazgin & R. Suter (Eds.), *Rewriting history in manga: Stories for the nation* (pp. 175–183). Palgrave Macmillan. https://doi.org/10.1057/978-1-137-55143-6_9

Tagame, G. (2016). *Brother's husband [弟の夫]*. Tokyo: Futabasha.

Tsai, Y.-S. (2016). The characteristics of manga fan communities—preliminary observations of 16 teenage manga readers in the UK. *Journal of Graphic Novels and Comics, 7*(4), 417–430. https://doi.org/10.1080/21504857.2016.1195759

Tsai, Y.-S. (2018). Close-ups: An emotive language in manga. *Journal of Graphic Novels and Comics, 9*(5), 473–489. https://doi.org/10.1080/21504857.2018.1 480502

Versaci, R. (2001). How comic books can change the way our students see literature: On teacher's perspective. *The English Journal, 91*(2), 61–67.

Wallner, L. (2019). Gutter talk: Co-constructing narratives using comics in the classroom. *Scandinavian Journal of Educational Research, 63*(6), 819–838. https://doi.org/10.1080/00313831.2018.1452290

Part 3

Reimagining Asia's literacy policy–practice nexus

9 Lived experiences of literacy learning in Singapore from the past to the present and lessons for the future

The relationship between familial and institutional habitus in situated contexts

Chin Ee Loh

Introduction

Singapore's unprecedented and rapid economic growth in the span of 50 years is well known. In 1965, Singapore's nominal Gross Domestic Product (GDP) per capita was around US$500, and by 2015 the GDP per capita was around US$56,000 (Menon, 2015). The phenomenal economic success is in part due to a centrally controlled education policy responsive to economic needs (Gopinathan, 2007; OECD, 2010) and Singapore's adoption of and emphasis on English as a language of trade and education that enabled the country to plug into global economic markets. Language policies and educational reforms are ways to "retool" the "productive capacity of the system" (Gopinathan, 2007, p. 59), and the success of Singapore's education policy can be seen in the rise in its literacy rate, from 60% in 1965, the year of independence (National Archives Singapore), to 97.3% in 2018 (Singapore Department of Statistics, 2019). However, while Singapore is often ranked highly on international assessments such as the Programme for International Student Assessment (PISA) and Progress in International Reading Literacy Study (PIRLS), there are concerns with the issue of equitable access to educational opportunities given the widening gaps in student achievement across different socio-economic backgrounds (Gopinathan & Abu Baker, 2013; Loh & Sun, 2020; Ng, 2013; Tan, 2008).

In this chapter, I seek to unpack issues of educational access in the area of literacy learning, especially reading, through the lenses of Bourdieu's (1977, 1984) concepts of cultural capital, habitus and field. More specifically, I engage with concepts of familial and institutional habitus to consider how individuals and families as actors move in relation to the changing fields in which they are embedded (Burke, Emmerich, & Ingram, 2013; Reay, 1998). In line with Bourdieu's approach to utilise empirical data to resolve conceptual issues (Burke et al., 2013; Weininger & Lareau, 2003), I draw on my own experience of literacy learning as an exploratory case study. My autoethnographic approach requires me to "describe and systematically analyse personal experience in order to understand cultural experience" (Ellis, Adams, & Bochner, 2011). Here, autoethnography serves as a reflexive tool (Bochner, 2012; Schön, 1991) for understanding how broad policies are enacted and experienced in everyday practice across time. In choosing to use autoethnography, I emphasise the role of narratives in helping us to make sense of our world (Bruner & Weisser, 1991; Mishler, 1999), and I present my own narrative as a starting point for opening up dialogue and further research about educational effectiveness, equity and reform.

Familial and institutional capital within national contexts

The triad of habitus, cultural capital and field conceptualised by Bourdieu provides a way to understand educational reproduction and transformation (Mills, 2008; Nash, 1990). While Bourdieu has been criticised for his tendency towards determinism in its focus on educational reproduction (Giroux, 1983), there is much profit to be had from focusing on the relational aspect of social structures and individual practices (Nash, 1990), leading to a more nuanced and complex view of educational practice. Specifically, in this chapter, I focus on the concept of habitus as a conceptual tool to understand how continuity is maintained and how changes occur over time (Reay, 2004). For Bourdieu, the social world is "accumulated history" (Bourdieu, 1986, p. 241), where individuals learn to make use of the capital valued within one's schooling and economic context to achieve other forms of value such as economic gain and social standing (Lareau & Weininger, 2003). Cultural capital, which may be embodied in the forms of dispositions of the mind, objectified in the form of cultural goods such as books and pictures owned, and institutionalised in the form of cultural capital (Bourdieu, 1986), can be seen as ways of consumption of culture transmitted by high socio-economic status (SES) parents to their offspring. However, research has found that reading as a form of cultural capital can be correlated to educational advantage for children, regardless of SES (Araujo & Costa, 2015; Chiu & Chow, 2010; De Graaf, De Graaf, & Kraaykamp, 2000), suggesting that factors other than parents' financial status may be of relevance for the acquisition of reading as a form of cultural capital.

To understand how reading as a form of cultural capital can be acquired across generations, I argue that the concept of habitus, particularly of the collective habitus in the form of familial and institutional habitus, can explain how cultural capital is actualised through home or schooling (Loh & Sun, 2020). The concept of habitus accords agency to individuals and groups, recognizing that habitus can be transformed through repeated practices over time. Reay notes:

> while habitus reflects the social position in which it was constructed, it also carries within it the genesis of new creative responses that are capable of transcending the social conditions in which it was produced.
>
> (2004, p. 435)

Repetition over time is thus key to sedimentation or transformation of practice valued within a field of play or the institutional and social arenas within which particular practices are accorded value and significance. The value of institutional and familial habitus as conceptual tools lies in their potential to reveal how groups collectively build capital within a particular field of practice. Burke et al. (2013) argue that the exploration of collective practices "reveals the complex interplay of not simply the individual in their sociocultural location, not simply of habitus and field, but of the collective and interrelated practices of *multiple individuals* within a particular field" (p. 166). Practically, the refinement of collective habitus into institutional and familial habitus allows engagement with empirical data to observe connections, transitions and variations across interactions, to deepen understandings of how change and continuity occur within a particular field. Furthermore, institutional habitus is not monolithic but constitutes a combination of official policy documents shaping national psyche, and implementation of these policies and practices at school levels and public institutions such as the public library, which support national and school objectives of literacy. The interplay of these different institutions with familial habitus in a particular field shifts across time, its impact either cumulative or dwindling.

Within the field of Singapore where English has been continually emphasised as the lingua franca for academic and economic advancement (Silver, 2005), individuals who maintain or gain proficiency in the language, whether through familial or institutional habitus, find themselves in better positions for securing educational and economic gains. Tracing familial habitus as responses to the demands of the field highlights how individuals within groups may mobilise various capital to improve their position within the field. At the same time, tracing shifts in educational policy and practice as elements of institutional habitus highlights how collective efforts affect national and personal trajectories. The intersection of complex homeschool practices reveals how schooling can complement or work against familial habitus in the lives of individuals and collectively.

Shifting familial and institutional habitus in Singapore

In the case of Singapore, where the official emphasis on English as a valued language of global business has permeated daily life, there is a trickle-down effect on familial practices, where families shift their focus and energies onto acquiring English language competence through home use and/or emphasis. Furthermore, in the context of the "manufacturing" mentality (Koh & Chong, 2014) of Singapore's education system, where education is closely shaped by economic needs, institutional habitus in the form of official (e.g. syllabus documents, assessments) and unofficial (e.g. classroom cultures, teacher talk) structures of practice at school and at the societal level interlace with home practices to collectively shape new trajectories ready for economic futures envisioned by the State. In this section, I offer a brief overview of language and educational policies that shaped the value of English in the field of Singapore between 1980 and the year 1999. I recount my lived experiences through the analytic lenses of familial and institutional habitus to examine the complex interplay between homeschool practices that directed the acquisition of English literacy as a valued competency in Singapore's context.

The bilingual policy in Singapore established English as a medium of instruction and first school language in 1987, and students were required to study one of three other official languages (Malay, Chinese and Tamil) as their Mother Tongue language (Pakir, 2004). English was selected as the first language, as it was seen as a "neutral language" that allowed for interethnic communication and acted as a tool to plug into the global community of business (Gopinathan, 1980, 1998; Silver, 2005). Officially, English was established as the official language of education and first language in 1987, but unofficially the demise of the other languages relative to English in the Singapore schooling system began much earlier. Although students could enrol in different medium schools then, there was a strong shift in parents' preferences towards English-medium schools by the late-1970s (Sim, 2016) in line with the government's emphasis on English as the language for trade and economic growth. By December 1983, less than 1% of those eligible for Chinese-medium schools enrolled in Chinese-medium schools.

My paternal grandmother was principal of Poicai Primary School, a Chinese-medium school in Sembawang. She retired and closed the school in 1980 due to falling enrolment. My father began his primary school education in 1957 in the same primary school and completed his secondary and post-secondary education in Thomson Secondary School, one of four Chinese government schools then. For individuals of my father's generation, the importance of English was already making its impact felt. His employment and subsequent promotions as a bank manager at United Overseas Bank depended in part on his capacity to communicate in English. My mother only completed her secondary school education but did well enough in her English and grades to be employed in the bank, where she met my father.

Policy-wise, a report on the shortcomings of the Singapore education system, the Goh report (Goh & Team, 1979), led to the implementation of the New Education System (NES) that led to the streaming of pupils into different courses at upper primary and lower secondary based on their language proficiencies and academic ability (HistorySG, n.d.). To address the issues raised by the Goh Report, the Curriculum Development Institute of Singapore (CDIS) was created in June 1980. Lim notes that the *English Syllabus 1981* was "reductive" (Lim, 2002, p. 86) compared to the previous syllabus, with speech activities and literacy enrichment removed from it. The reduction in core skills resulted from the focus on functional literacy, to ensure that Singapore pupils would acquire the minimum core language requirements to form a literate workforce for Singapore's globalising ambitions. CDIS also marked the transition from the use of commercial materials to materials fully developed by the Singapore Ministry of Education (MOE). By mid-1980, the influence of the communicative language movement and emphasis on reading led to an increased emphasis on print-rich classrooms and reading in the form of programmes such as the *Reading and English Acquisition Programme* (REAP) in lower primary classes, the *Active*

Figure 9.1 My grandmother (centre, in a sleeveless dress) with her teachers and students

Communicative Teaching (ACT) in upper primary classes and the *Project to Assist Secondary Schools in English Skills (PASSES)* (Lim, 2002; Loh, 2018).

Within the Singapore context, national policy and economic circumstances thus conspired to establish the value of English as cultural capital that could translate into economic gain in the form of academic credentials, higher paying jobs and social mobility. Institutionally, policy changes sought to transform official policy into enacted practice through the development of materials that would guide teachers' work. The curriculum documents and programmes designed by MOE could be seen as a national attempt to shape the institutional habitus of school, to complement or fill in where the familial habitus was one that was not necessarily in line with the perceived global demands of literacy. In 1980, only 11.6% of the population spoke English as the dominant language and most children communicated in languages other than English within their homes and with their peers.

Within my familial habitus, I was exposed to a mixture of Chinese and English at home, with exposure to the Chinese dialects of Hakka and Teochew when I met with my paternal grandparents and maternal great-grandmother and relatives respectively. On radio and broadcast television, I was exposed to both English and Chinese channels. At a personal level, the increasing value accorded to being able to read and communicate in English was emphasised, and my father, himself educated in a Chinese-medium school, told me to "just do well in your English and pass your Chinese". This emphasis on the acquisition of English literacy proficiency was supported by regular public library visits as well as explicit instruction at home. I remembered completing English assessment books and reading my mother's copy of *Word Power Made Easy*, a classic vocabulary builder by Norman Lewis. Books such as these could be seen as the objectified cultural capital in homes, acquired to encourage greater familiarity with the English language.

Language-wise, the institutional habitus of school was one where English was the default language of communication between teachers and students and among friends, at least from Primary 2 onwards. I initially enrolled in Nanhua Primary school for my Primary 1 education in 1981 but moved to Marymount Convent School in 1982 when we relocated from North Bridge Road to Upper Thomson Road. I remembered using the textbooks created by CDIS, laughing about the antics of characters named Mr Wollie, Mr Yakki and Miss Lala as I read the texts in class or on my own. School-wise, a general interest in "book flood" methods of providing students with high-interest books to encourage pleasure reading during that period of time (Elley, 2000) may have supported the general culture of school library visits. A significant memory of reading for me was visiting the primary school library and looking for books from my favourite authors or series, including Enid Blyton, the *Nancy Drew* series and *Anne of Green Gables* (Loh, 2016). The institutional habitus thus comprised school cultures of valuing English, textbooks used, lessons and library materials made available to students.

Home habitus aligned with school habitus for me insofar as the reading of English books (textbooks, storybooks) was encouraged at home. Reading books in English was prescribed by my parents, since they saw English as a vital language that I needed to master for future work. The repetition of practices (Bourdieu, 1986)—in this case, the view and practice of reading as a valued disposition—was passed down from previous generations. In an informal interview, my grandmother, aged 97, recounts the generosity of a second-hand bookseller who allowed her to read books in his shop even though she could not afford to purchase them. Across the generations, aided by institutional habitus, the habit of reading was sedimented, embodied and inscribed in my personal preferences and habits, though my preference was to read in English rather than in Mandarin.

At the level of institutional habitus, the Singapore national library played and continues to play a significant role in the national push towards language learning and knowledge building, with extensive public funding allocated to library development and materials then (Ramachandran, 1999) and now (Hong, 2019). Bookstores too played a significant role in Singapore's literacy history (Loh, 2016). As a teenager, I bought second-hand books where possible and made regular visits to the public library to feed my reading habits. I visited the now demolished National Library at Stamford Road (where I remember reading Joan Aiken books and historical romances and adventures) and Ang Mo Kio Public

Library (which I frequented after school with my best friend), the closest library to my home, making use of national resources to support my reading habit.

The accumulation of cultural capital over time

Cultural capital holds value depending on its place in the field, "a network . . . of objective relations between positions" (Bourdieu & Wacquant, 1992). The field is often compared to a game, where positions may be strengthened, weakened or maintained over time. Where the relative value of various capital holds its position within a consistent field, and individuals act to maintain or increase its value through socialisation, it is possible for individuals to accumulate cultural capital across generations (Bourdieu & Wacquant, 1992), resulting in a multiplier effect. The familial accumulation of reading as a form of cultural capital was particularly significant in Singapore as it moved towards a knowledge-based economy (Chia, 2001), where higher standards of literacy were expected to create skilled knowledge workers. Globally, the digital revolution meant that reading as a core literacy skill is even more crucial currently for individuals who seek to engage in other forms of literacy, from writing to coding (Brandt, 2015; Schwab, 2017).

English retained a key position in the nation's economic and educational plans. This official emphasis is institutionalised in syllabus documents, with the 2010 English syllabus stating that

> The majority of our pupils will attain a good level of competence in English, both in speech and writing. . . . At least 20% will attain a high degree of proficiency in English . . . to help Singapore keep its edge in a range of professions, and play an important role in teaching and the media. . . . A smaller group of Singaporeans to achieve mastery in their command of the language that is no different from the best in English-speaking countries.
>
> (CPDD, MOE, 2010, p. 6)

Within the Singapore field, English had acquired an advantageous position and was sedimented in the institutional habitus, so much so that English teachers often felt emotionally burdened at having to help their students achieve passes and high grades in English high-stakes examinations (Loh & Liew, 2016).

The success of the bilingual policy is reflected in an increase in more families choosing to use English as the dominant home language across the years (see Table 9.1). The trend in Singapore moved towards "English-knowing bilingualism" (Pakir, 1991), where Singaporeans were becoming increasingly bilingual with English as the dominant language across different ethnic groups. By 2015, English had become the most common language spoken at home (Lee, 2016). The demands of the field and institutional emphasis on English had influenced home language practices.

My own language biography reflected that of a Singaporean who made the transition from a home where both Mandarin and English were spoken in equal parts to one who communicated predominantly in English with her peers across

Table 9.1 Resident population aged 5 years and over, by language most frequently spoken at home

Language	1980	1990	2000	2010	2015
English	11.6	18.8	23.0	32.3	36.9
Mandarin	10.2	23.7	35.0	35.6	34.8
Chinese dialects	59.5	39.6	23.8	14.3	12.9
Malay	13.9	14.3	14.1	12.2	10.7
Tamil	3.1	2.9	3.2	3.3	3.3
Others	1.7	0.8	0.9	1.1	0.9

Sources: Census of Population, 1980, 1990, 2000 & General Household Survey 2015. Singapore: Department of Statistics.

her social network. In 1994, I enrolled in law school at the National University of Singapore, where I mingled with mostly English-speaking peers, completed pupillage in a law firm (mostly English-speaking again) and was called to the Singapore Bar in 1999. It was then I decided that teaching rather than law was my calling and trained as a secondary school English language and literature teacher at the National Institute of Education, then located at the Bukit Timah campus, from 1999 to 2000. I taught in three different schools between 2000 and 2006, with a one-year interlude to complete my master's in literary linguistics at the University of Nottingham. I later pursued my PhD in curriculum and instruction in the State University of New York at Albany, where I graduated in 2010. In both England and the United States, I was often told that I spoke "good English". By the time my son was born in 2009 and my daughter in 2011, my husband and I belonged to the group of Singaporeans who communicated primarily in English as the home language. Our concern was not whether our children would speak well in English but whether they would learn Mandarin well enough as their Mother Tongue, which we did not use often enough in the home.

Within my children's home context, the learning of English was not so much a necessary enforcement but a pleasurable experience. Competence in terms of knowledge of books results from "unintentional learning made possible through domestic or scholastic inculcation of a legitimate culture" (Bourdieu, 1984, p. 28). Our home practices of "intensive immersion" (Loh & Sun, 2020) in a habitus of an English literacy-rich environment comprised a home filled with books, regular visits to the public libraries, parent–child book sharing practices and constant engagement with books and reading, a practice more typical of a Singapore middle-class home (see Figure 9.2). In a survey of English reading habits and preferences of 6,005 students from six Singapore secondary schools, my colleague and I found that adolescent students from middle-class homes were more likely to enjoy reading, have more books at home, have access to more reading role models and borrow more books from the public library (Loh & Sun, 2018, 2020). Habits of engaged reading are cultivated through home habitus. Parents' educational levels (institutional cultural capital), dispositions towards

Figure 9.2 Images of my children reading English books. From left to right: My daughter "reading" an electronic nursery rhyme book; my son (age 7) reading a book on World War 1 during his lunch; my children at the Ang Mo Kio public library.

reading (embodied cultural capital) and objectified cultural capital (books and other reading-related resources) are invested in their children. Reading as cultural capital is amplified as the child uses what is available to bootstrap his or her linguistic proficiencies for a global, information-saturated future.

Institutional habitus and educational inequity?

Context is imperative for understanding the operation of cultural capital and habitus within the field (Byun, Schofer, & Kim, 2012; Koh & Kenway, 2012; Weininger & Lareau, 2003). The exponential and speedy growth of Singapore's economy resulted in what has been termed a "middle class society" (Lee Kuan Yew, 1987 in Tan, 2015), in that 80% of Singaporeans owned the residential property they lived in. The widening income gaps between individuals from different social backgrounds make questionable the sufficiency of existing models of meritocracy to handle inequality in Singapore (Bhaskaran et al., 2012; Lien Centre for Social Innovation, 2015). For the post-independence generation growing up in developing Singapore, the differences in home resources may be less stark compared to contemporary Singapore. The current playing field continues to reward individuals who are competent in the English language. However, rising standards and middle-class parents' increasing capacity to invest in their children's education contribute to uneven starting points for children, even before they enter school (Ng, 2013; Teo, 2018), similar to situations in other developed nations (Currid-Halkett, 2017; Park, 2008). Families from different SES have widely differing means and resources to provide for their children, in terms of time, money and resources. In the area of reading, middle-class parents are typically able to provide more books, serve as reading role models and enrol their children in extra classes (Loh & Sun, 2020).

The Singapore education system between the 1980s and the end of the 1990s, which I grew up in, was an "efficiency-driven" education system which was highly centralised, standardised and competitive (Sharpe & Gopinantha, 2002). Systemically, the streaming or tracking system that began under the New Education System, refined into an efficient system of sorting (Ng, 2013; Tan, 2010), tended to privilege students proficient in English, as it was the official language of teaching and learning. Thus, students who had access to reading in English as cultural capital tended to profit from the investment and to invest similarly in their own children. The investment tended to have a multiplication effect as successive generations acquired more capital, and literacy expectations rose. The capacity to engage in independent self-directed reading resulted from proficiency and practice, which for middle-class children, was gained from familial habitus (Loh & Sun, 2020).

In 1997, the Singapore education system shifted into the "ability-driven" paradigm, with explicit focus on the development of individual abilities and talents to meet the challenges of a knowledge-driven economy (Tan, 2005). The promise of meritocracy as an overarching principle of governance and educational distribution assumes equal access and opportunities for all students (Lim, 2013). Yet the egalitarianism promised by meritocracy does not account for the unequal starting points of individuals from different SES. Applied to literacy learning, the cumulative effect of my early literacy investments ensured a multiplier effect for my children. In contrast, students from less well-resourced backgrounds begin with less and find it harder to reach the benchmark of engaged reading even as the global and national economy demands ever-higher levels of literacy.

I witnessed this differential access to literacy practices in my teaching across both elite schools and government schools across different streams between 2000 and 2006. For example, while I could assume that 13-year-olds in the top schools I taught had read Roald Dahl and were familiar with Sherlock Holmes by the time they arrived in Secondary One, the same 13-year-olds in another school would have difficulty understanding the British context in which Sherlock Holmes is set. Students in the top schools were more likely to have wide exposure to English language storybooks at home that helped them connect with the cultural and linguistic knowledge required to understand and enjoy what might seem to be a culturally distant text (Loh, 2013). Students from different backgrounds had differential access to English reading materials and dispositions, in part from their familial and primary school institutional habitus, which supported their familiarity or lack of familiarity with engaged reading practices (Lareau, 1989; Loh, 2013, 2015). However, the tendency of schools and educators to frame English language learning as a hierarchical, decontextualised skills-focused subject (Kramer-Dahl & Kwek, 2011) ignores or "misrecognizes" (Bourdieu, 1977) the place of the affective, the cultural and social embedded in the act of learning to read and of reading particular kinds of texts. Neglecting the affective or the cultural disposition of engaged reading in curriculum planning and instruction leaves out a crucial element—the will and desire to read—as an important factor for teaching and learning to read. If the affective is not included in school policies and practices of reading, a key component of institutional habitus for supporting motivated reading is left out of the equation.

Conclusion

Examining past literacy practices and the field in which they were enacted and lived out allows critical reflection on current and future roles of literacy (Graff, 1987). Examining my personal literacy practices as a child, parent, teacher and researcher helped me to see how my habitus, "structuring structures" (Bourdieu & Passeron, 1990), shaped my identity as a reader and had implications for my educational and economic futures. My narrative, set against policy emphasis and school practices, make visible the enactment of policy in everyday practice. The narrative and historical tracing of my literacy practices shows how cultural capital has the capacity to be multiplied even as contexts shift, *if* the value of the capital remains the same or increases, and the collective habitus of familial and/or institution are applied to socialise individual acquisition of the relevant cultural capital. In this case, my narrative of the earlier acquisition of literacy in the 1980s to 1990s demonstrates how familial and institutional habitus collectively impact individual acquisition of English language literacy, relevant for Singapore's national interests and global markets. The continuity in my family's emphasis on reading in English aligned with national directions, enabling the multiplication of cultural capital across generations in my family context.

There is insufficient room in this chapter for discussion of the complexity of institutional habitus, but what needs to be highlighted is the multiplicity and relational aspects of institutional habitus. Institutional habitus exists at various interrelated levels: at the level of national policies, school policies and practices and public institutions such as the public library. At a policy level, there needs to be an understanding that the collective habitus of home and institution intersect with differing results in each milieu. Although Singapore's educational system premised on meritocracy has allowed a large proportion of its population to improve literacy and economic standards, the changing global system and dynamics necessitate a reconsideration of whether changes need to be made for a more equitable educational system. The growing middle-class invest in reading resources and practices to multiply their children's access to reading as a form of cultural capital (Loh & Sun, 2020; Ng, 2013), even as the educational system demands more from students. Beyond print reading, proficient online reading is dependent on navigation ability and critical literacy skills, and research demonstrates that early home literacy practices are associated with adolescent online digital reading proficiency (Notten & Becker, 2017). Low-SES parents, unable to provide the familial habitus for acquiring reading due to lack of resources, time and energy, may see their children fall behind if the schooling system does not do more to help those with less access to resources (Teo, 2018).

In the area of reading, understanding that reading engagement is the core embodied cultural capital that middle-class families cultivate, and that it is valued in school and for self-directed independent learning, may allow educators to understand why, at least in Singapore, the reading gap between low and high achievers continues to widen even as more effort is pumped into helping all

---

students learn (Loh & Sun, 2020). A skills-focused approach in school that does not account for the affective elements of reading engagement fails to understand that pleasure or motivation to read is a key component to encourage students towards higher-level critical reading. Resourcing issues should not be limited to physical resources and skills training. Instead, educational policies need to redirect the attention of the focus of literacy teaching and learning away from a decontextualised skills-only approach towards a model that attends to the affective, social and cultural elements of learning to read. Acknowledging that literacy learning is varied and multiple and constitutes more than decoding and comprehension skills is one way to begin rethinking how policy and practice can tackle the cultural inequity of learning for students from different SES.

As an analytic lens, Bourdieu's concept of habitus has the potential to reveal schooling's transformative possibilities. Carmen Mills (2008) highlights that habitus constitutes both reproductive and transformative traits, and I have argued in this chapter that analysing the familial and institutional habitus in application to empirical data may reveal entry points for new ways of thinking about literacy learning for greater equity. Certainly, more narratives of literacy learning should be gathered to generate insight about how to plan for future reading. This singular narrative, while limited, highlights that educational transformation requires structural intervention and not just individual effort. Recognising the structural factors that contribute to learning inequities should prod policy makers and educators to rethink what counts as literacy education and how reading should be taught and learnt in schools.

While even more complex issues of bi- and multilingual literacy learning and digital literacy skills are not addressed in this chapter, the chapter emphasises that policy makers and practitioners concerned with ensuring equitable access to higher literacy demands of the future must engage with some pressing questions: What counts as literacy in this technological, global and multilingual world? How do we ensure that students from different backgrounds have equitable access to resources for learning? How do we measure the success of our education system for equity? How the reading futures of our children pan out will depend on how we address these difficult questions.

References

Araujo, L., & Costa, P. (2015). Home book reading and reading achievement in EU countries: The progress in international reading literacy study 2011 (PIRLS). *Educational Research and Evaluation, 21*(5–6), 422–438.

Bhaskaran, M., Ho, S. C., Low, D., Tan, K. S., Vadaketh, S., & Yeoh, L. K. (2012). *Inequality and the need for a new social compact.* Paper presented at the Singapore Perspectives 2012, Singapore.

Bochner, A. P. (2012). On first-person narrative scholarship: Autoethnography as acts of meaning. *Narrative Inquiry, 22*(1), 155–164.

Bourdieu, P. (1977). *Outline of a theory of practice* (R. Nice, Trans.). Cambridge: Cambridge University Press.

Bourdieu, P. (1984). *Distinction: A social critique of the judgement of taste* (R. Nice, Trans.). Boston: Harvard University Press.

Bourdieu, P. (1986). The forms of capital (R. Nice, Trans.). In J. E. Richardson (Ed.), *Handbook of theory of research for the sociology of education*. Westport, CT: Greenwood Press.

Bourdieu, P., & Passeron, J.-C. (1990). *Reproduction in education, society and culture* (R. Nice, Trans.). London: Sage.

Bourdieu, P., & Wacquant, L. J. D. (1992). *An invitation to reflexive sociology*. Chicago: The University of Chicago Press.

Brandt, D. (2015). *The rise of writing: Redefining mass literacy*. Cambridge: Cambridge University Press.

Bruner, J., & Weisser, S. (1991). The invention of self: Autobiography and its forms. In D. R. Olson & N. Torrance (Eds.), *Literacy and orality* (pp. 129–148). Cambridge: Cambridge University Press.

Burke, C. T., Emmerich, N., & Ingram, N. (2013). Well-founded social fictions: A defence of the concepts of institutional and familial habitus. *British Journal of Sociology of Education, 34*(2), 165–182. doi:10.1080/01425692.2012.746263

Byun, S. Y., Schofer, E., & Kim, K. K. (2012). Revisiting the role of cultural capital in East Asian educational systems: The case of South Korea. *Sociology of Education, 85*(3). doi:10.1177/0038040712447180

Chia, S. Y. (2001) Singapore: Towards a knowledge-based economy. In S. Masuyama, D. Vandenbrink, & S. Y. Chia (Eds.), *Industrial restructuring in East Asia: Towards the 21st century*. Singapore: Institute of Southeast Asian Studies.

Chiu, M. M., & Chow, B. W. Y. (2010). Culture, motivation, and reading achievement: High school students in 41 countries. *Learning and Individual Differences, 20,* 579–592.

CPDD, MOE (2010) *English language syllabus 2010: Primary & secondary (express/ normal [academic])*. Singapore: Curriculum Planning & Development Division, Ministry of Education.

Currid-Halkett, E. (2017). *The sum of small things: A theory of the aspirational class*. Princeton, NJ: Princeton University Press.

De Graaf, N. D., De Graaf, P. M., & Kraaykamp, G. (2000). Parental cultural capital and educational attainment in the Netherlands: A refinement of the cultural capital perspective. *Sociology of Education, 73,* 92–111.

Elley, W. B. (2000). The potential of book floods for raising literacy levels. *International Review of Education, 46*(3–4), 233–255.

Ellis, C., Adams, E. & Bochner, P. (2011). Autoethnography: an overview. *Forum Qualitative Social Research 12*(1). https://www.qualitative-research.net/index. php/fqs/article/view/1589/3095.

Giroux, H. A. (1983). Theories of reproduction and resistance in the new sociology of education. *Harvard Educational Review, 53*(3), 257–293.

Goh, K. S., & Team, T. E. S. (1979). *Report on the ministry of education 1978*. Singapore: National Archives of Singapore. Retrieved from www.nas.gov.sg/archiveson line/data/pdfdoc/956-1979-02-10.pdf

Gopinathan, S. (1980). Language policy in education: A Singapore perspective. In E. A. Afendras & E. L. Y. Kuo (Eds.), *Language and society in Singapore* (pp. 175–202). Singapore: Singapore University Press.

Gopinathan, S. (1998). Language policy changes 1979–1997: Politics and pedagogy. In S. Gopinathan, A. Pakir, W. K. Ho, & V. Saravanan (Eds.), *Language, society and education in Singapore: Issues and trends* (pp. 19–44). Singapore: Times Academic Press.

Gopinathan, S. (2007). Globalisation, the Singapore developmental state and educational policy: A thesis revisited. *Globalisation, Societies and Education*, 5(1), 53–70.

Gopinathan, S., & Abu Baker, M. (2013). Globalization, the state and curriculum reform. In Z. Deng, S. Gopinathan, & C. Lee (Eds.), *Globalization and the Singapore curriculum*. Dordrecht: Springer.

Graff, H. J. (1987). *The legacy of literacy: Continuities and contradictions in Western culture and society*. Bloomington: Indiana University Press.

HistorySG. (n.d.). *Report on the ministry of education (Goh Report)*. National Library Board. Retrieved from http://eresources.nlb.gov.sg/history/events/8f0a445f-bbd1-4e5c-8ebe-9461ea61f5de

Hong, X. (2019). *The remaking of Singapore's public libraries*. Singapore: National Library Board.

Koh, A., & Chong, T. (2014). Education in the global city: The manufacturing of education in Singapore. *Discourse: Studies in the Cultural Politics of Education*, 35(5), 625–636.

Koh, A., & Kenway, J. (2012). Cultivating national leaders in an elite school: Deploying the transnational in the national interest. *International Studies in Sociology of Education*, 22(4), 331–351.

Kramer-Dahl, A., & Kwek, D. (2011). 'Reading' the home and reading in school: Framing deficit constructions as learning difficulties in English classrooms. In C. Wyatt-Smith, J. Elkins, & S. Gunn (Eds.), *Multiple perspectives on difficulties in learning: Literacy and numeracy* (pp. 159–178). Dordrecht: Springer.

Lareau, A. (1989). *Home advantage: Social class and parental intervention in elementary education*. New York: The Falmer Press.

Lareau, A., & Weininger, E. B. (2003). Cultural capital in educational research: A critical assessment. *Theory and Society*, 32(5/6), 567–606.

Lee, P. (2016, March 10). English most common home language in Singapore, bilingualism also up: Government survey. *Straits Times*. Retrieved from www.straitstimes.com/singapore/english-most-common-home-language-in-singapore-bilingualism-also-up-government-survey

Lien Centre for Social Innovation. (2015). *A handbook on inequality, poverty and unmet social needs in Singapore*. Singapore: Lien Foundation.

Lim, L. (2013). Meritocracy, elitism, and egalitarianism: A preliminary and provisional assessment of Singapore primary education review. *Asia Pacific Journal of Education*, 33(1), 1–14.

Lim, S. C. (2002). Developments in the English language syllabus in Singapore. *Asia Pacific Journal of Education*, 22(2), 81–95.

Loh, C. E. (2013). Singaporean boys constructing global literate selves through their reading practices in and out of school. *Anthropology and Education Quarterly*, 44(1), 38–57.

Loh, C. E. (2015). Building a reading culture in a Singapore school: Identifying spaces for change through a socio-spatial approach. *Changing English*, 22(2), 209–221.

Loh, C. E. (2016). In remembrance of reading. *Biblioasia*, 12(1), 46–53.

Loh, C. E., & Liew, W. M. (2016). Voices from the ground: The emotional labour of English teachers' work. *Teaching and Teacher Education*, 55, 267–278.

Loh, C. E., & Sun, B. (2018). *Report on the reading habits of Singapore teenagers 2017.* Singapore: National Institute of Education, Nanyang Technological University.

Loh, C. E., & Sun, B. (2020). Cultural capital, habitus and reading futures: Middle-class adolescent students' cultivation of reading dispositions in Singapore. *British Journal of Sociology of Education, 41*(2), 234–252. https://doi.org/10.1080/014 25692.2019.1690426

Loh, J. (2018). Implementing and sustaining curriculum reform in Singapore primary schools. In G. E. Hall, L. F. Quinn, & D. M. Gollnick (Eds.), *The Wiley handbook of teaching and learning.* Singapore: John Wiley & Sons Inc.

Menon, R. (Producer). (2015, December 26). *An economic history of Singapore: 1965–2065 [Transcript].* The Bank for International Settlements. Retrieved from www.bis.org/review/r150807b.htm

Mills, C. (2008). Reproduction and transformation of inequalities in schooling: The transformative potential of the theoretical constructs of Bourdieu. *British Journal of Sociology of Education, 29*(1), 79–89. doi:10.1080/01425690701737481

Mishler, E. G. (1999). *Storylines: Craft artists' narratives of identity.* Cambridge, MA: Harvard University Press.

Nash, R. (1990). Bourdieu on education and social and cultural reproduction. *British Journal of Sociology of Education, 11*(4), 431–447.

National Archives Singapore. *Singapore in August 1965.* Retrieved from www.nas.gov. sg/1stCab/PanelPDF/Section%201%20-%20Singapore%20in%201965.pdf

Ng, I. Y. H. (2013). Education and intergenerational mobility in Singapore. *Educational Review, 66*(3), 362–376.

Notten, N., & Becker, B. (2017). Early home literacy and adolescents' online reading behavior in comparative perspective. *International Journal of Comparative Sociology, 58*(6), 475–493. doi:10.1177/0020715217735362

OECD. (2010). *Singapore: Rapid improvement followed by strong performance.* France. Retrieved from www.oecd.org/countries/singapore/46581101.pdf

Pakir, A. (1991). The range and depth of English-knowing bilinguals in Singapore. *World Englishes, 10*(2), 167–179.

Pakir, A. (2004). Medium-of-instruction policy in Singapore. In J. W. Tollefson & A. B. M. Tsui (Eds.), *Medium of instruction policies* (pp. 117–131). Mahwah, NJ: Lawrence Erlbaum Associates, Publishers.

Park, H. (2008). Home literacy environments and children's reading performance: A comparative study of 25 countries. *Educational Research and Evaluation, 14*(6), 489–505.

Ramachandran, R. (1999, August). *The "national" role of the national library board of Singapore.* Paper presented at the IFLA Council and General Conference, Bangkok, Thailand.

Reay, D. (1998). 'Always knowing' and 'never being sure': Familial and institutional habitues and higher education choice. *Journal of Education Policy, 13*(4), 519–529.

Reay, D. (2004). 'It's all becoming habitus': Beyond the habitual use of habitus in educational research. *British Journal of Sociology of Education, 25*(4), 431–444.

Schön, D. A. (1991). Introduction. In D. A. Schön (Ed.), *The reflective turn: Case studies in and on educational practice* (pp. 1–12). New York: Teachers College Press.

Schwab, K. (2017). *The fourth industrial revolution.* New York: Crown Business.

Sharpe, L., & Gopinantha, S. (2002) After effectiveness: New directions in the Singapore school system? *Journal of Education Policy, 17*(2), 151–166.

Silver, R. E. (2005). The discourse of linguistic capital: Language and economic policy planning in Singapore. *Language Policy, 4*, 47–66.

Sim, C. (2016). *Bilingual policy.* National Library Board. Retrieved December 26, 2019, from https://eresources.nlb.gov.sg/infopedia/articles/SIP_2016-09-01_093402.html

Singapore Department of Statistics. (2019). *Education, language spoken and literacy.* Singapore. Retrieved from www.singstat.gov.sg/find-data/search-by-theme/population/education-language-spoken-and-literacy/latest-data

Tan, C. (2005). The potential of Singapore's ability driven education to prepare students for a knowledge economy. *International Education Journal, 6*(4), 446–453.

Tan, E. S. (2015). *Class and social orientations: Key findings from the social stratification survey 2011.* Scholar Bank@NUS Repository. https://doi.org/10.25818/ycg7-dpns

Tan, J. (2008). The marketisation of education in Singapore. In J. Tan (Ed.), *Thinking schools, learning nation: Contemporary issues and challenges* (pp. 19–38). Singapore: Pearson Education.

Tan, J. (2010). Education in Singapore: Sorting them out? In T. Chong (Ed.), *Management of success: Singapore revisited* (pp. 288–308). Singapore: Institute of Southeast Asian Studies.

Teo, Y. Y. (2018). *This is what inequality looks like.* Singapore: Ethos Book.

Weininger, E. B., & Lareau, A. (2003). Translating Bourdieu into the American context: The question of social class and family-school relations. *Poetics, 31*, 375–402.

10 English language and literature education in the biliterate and trilingual Hong Kong

A walk through the post-war era

Faye Dorcas Yung

Introduction

On 31 August 1945, Hong Kong was liberated from Japanese occupation which had begun on 25 December 1941. Like many societies, Hong Kong experienced drastic changes during the post-war decades, navigating itself amidst the region's political instability. The British colonial government has responded to the social and economic changes with a different approach to governance in comparison to the century of colonial rule before the Japanese occupation. It was during that transformative times of the early 1950s that my parents were born. They received education in the years of a rapidly, and at times chaotically, expanding education sector in the 1960s and 1970s, a time where educational resources were still scarce. They later on joined the ranks of secondary school teachers in the mid-1970s. It was at the turn of the 1970s and 1980s that my elder brother and I were born. Our educational experiences were quite different from our parents' as the government offered universal free nine-year education at primary and junior secondary level in the year before my brother was born. During our secondary school years, we witnessed Hong Kong's change of sovereignty in 1997 from Britain to the People's Republic of China. I became a secondary school English teacher in the new millennium and experienced the second wave of education reform. Compared to my students, my brother and I were the last generation fully educated under British colonial rule. The language landscape we grew up with has always been occupied by both English and Chinese. The ambiguous term "Chinese" during our school years referred to Cantonese[1] in speech and Traditional Chinese characters in written text, but it has changed gradually over the years to include Putonghua. The marginal presence of Putonghua during my school years was overtly changed after the change of sovereignty in 1997. In his first policy address, the first Chief Executive introduced a new aspiration of Hongkongers' language learning goal:

> Confidence and competence in the use of Chinese and English are essential if we are to maintain our competitive edge in the world. The Education Commission Report No.6 has already laid down a framework to achieve our

goal for secondary school graduates to be proficient in writing English and Chinese and able to communicate confidently in Cantonese, English and Putonghua.

(Hong Kong SAR Government, 1997, para. 84).

This aspiration was reiterated in the *Medium of instruction: Guidance for Secondary Schools*, stating that "[o]ur aim is for our students to be biliterate (i.e. master written Chinese and English) and trilingual (i.e. speak fluent Cantonese, Putonghua and English)" (Education Department, 1997). By inference, the government's vision for literacy refers to students' (and the general population's) ability to read and write, whereas one's "trilingual" ability refers to one's competency in speaking the languages.

This chapter gives a historical overview of the development of the English language and literature education in Hong Kong within the competitive educational space towards biliteracy and trilingualism in the post-war years up to the present day. It also offers a perspective from a rather typical Hong Kong family who live through these changes. I retrace my parents' footsteps in the 1950s to the 1970s amidst the tides of a changing society and educational policies, and how they raised a family in the 1980s and 1990s which led up to the political paradigm shift. My own career path as a secondary school English teacher and subsequently an English teacher trainer is also referenced to illustrate the impact of various educational policies.

The English language in Hong Kong society

The development of the education system in Hong Kong was very different before and after the Japanese occupation period between December 1941 and August 1945 (Sweetings, 1993, 2004; Evans, 2011; Lee, 2005). Before the Japanese Occupation, Hong Kong had already been a Crown Colony of Britain for a century. Since the beginning of Hong Kong's colonial existence in 1842, the English language has been the official language of governance and the language for international trade in this growing trading outpost. Even though the population has always been largely Cantonese-speaking Chinese, it was not until 1974 that the colonial government enacted the Official Languages Ordinance to make both English and Chinese "the official languages of Hong Kong for purposes of officers and members of the public," giving equal status to both in officialdom. The long colonial governance may lead people to think that English had dominated Hong Kong's general society and the education system, but as So (1996) observes, "[T]he spread of English has been restricted to the local elite who acquire the language mostly by way of formal education" (p. 41). Evans (2013) also points out that "it is necessary to distinguish the spoken and written language" (p. 308), as he observes that, in business communication and socially inspired digital communications, Hongkongers often read and write in English but speak Cantonese. Even though

Cantonese remains by and large the everyday language among the relatively homogenous population, the linguistic space is shared between English and Cantonese in a way that serves the formality requirement and the pragmatic everyday ease of usage.

My parents' learning of English outside of formal education reveals another façade of English in the Hong Kong society that truly characterises the city's international vibe and free flow of information and people. To them, the appeal of English was not just for the language's political status, economic promises or social prestige. In the 1950s and 1960s, until the mid-1970s, pop music in Hong Kong was mainly in English. It was the time of Elvis Presley and The Beatles. Looking at the old photos of my father in his late teen years with his sideburns, I could imagine him singing and dancing to Elvis in his bellbottoms jeans. English films were also really popular in those days. When asked how he learnt his English, my dad cited his habit of going into the cinema with a little notepad. He would scribble down words or phrases, at least phonetically, which were new to him and he would check his scribbles against the dictionary afterwards. For someone who grew up in a public housing estate from a typical working-class family which sometimes struggled to put food on the table, the English-language pop culture readily available to him seemed to also be part of the general public's entertainment repertoire. Those were sources of my father's English education outside of formal education. Apart from pop culture and entertainment, religious organisations also provided exposure to English outside to the public. As my mother recalled, she accredited her extracurricular English literacy development to the Salvation Army, where she attended Sunday school taught by American missionaries. Some of her older siblings attended the English church services in which her father often served as the Cantonese interpreter. My parents' experiences show a side of the everyday life of ordinary Hongkongers, who were exposed to English in the realms of entertainment and religious activities, showing where English appears outside of the realm of the elite world and officialdom and coexists alongside Chinese.

As Sweeting and Vickers note, "As far as language was concerned, there was no coherent overall 'policy' for at least the first three and a half decades of Hong Kong's colonial existence" (2007, p. 12). During the first century of the colonial rule, the colonial government adopted a *laissez-faire* approach to education which was mostly decentralised and reactionary to the changing political and social situations (Evans, 1998; Sweeting & Vickers, 2005, 2007; Jeon, 2016). It was a myth to assume the relatively prestigious status of the English language in Hong Kong is simply the result of Britain's imperialistic presence. Instead, it was a dynamic interplay between the interests of many parties, including the government, the various school funding bodies (mostly missionaries who arrived in Hong Kong in the late nineteenth century to early 20th century, and then local charitable organisations in the post-war decades), the local elites and the general public.

The growing Hong Kong and her growing education system: grant schools and their impact on the status of English

Hong Kong experienced a rapid surge in population during the first three decades after World War II. From a population of merely 600,000 in 1945, the population tripled to 1.8 million by 1947. The population increased by almost 1 million per decade in the following year, reaching 2.8 million at 1957, 3.9 million at 1967, and 4.4 million by 1976 (Census & Statistics Department, 1969, 1981). As the political situation in China remained unstable until the late 1970s, Hong Kong had been a steady destination for migrants and refugees. The growth in the 1940s to 1960s consisted of mainly immigrants from China who were mostly young people. Different from the general baby-boom phenomenon in other countries, the population structure in Hong Kong skewed towards the younger age-bands. The population was also changing from a transient to a "settled, indigenous population" with very high levels of female employment in the manufacturing sector (Sweeting & Morris, 1993). The steadily developing economy with a strong manufacturing sector made people more affluent. These factors contributed to the high demand for kindergarten and primary education. The colonial government's approach to education could no longer focus only on serving the elites, as it had been during the first century of her colonial rule. The rapidly growing population also presented significant governance challenges to the colonial government which could no longer be handled by the *laissez-faire* approach adopted during the pre-war century. Therefore, the government in the post-war era had to make active attempts to centralise and standardise education. Language policy, encompassing the medium of instruction and the English language as a subject, has been one of the most controversial and unsettled issues amongst the many educational policies since the dawn of mass education in Hong Kong.

The status of English, both as a subject and as a medium of instruction in the education system, has a strong correlation to the types of schools set up in the earlier colonial days. Schools set up before the occupation period were what Sweeting (1993) terms a "quadripartite 'system'" (p. 7) and involve four funding and operation models: *government schools, grant schools, subsidised schools* and *private schools*. While the early government schools were set up as models for English-medium (Anglo-Chinese) education, whose curricula were adopted by the grant schools, the subsidised and private schools were mainly Chinese-medium schools set up in the 1960s through the 1970s to meet the needs of the influx of migrants from China. Most grant schools were founded by missionary bodies which mostly arrived in the nineteenth century. In comparison to subsidised and private schools, the grant schools' long history and prestige gave them more influence on the government's education initiatives and "played an instrumental role in both the development of the colony's education system and the provision of English Language education in Hong Kong [during the course of the 19th century]" (Evans, 1998, p. 160). The Grant School Council has been a strong proponent of the importance of English education as schooling system and syllabus, as a language subject and as a medium of instruction. For instance, the Grant School Council was adamant about the Education Department's General Circular No. 19 on 20 August, 1946, which suggested the teaching of English in schools should take a utilitarian approach and teach pupils English to a level that was likely to be needed for whatever career prospect available to them at the time (Sweeting, 1993; Fung & Chan-Yeung, 2009). The grant schools rejected the government's appeal to offering a vernacular education, claiming that parents chose to send their children to these schools for a good English education (Sweeting, 1993). The prestige of the grant schools and their traditionally selective and elite student intake, which produce graduates with promising careers in business and the government, reinforced the general public's perception on the superiority of an English-medium education. The number of English-medium schools increased from "54% in 1955, to 68% in 1965, to 80% in 1975, to 91% in 1985 and to 94% in 1997" (Education Department 1995–1997, cited by Lee, 2005, p. 36). This phenomenon, as Evans (1996) argues, "was entirely driven by parents, who perceived that access to further education or careers in business and government depended on proficiency in English" (p. 38). He argues that the model for mass education, mainly to serve an increasingly Chinese-speaking population in the post-war, years has inappropriately modelled upon a model developed in the earlier colonial days "designed to produce an education (of) Hong Kong Chinese elite" (Evans, 1996). In practice, however, most English-medium schools were only believed to be operating as such in name (Evans, 1998, 2002, 2008, 2016; Tsui, 2004). Due to the dominating Cantonese speaking masses, teachers were often found to employ code-mixing in teaching: lessons are conducted in Cantonese, while textbooks, assignments, tests and exams are in English. Even though English is not an everyday language in Hong Kong for the vast majority, the hierarchy between English and Chinese is apparent to all in the society.

This hierarchy of languages was picked up by my then 5-year-old mind. When I learnt that I was not going to enter into the English medium primary school like most of my kindergarten classmates would, I remember clearly the realisation that I belonged to the bottom of the heap. Being sent to a Chinese primary school was a lesser option. Seeing my brother attending an English-medium primary school and proceeded smoothly from book to book along the Ladybird Keyword Reading Scheme at home reinforced that hierarchy in my young mind. It was a phenomenon so prevalent that even a young child could perceive it. What was observed by the scholars were also true in my parents' generation. During her primary school years, my mother switched to an English primary school after studying one year in a neighbourhood primary school. The reason was that the first school she enrolled in did not offer English until Primary 3. In the late 1950s and 1960s, there were not many choices of English textbooks, and most schools adopted *The Oxford English Course for Hong Kong* (1956), which was adapted from *The Oxford English Course for Malaya* (1940). She still remembers the first chapter of the English textbooks that everyone in that generation uses, "This is a man. This is a pan. A man and a pan."

Figure 10.1 The Oxford English Course for Hong Kong—First Year Part Two: Reading
(1956)

Source: Private collection of Mr Lau Chi Chung, collector and founder of Old Textbooks.

English vs the vernacular: the medium of instruction policies

Growing up with an awareness (and an ignorant certainty) of the supremacy of English in society, the history of my own *alma mater* surprised me with a time when English was not as dominating as it was during my own school years. The development of mass education in 20th-century Hong Kong has followed on the two tracks: Anglo-Chinese (i.e. English) and Vernacular (i.e. Cantonese). My alma mater was among the few girls' schools that used to offer a vernacular education modelled after the schools of the Republic of China in its earlier days since founded in 1936 (Chiu, 2020). During the pre-war years, its curriculum prepared students for further education opportunities in China. This arrangement echoed the appeal by the British Inspector of Schools Edmund Burney, who in 1935 recommended the use of Chinese as the medium of instruction and English to be taught as a subject for vocational purposes. (His suggestion was the cause of the eventually rejected August 1946 circular no. 19 mentioned earlier.) However, the dynamics of the two languages changed as the path to further studies in China gradually closed down in the 1950s onwards, and the alternative to tertiary education in the only university in Hong Kong operated in English. The demand for an English education increased, and my alma mater began to transition into an Anglo-Chinese school in the 1950s. By the 1960s, the vernacular section was completely phased out. It seems to suggest that choice of medium of instruction in secondary schools was largely a strategic decision responding to the opportunities presented to their students upon graduation, be it employment or further studies. The University of Hong Kong (HKU) had been the only university in the city which used English as the medium of instruction until the establishment of Chinese University of Hong Kong (CUHK) in 1963, a vernacular university. CUHK was partly an answer to the increased number of secondary graduates from the expanding mass education system of vernacular schools who demanded tertiary education in Chinese; another factor which led CUHK to be a vernacular university is that its founding members were mostly scholars self-exiled from the Communist regime in China. By the 1980s and 1990s, Hong Kong's position as an international financial centre was well established, and the demand for a work force with good English proficiency was high. It was the social consensus that English was the more esteemed language and the preferred choice for medium of instruction (Tung, Lam, & Tsang, 1997; Jeon, 2016). Upon the handover of sovereignty in 1997, the policy on the medium of instruction took centre stage again, only this time the government implemented it forcibly (Cheng, 2009; Poon & Lau, 2016) and the reason appears political rather than the wonted pragmatic concerns.

The Education Department (ED) issued the Medium of Instruction Guidance for Secondary School (1997). Schools need to prove (1) their students' ability to learn in English, (2) teachers' capability to teach through English and (3) having adequate support strategies/measures in place to help students learn in English in order to maintain the use of English as the medium of instruction. However, the "coercively implemented" (Cheng, 2009, p. 71) policy was under much criticism and "aroused strong emotional reaction from every sector of the community" (Tsui, 2004, p. 99). Choi calls it:

> an elitist language selection policy. . . [which] was designed to be a cost-effective way of training in English skills for those who had the economic and cultural capital to benefit from it. Meanwhile, the majority of students were barred from sufficient exposure to English, the language of power and wealth.
>
> (2005, p. 147)

I was in my senior secondary years when the policy was introduced, and I was, in Choi's words, the "elite" benefiting from this policy. As a teenager with limited understanding of the bigger education context, the nuances amongst these 94% of English medium schools was unknown to me. I thought all English medium schools were similar: all would have teachers who ranged from being perfectly comfortable to teach in English to struggling to do so, but overall teaching could be carried out effectively in English. I remember during the time leading up to the implementation of the policy, our school principal reminded all of us to speak English at all times during lessons. All teachers were to use 100% English to teach in preparation for sudden visits of school inspectors. It turned out that not all of the 94% English medium schools wanted to continue to use English as the medium of instruction. Upon the implementation of the policy, only 124 schools out of 421 applied to use English as the medium of instruction. The government granted approval to 100 schools, my alma mater being one of them. Twenty of the disapproved schools appealed the decision and in the end 114 schools were granted approval. These 114 schools were labelled as EMI schools (English as medium of instruction) with an added layer of prestige. The remaining 307 schools were labelled CMI schools (Chinese as medium of instruction) (Tsui, 2004; Evans, 2016).

As the policy came under mounting criticism from various sectors of the community, including principals, teachers, parents, school sponsoring bodies and the business sector, the government conceded to issue a fine-tuning arrangement in 2009. The government argues that the fine-tuning arrangements worked towards "the policy goal of 'upholding mother-tongue teaching while enhancing students' proficiency in both Chinese and English" (EDB, 2010, p. 4) so as to enhance their ability to learn in English and to better prepare them for future studies and work in the future. In essence, the 1997 policy has been abandoned as CMI schools can "provide students with diversified MOI arrangements, starting from Secondary One (S1)" (EDB, 2010, p. 2) according to the students' ability. The school-based decision is still dependent upon the three criteria set out in the 1997 policy (but much less stringently enforced), namely, that schools are expected to make professional judgment on the most appropriate MOI arrangements for their students in accordance with their own circumstances (including teachers' capability to teach in English, school support measures, etc.) and students' needs (EDB, 2010). In other words, due to the strong push back from society, the government has once again backed down from officialising vernacular education, leaving the decision of MOI arrangements to school management.

The development of the English language as a subject: syllabus aims, pedagogy and assessment

The issue of medium of instruction throughout the post-war decades basically laid the ground for how English is to be positioned in Hong Kong's education system. The fact is that English remains the ticket to better higher education opportunities and better job prospects. English as a language subject has always been expected to respond to society's changing needs while serving the cross-curricular demands. Also, the rebuilding and expansion of the education system in the post-war period slowly funnelled into a more centralised endeavour. The establishment of the Hong Kong Examinations Authority in 1977 (renamed Hong Kong Examinations and Assessments Authority in 2002) was one of the important milestones of the government's effort in centralising and standardising education since public exams had been an effective tool. The three phases of curricula as well as assessment designs in the 1970s, 1980s and late 1990s reflect these developments. They also reflected the ever-developing trends in ESL pedagogy. The pedagogy favoured in the syllabi changed from the audio-lingual approach (1975, 1976), to a communicative approach (1981, 1983), and then to a task-based approach (CDC, 2002, 2017a; CDC & HKEAA, 2007).

The 1975 (secondary) and 1976 (primary) syllabi

Since the government achieved free, universal and compulsory primary education in September 1971, and aimed at extending this up to three years of junior secondary education by 1979 (a target met one year ahead of planned in 1978), the 1975 and 1976 syllabi were the first English language syllabi written for mass education intending to address students of a much wider range of abilities (Walker, 2000) and more varied career prospects. It aimed at training students to acquire "basic level of everyday English in nine years of schooling" (Tong & Adamson, 2013, p. 24). One of the most prominent features of the 1975 English syllabus for secondary school was that it was divided into Syllabus A and Syllabus B. The former was an easier syllabus intended for students attending Chinese-medium schools, "designed to cater for the mass of students who were expected to leave school after Form Three" (p. 25), whereas the latter was designed for English-medium schools in which students were more likely to be pursuing further education in the senior secondary and tertiary levels. The syllabus prescribed an "oral structural teaching method" which focused on structural knowledge and accuracy and placed more focus on fluency in speaking than on writing (Walker, Tong, & Mok-Cheung, 2000). The 1979 oral examination paper gave us a hint into the days where English language learning placed more emphasis on formal accuracy than communicative success. Candidates were required to read out a short passage of about 150 words, and their oral competency was judged for their accuracy and fluency by two examiners.

The 1981 (primary) and 1983 (secondary) syllabi

The 1980s English language teaching was characterised by the Communicative Language Teaching (CLT). This curriculum showed attention shifting towards the communicative value of language learning, instead of focusing on the accuracy of reproducing the language. The importance of language teaching and learning being purposeful and meaningful was highlighted, addressing students' need to use the language in real communicative situations. This was the beginning of moving towards a more *communicative approach*. The traditional oral-structural approach was no longer encouraged. The change was caused by Hong Kong's changing economic situation: the growing tertiary sector demands a workforce with a higher English competency. The syllabus document recognises that English is not only the official language, a language for education, business, commerce, science and banking—its value for personal enjoyment was also highlighted (CDC, 1981). A new emphasis was placed on the *use* of the language.

However, some critics regarded this approach as a failure due to the mismatch between the curriculum intentions and the resources available for teachers at the time. This change, as Evans argued, "was not underpinned by research conducted in Hong Kong classrooms; it merely repeated criticism of structural approaches which appeared in the communicative literature since the early 1970s" (1998, p. 33). When CLT was introduced into the Hong Kong syllabus, it was met with criticism from teachers, citing the examination-driven Hong Kong education system, the big class size (often over 40 students per class) and the lack of teaching materials and training for teachers. It has taken many more years before the CLT has had a significant impact on the English language classroom.

The 1997 (primary) and 1999 (secondary) syllabi

These syllabi were produced after the introduction of Targets and Target-related Assessment (TTRA) in the early 1990s, which was renamed Target Oriented Curriculum (TOC) in 1993. The concepts of learning targets are introduced into the curriculum framework and syllabus design. Implemented in 1995, schools participating in the TOC incorporated its framework into the 1981 syllabus. By 1997, 90% of the primary schools participated in the TOC, prompting the Education Department to formalise it into the curriculum (Pang & Wong, 2000). When TTRA was first announced in the early 1990s, it was a time when the education system was still struggling to staff all schools with qualified teachers. Teachers understandably found the new concept challenging, even though some of the reluctance against the change was due to misunderstanding (the word "assessment" in TTRA was misleading, thus prompting the name change later). My mother recalled that in those days when the reform was introduced, the teachers jokingly said the TTRA stood for "teachers-totally-ran-away".

Nonetheless, the pace of reform did not slow down. Within two decades, English Language teaching changed significantly in the theoretical orientations about language and language teaching and learning. The scope and purposes of learning also changed from the relatively narrow view in the 1970s, aiming to mainly develop pupils' oral proficiency, to a broadened aim in the 1981 syllabus to nurture pupils' bilingual competence. Approaching the new millennium, the 1997 syllabus aimed to enable every child living into the 21st century to have a multidimensional language education.

The current English Language syllabus (based on the 2002 to 2017 curriculum documents)

The current syllabus (CDC, 2017a) is largely based on the 1997/1999 syllabus, adopting the framework of TOC. Each new syllabus and its revision aim at enriching the elements of reading, IT in education and the promotion of varied forms of assessments. The curriculum documents promote the use of a task-based approach and encourage schools to:

> make flexible use of lesson time (e.g. the inclusion of more double or even triple periods per week or cycle in the school timetable) to facilitate a task-based approach to language learning and allow for continuous stretch of

time for English tasks and projects as well as co-curricular activities (e.g. watching videos or movies, taking part in drama workshop).

(CDC, 2017a, p. 29)

The 2007 reform of the senior secondary English syllabus paved the way for the change of the schooling system from four years of senior secondary to three years. It also introduced the school-based assessment component into the secondary school leaving examination, Hong Kong Certificate of Education Examination (HKCEE) (Hong Kong Examination and Assessment Authority, 2006). The subsequent New Senior Secondary (NSS) syllabus implemented in 2009 (EMB, 2007) and the corresponding final exam, the Hong Kong Diploma of Secondary Education (HKDSE) retained this component. The school-based assessment component claims to "promote a *positive impact or 'backwash effect'* designed to motivate students by requiring them to engage in extensive reading and viewing that will help develop their overall language ability" (EMB, 2007, p. 119). But three years of reading only accounts for 10% of the total grade in the assessment, which does not incentivise the students to read (because they often only need one book and one film to fulfil the assessment requirement), let alone read widely. The NSS curriculum also added eight elective components to the syllabus, encouraging teachers to spend class time on theme-based content under two categories: language arts and non-language arts. It also relies on the public exam to create a positive backwash effect to encourage an exposure to a wider variety of content, but the exam only consists of a 400-word writing task on topics that are vaguely related to the contents of the elective components. The extent to which the well-intended design enriches students' breadth and depth of English literacy is questionable.

English literacy without reading: the abolishing of the extensive reading scheme and the dwindling literature in English

With biliteracy being the overarching goal, together with placing reading as one of the Four Key Tasks in the whole curriculum (CDC, 2014, 2017b), one would expect to see an increase in efforts and resources in promoting reading. Therefore, the termination of the grant for the Extensive Reading Scheme (ERS) in 2016 was perplexing. Modelled after the Edinburgh Project of Extensive Reading (EPER), the scheme was introduced in 1991 to fund reading programmes in schools for both Chinese and English. The government's justification for axing this grant is that promotion of reading has already been done proactively since "Reading to learn" has been set as one of the Four Key Tasks. The grant for ERS, as a supporting measure, is deemed unnecessary (LC, 2016). Schools are encouraged to seek alternative funding for programmes to promote reading when needed.

The waning of the subject Literature in English is also unfavourable to English literacy. Whereas English Language has almost always been taught as a mandatory subject from primary one onwards, Literature in English is taught to a much smaller student population. Very few schools, both primary and secondary, offer it as a subject. It ambiguously overlaps with what the curriculum documents refer to as *language arts*, which also diminishes the need for schools to offer it as a separate subject. In 1994, 54 secondary schools offered English Literature for HKCEE and 25 schools offered it for Hong Kong Advanced Levels Examination (HKAL) (Wilcoxon, 1994). In 1981, 2,782 and 466 students studied for HKCEE and HKAL English Literature respectively; the numbers dropped to 1,010 and 210 in 1991, and further down to 721 and 132 in 2001. In 1981, it only made up 4.7% and 2.75% of the day school candidates of HKCEE and HKAL respectively; the percentage dropped to 1.63% and 1.09% in 1991 and 0.46% and 0.78% in 2001. The student percentage for HKCEE and HKAL candidacy remained at a similar level until both subjects were phased out after their respective last seating in 2010 and 2012. The number of candidates taking the subject for HKDSE at its launch in 2012 was 451. It dropped to 380 in 2016 and 283 in 2019. The corresponding percentages of day school candidates were around 0.6% to 0.7%. Wilcoxon's concern that "the iron lung of the established programmes and examinations may give out any time" (1994, p. 88) seems increasingly vivid today. Currently, only 37 out of 446 secondary schools are preparing students to sit for the Literature in English in HKDSE. These are mostly schools which are perceived to be traditionally prestigious ones, since it is perceived that students need to possess a certain level of English to be able to study Literature in English. My alma mater is one of the few schools that offers Literature in English to all years, but the fact (during my student days there) that they did not offer English Literature to the academically weakest class reflects this perception.

With such a small reach amongst the student population, it is understandable that very little research has been done about the teaching and learning of the subject. The subject has always been overlooked in the pragmatic society of Hong Kong for two reasons. Firstly, it does not have an obvious career prospect related to the subject. Even if one aspires to become an English teacher, knowledge in literature is not necessary, given the local university programmes that train ESL/EFL teachers put very little emphasis on literature. Secondly, before the government merged the secondary leaving exam (HKCEE) and the matriculation exam (HKAL) into one secondary leaving exam (HKDSE), more students had studied Literature in English during their secondary education. The single secondary education leaving exam (HKDSE) has significantly increased the stake of this exam, deterring students to take this "risky" subject which is seen as difficult and less predictable to achieve good grades. Fewer students will grow up knowing how to appreciate literature, and few will see the value in it. Those who choose to pursue a career in English language education will also have minimal exposure to literature, leading English language education down the path of pure function.

Conclusion

This chapter focused on English in Hong Kong's education, but that is just half of the story. The English language has always been competing with Cantonese and written Chinese for the precious attention and energy of the young minds in this demanding society. History and globalisation may have given English an elevated position in Hong Kong, but the everchanging political, social and economic factors continue to influence the dynamics between the languages in the city. Upon the change in sovereignty in 1997, the Biliterate and Trilingual policy officiated Putonghua (Mandarin) into the crowded linguistic space in schools. It is within such a context that this chapter spelt out the development of the English language and Literature education from the post-war period to the present day. This chapter discussed the broader contexts which determined the status of English in the education system as a medium of instruction. I then discussed the development of English as a language subject and changing pedagogical trends, moving towards a more meaning focused approach and more emphasis on reading. The final observations on the termination of the Extensive Reading Scheme and the diminishing of the Literature in English subject dampens the aspirations expressed in the government's policy addresses and the curriculum documents. This chapter also pointed out some inconsistencies in government policies which do not align with the biliteracy goal. My family and my experiences may not be representative of the masses; they are one example of how individuals lived with the changing policies and found their own path of literacy development. A better testimony of Hong Kong's English literacy is perhaps the international presence of Hong Kong's civil society in the year 2019 to 2020. The fruits of Hongkongers' English literacy has been evident in numerous international media, in the US Congress, the UN Human Rights Council and many more. The future of Hong Kong's language policy in education will be shaped by the ongoing social and political factors, as it has always been since the beginning of the British colonial rule. The unique history and position of Hong Kong in this globalised world and the expansive digital world give strong reasons for English literacy education to stay and to change for the better.

Note

1 Cantonese is the mother tongue of around 90% of Hong Kong's population since the 1971 census (Bacon-Shone & Bolton, 1998). The census reported that Cantonese is the mother tongue of 88.8% of the population (Census & Statistics Department, 2019).

References

Bacon-Shone, J., & Bolton, K. (1998). Charting multilingualism: Language censuses and language surveys in Hong Kong. In M. C. Pennington (Ed.), *Language in Hong Kong at century's end* (pp. 43–90). Hong Kong: Hong Kong University Press.
Census & Statistics Department. (1969). *Hong Kong statistics 1947–1967*. Hong Kong: Government Printer. Retrieved from www.censtatd.gov.hk/fd.jsp?file=hist/1961_1970/B10100031967AN67E0100.pdf&product_id=B1010003&lang=1

Census & Statistics Department. (1981). *Hong Kong annual digest of statistics (1981 edition)*. Hong Kong: Government Printer. Retrieved from www.censtatd.gov.hk/fd.jsp?file=hist/1981_1990/B10100031981AN81E0100.pdf&product_id=B1010003&lang=1

Census & Statistics Department. (2019). *Thematic household survey report no. 66*. Retrieved from https://www.censtatd.gov.hk/fd.jsp?file=B11302662019XXXXB0100.pdf&product_id=C0000086&lang=1

Cheng, Y. C. (2009). Hong Kong educational reforms in the last decade: Reform syndrome and new developments. *International Journal of Educational Management, 23*(1), 65–86.

Chiu, P. P. K. (2020). *Promoting all-round education for girls: A history of Heep Yunn School, Hong Kong*. Hong Kong: Hong Kong University Press.

Choi, P. K. (2005). The best students will learn English: Ultra - utilitarianism and linguistic imperialism in education in post - 1997 Hong Kong. In Ho, L. S., Morris, P., & Chung, Y. P. (Eds), *Education reform and the quest for excellence: The Hong Kong story*. Hong Kong: Hong Kong University Press.

Curriculum Development Committee (CDC). (1981). *English: Primary 1–6*. Hong Kong: Curriculum Development Committee.

Curriculum Development Committee (CDC). (2002). *English language education key learning area curriculum guide (primary 1 – secondary 3)*. Hong Kong: Curriculum Development Council. Retrieved from https://www.edb.gov.hk/attachment/en/curriculum-development/kla/eng-edu/cdc_ele_kla_curriculum_guide_(p1-s3)_2002.pdf

Curriculum Development Council. (2014). *3B: Reading to learn. Basic education curriculum guide: To sustain, deepen and focus on learning to learn (primary 1–6)*. Hong Kong: Curriculum Development Council. Retrieved from https://cd.edb.gov.hk/becg/english/chapter3B.html

Curriculum Development Council. (2017a). *English language education: Key learning area curriculum guide (primary 1—secondary 6)*. Hong Kong: Curriculum Development Council. Retrieved from www.edb.gov.hk/attachment/en/curriculum-development/kla/eng-edu/Curriculum%20Document/ELE%20KLACG_2017.pdf

Curriculum Development Council. (2017b). Booklet 6B: Reading to learn: Towards reading across the curriculum. In *Senior Secondary Curriculum Guide*. Hong Kong: Curriculum Development Council. Retrieved from www.edb.gov.hk/attachment/en/curriculum-development/renewal/Guides/SECG%20booklet%206B_en_20180831.pdf

Curriculum Development Council and Hong Kong Examination and Assessment Authority. (2007). *English language curriculum and assessment guide (secondary 4–6)*. Hong Kong: Curriculum Development Council.

Education Bureau (EDB). (2010, April). *Enrich our language environment realizing our vision: Fine-tuning of medium of instruction for secondary schools*. Hong Kong: Government Printer.

Education Department. (1997). *Medium of instruction guidance for secondary schools*. Hong Kong: Government Printer.

Education and Manpower Bureau. (2007). *English language curriculum and assessment guide (Secondary 4–6)*. Hong Kong: Curriculum Development Council.

Evans, S. (1996). The context of English language education: The case of Hong Kong. *RELC Journal, 27*(2), 30–55.

Evans, S. (1998). The beginnings of English language education in Hong Kong, 1842–1859. *Educational Research Journal, 13*(2), 151–176.

Evans, S. (2002). The medium of instruction in Hong Kong: Policy and practice in the new English and Chinese streams. *Research Papers in Education, 17*(1), 97–120.

Evans, S. (2008). The medium of instruction in Hong Kong revisited: Policy and practice in the reformed Chinese and English streams. *Research Papers in Education, 24*(3), 287–309.

Evans, S. (2011). Historical and comparative perspectives on the medium of instruction in Hong Kong. *Language Policy, 10,* 19–36.

Evans, S. (2013). The long march to biliteracy and trilingualism: Language policy in Hong Kong education since the handover. *Annual Review of Applied Linguistics, 33,* 302–324.

Evans, S. (2016). *The English language in Hong Kong: Diachronic and synchronic perspectives.* London: Palgrave Macmillan.

Fung, Yee Wang & Chan-Yeung Mo Wah Moira. (2009). *To serve and to lead: History of the diocesan boys' school in Hong Kong.* Hong Kong: Hong Kong University Press.

Hong Kong Examination and Assessment Authority. (2006, October). *2007 HKCE English language examination: Introduction to the school-based assessment component.* Hong Kong: Hong Kong Examination and Assessment Authority.

Hong Kong Special Administrative Region (HKSAR) Government. (1997). *Policy address: Building Hong Kong for a new era.* Retrieved from www.policyaddress.gov.hk/pa97/english/patext.htm

Jeon, M. (2016). English language education policy and the native-speaking English teacher (NET) scheme in Hong Kong. In R. Kirkpatrick (Ed.), *English language education policy in Asia.* Cham: Springer.

Lee, I. (2005). English language teaching in Hong Kong special administrative region (HKSAR): A continuous challenge. In G. Braine (Ed.), *Teaching English to the world: History, curriculum, and practice.* New York: Routledge.

Legislative Council. (2016, November 23). Question 15: Promoting reading culture. *Official Record of Proceedings.* Retrieved from www.legco.gov.hk/yr16-17/english/counmtg/hansard/cm20161123-translate-e.pdf

Pang, Ying Mei May & Wong Shiu Yu Winnie. (2000). An analysis of the primary English curriculum: Mismatches and implications. In Y. C. Cheng, K. W. Chow, & K. T. Tsui (Eds.), *School curriculum change and development in Hong Kong* (pp. 295–310). Hong Kong: Hong Kong Institute of Education.

Poon, A. Y. K., & Lau, C. M. Y. (2016). Fine-tuning medium-of-instruction policy in Hong Kong: Acquisition of language and content-based subject knowledge. *Journal of Pan-Pacific Association of Applied Linguistics, 20*(1), 135–155.

So, D. W. C. (1996). Hong Kong: Language policy. In P. Dickson & A. Cummings (Eds.), *Profiles of language education in 25 countries.* Slough: National Foundation for Educational Research.

Sweeting, A. (1993). *A phoenix transformed: The reconstruction of education in post-war Hong Kong.* Oxford: Oxford University Press.

Sweeting, A. (2004). *Education in Hong Kong, 1941 to 2001: Visions and revisions.* Hong Kong: Hong Kong University Press.

Sweeting, A., & Morris, P. (1993). Educational reform in post-war Hong Kong: Planning and crisis intervention. *International Journal of Education Development, 13,* 201–216.

Sweeting, A., & Vickers, E. (2005). On colonizing 'colonialism': The discourses of the history of English in Hong Kong. *World Englishes, 24*(2), 113–130.

Sweeting, A., & Vickers, E. (2007). Language and the history of colonial education: The case of Hong Kong. *Modern Asian Studies, 41*(1), 1–40.

Tong, A., & Adamson, B. (2013). Educational values and the English language curriculum in Hong Kong secondary schools since 1975. *International Journal of Society, Culture & Language, 1*(1), 22–36.

Tsui, A. B. M. (2004). Medium of instruction in Hong Kong: One country, two systems, whose language? In J. W. Tollefson & A. B. M. Tsui (Eds.), *Medium of instruction policies: Which agenda? Whose agenda?* London: Lawrence Erlbaum Associates.

Tung, P., Lam, R., & Tsang, W. K. (1997). English as a medium of instruction in post-1997 Hong Kong: What students, teachers and parents think. *Journal of Pragmatics, 28*(4), 441–459.

Walker, E. (2000). An analysis of changes in the aims and objectives of secondary English syllabi (1975–1999). In Y. C. Cheng, K. W. Chow, & K. T. Tsui (Eds.), *School curriculum change and development in Hong Kong* (pp. 227–257). Hong Kong: The Hong Kong Institution of Education.

Walker, E. A., Tong, S. Y. A., & Mok-Cheung, H. M. A. (2000). Changes in secondary school English teaching methodologies and contents (1975–1999). In K. W. C. Yin Cheong Cheng & K. Tung Tsui (Eds.), *School curriculum change and development in Hong Kong* (pp. 259–293). Hong Kong: The Hong Kong Institute of Education.

Wilcoxon, H. C. (1994). Assessment in literature teaching. In J. Boyle & P. Falvey (Eds.), *English language testing in Hong Kong* (pp. 87–108). Hong Kong: Chinese University Press.

11 A case study of the language use and literacy practices of Brunei students

New perspectives on cultural literacy

Malai Zeiti Sheikh Abdul Hamid

Introduction

In this chapter, I will explore the language use and literacy of students from Brunei Darussalam, a small Islamic state located on the island of Borneo. I take the view that literacy is a social practice embedded within and negotiated by a sociohistorical context (Barton, 2007; Cook–Gumperz, 1986; Wagner, Venezky, & Street, 1999). Throughout the chapter, I will refer to the term " 'literacy" as students' abilities in reading and writing in English.

Brunei is perched between the two Malaysian states of Sabah and Sarawak, with a population of 459,500 which is composed of 65% Brunei Malays, 11% Chinese and 23% indigenous groups (DEPS, 2019). In 1985, Brunei introduced the *dwibahasa* (dual language) or Bilingual Education Policy, in which two different languages, the Malay Language and the English Language, was introduced into the system. The Malay Language is the official language in Brunei, while English is the second language. Any reference to literacy in this chapter will also refer to the role of English and literacy skills in the second language.

As of 2019, the Department of Planning, Development and Research, Ministry of Education (MOE), Brunei has listed 251 schools and institutions, with an enrolment of 108,553 students and 10,934 educators in government and private sectors ranging from primary, secondary to tertiary education. Within the student population, there is similar enrolment of boys and girls entering Brunei schools and institutions, that is, 54,585 and 53,968 respectively. In contrast, there are nearly three times the number of female educators entering the teaching profession compared to the male counterparts—7,933 female teachers and 3,001 male teachers, according to figures released by MOE.

Over the last 20 years, Brunei students have achieved low literacy rates and encountered failing standards of the English Language (Azaraimy, 2003; Nicol, 2004; Coluzzi, 2011). It has been established that English Language teaching in Brunei over the years focused on elevating students' proficiency in English, so educational initiatives have been targeted to increase literacy skills in this language. In Brunei, similar to Singapore's linguistic background, specific English Language Teaching (ELT) initiatives have been introduced into the school curriculum (Martin & Abdullah, 2004; Lim, 2000), but Brunei ELT initiatives over the last two decades have shown less impact in raising students' competencies. In 2009, as one of the grand initiatives to improve the failing language situation of English, Brunei restructured its education system and introduced literacy into its education through the latest education reform, known as *Sistem Pendidikan Negara Abad Ke-21* or SPN21 (The National Education System for the 21st century).

In this chapter, I maintain that language and culture are closely related, so any reference to literacy in Brunei is closely related to factors that affect the cultural and literacy practices of the Bruneian people. I reflect on my ongoing research studies in literacy and include cultural literacy as one of the factors that must be considered in improving literacy in Brunei. This chapter has two main focuses. Firstly, I will review the historical trajectory of literacy studies in Brunei and secondly, I will describe ongoing literacy initiatives in Brunei. I will reflect on my own research studies in literacy and review current policies that could be maintained and reviewed in Brunei.

Perspectives from historical trajectory of literacy in Brunei

The use of English in Brunei has been a consequence of the British influence prior to independence when Brunei was a British Protectorate (from 1888 to 1983). In Brunei, obtaining a credit pass in the Cambridge Ordinary Level ("O" level) English is essential for entry into higher education, in securing scholarships and for obtaining better job opportunities. English in Brunei is often used as the language for business, international banking and trading. According to media reports, the average success rates of students of obtaining satisfactory credit passing rates (Grades A–C) in Brunei government schools is 12.8% in the O level English examinations (Azaraimy, 2003; Bourke, 1999). According to Simmons, Davis, Bakkum, Hessel, and Walter (2014), it has been reported that attainment of students in obtaining credit passing rates at "O" level English from 1996 to 2012 have risen from 15.4% (in 2006) to 39.9% (in 2012). The increase, however, is still considered as very low. Credit passes in the English O level have been used for the past two decades as standard indicators of students' proficiency in reading and writing in English.

One of the reasons for the raised concerns is the perceptual decline in standards of achievements in the English "O" level examinations. In comparison to Singapore, which has been ranked as one of the best performers in education globally, Brunei students continue to struggle in obtaining high educational standards, particularly in reading and writing skills. In PISA 2018, for example, about 52% of Brunei participants achieved less than Level 2 in Reading, which is the baseline level of proficiency for students to demonstrate their competencies in participating effectively and productively in life as continuing students, workers and citizens (OECD, 2017).

The high expectations of achieving credit passes in public examinations through Cambridge Examinations, which are designed for first language users of English, have led to a mismatch between students' actual performance and expectations of MOE. Low proficiency levels in English results are likely to place students at a disadvantage and prevent them from excelling in schools. One of the main reasons is due to the increase in the use of English to deliver lessons as students approach upper primary and onwards. Brunei students therefore, require sufficient mastery and proficiency of English to understand difficult concepts and for grasping information, which entails that the students must have competencies in comprehension skills in a language that is not commonly used, despite being the second language for educational purposes.

While adult literacy rates of 97.6% are considered as high, students in Brunei primary and secondary schools however, still struggle to excel in reading and writing skills. These factors have been reported elsewhere in my other papers. In terms of building understanding, I emphasise that Brunei students usually receive information that is within their cultural knowledge as second language users of English, not first language users—unlike Singapore, which is the closest to Brunei in terms of educational history, economics and standards of living. Yet the national language, Malay in Brunei's case, takes precedence in all aspects of the Bruneian way of life, from home, work and as societal language.

Under the *dwibahasa* (dual language) or Bilingual Education Policy, Brunei students go through 12 years of education, with seven years in preschool and primary education and five years in lower secondary and upper secondary school. Subjects at preschool and lower primary (for students aged 5–8 years) were taught in Malay except for English. At upper primary level (for students aged 9–12 years), all school subjects were taught in English, with the exception of Malay Language, Islamic Religious Knowledge, Physical Education, Art and History (The Government of Brunei Darussalam, 1985). The National Education System for the 21st Century (SPN21) then replaced the bilingual system in 2009 to meet challenges in globalisation (Garcia, 2009).

The SPN21 Curriculum and Assessment was also introduced to achieve the Ministry of Education's Strategic Plan on Quality Education. Nine key learning areas have been identified in SPN21: Islamic Religious Education, Nationhood Education, Languages, Mathematics, Science, Physical and Health Education, Social Sciences and Humanities, Technology, and Arts and Culture (Ministry of Education, 2019). Through these areas, students have opportunities to participate in student-centred learning and offered multiple pathways at upper secondary education with specialisation in science, arts and technical fields. High achievers at secondary levels undertake the Cambridge GCE Ordinary and Advanced examinations, while less capable students are offered vocational and technical educational pathways.

Move towards mastery framework in literacy

In 2018, Brunei participated in the Programme for International Student Assessment (PISA), which represented 6,828 students from 55 schools and colleges. Brunei was reported to rank among the top three ASEAN countries in three domains: Reading, Mathematics and Science (Izah, 2019). From the assessment, Brunei female students outperformed boys in the three domains. The most significant result, however, was attainment in reading scores, which matched research in literacy as early as primary schools with gender differences found. According to my previous study, I found that there were gender differences and that girls were keen to participate in literacy activities compared to boys (Hamid, 2020). The gender differences are likely to have an impact on the academic performance as girls in Brunei continue to outperform boys which begins as early as primary school years and likely to continue to higher levels of education. According to statistics from the Ministry of Education (2018), for example, there are 4,701 male students, with a significantly higher number of about 6,705 females who enrolled at higher education.

In preparation for PISA 2018, MOE had partnered with the Centre for British Teachers (CfBT) Brunei to implement the Literacy and Numeracy Coaching Programme (LNCP). The programme began in September 2018 and ended in mid-2019. It has three parts: (1) a capacity building programme building the skills of central office leaders with cluster heads, (2) the recruitment and deployment of 60 international coaches in all schools and (3) a local coach identification, training and accreditation component (Teaching for English Literacy Framework, 2017). Through LNCP, the main objective was to assist Brunei teachers in acquiring pedagogical skills that aid knowledge on content matter and raise learning standards in literacy. The best teaching practices in the teaching of English literacy were then disseminated through the *Teaching for English Mastery Framework*. Best practices of teaching English literacy were then applied to every Brunei government school. Referring to the *Teaching for English Literacy Framework*, the expectation is to ensure effective teaching of English literacy by adhering to the pedagogical themes as follows:

(1) Structuring and organising lessons
(2) Teaching content dialogically
(3) Designing effective learning tasks
(4) Assessing learning continuously
        (Extracted from *Teaching for English Literacy Framework*, 2017, p. 2)

One of the most promising areas in the *Teaching for English literacy framework* is *dialogic teaching and learning*, which is described as promoting student talk. This method offers students the opportunity to express their thoughts and opinions. Another interesting aspect of the literacy framework was the focus on teacher questions, namely, testing, focusing and genuine enquiry. The framework offers

Brunei teachers guidance for improving student outcomes, as students receive opportunities to speak and increase their communication with less focus on rote learning. The literacy framework therefore is designed to give Brunei teachers some guided structure for improving current teaching methods through best practices in literacy teaching. There is also strong indication the above strategy to improve literacy would continue, in preparation for the next round of PISA assessment if Brunei decides to participate in the future.

Nationally, various government departments have also taken various initiatives to improve literacy levels and teaching quality. The initiatives include dissemination of the Early Literacy Packs to newborns, which in collaboration with the Ministry of Culture, Youth and Sports (MCYS), the Ministry of Health (MOH), the Ministry of Religious Affairs (MORA) and Ministry of Home Affairs (MOHA). Other programmes were, the Ministry of Education National Reading Campaign and the yearly Brunei Book Fair Carnival, organised by the Ministry of Culture, Youth and Sports. Currently, the leading non-governmental organisation (NGO) in Brunei that promotes reading and writing activities with other educational initiatives, is the Reading and Literacy Association (ReLA) of Brunei Darussalam, with the goal of "One Book, One Child Per Lifetime". ReLA has been established over 27 years and targets to provide free books to every child in the country. With initiatives undertaken by both government and non-governmental agencies to promote reading, these initiatives are crucial for producing "well educated and highly skilled people" one of the goals of Brunei *Wawasan* 2035 (Brunei Goal 2035), amongst others.

Literacy as sociocultural practice amongst the Brunei community

Literacy has been viewed as a social practice in Anglophone countries, such as the UK and USA. As children find themselves in favourable reading environments and participate in literacy activities, the culture of bedtime reading and reading to children become common literacy practices amongst cultures in the West. Yet the situation is different from other cultures, particularly among Asian cultures and countries in the East, including Brunei.

There has been little research to indicate that there is a supportive environment for reading in Brunei homes to facilitate literacy development. Brunei is a highly cultural community and rich with values, customs and traditions that have been passed down from generation to generation. It is composed of a tightly knit community in which family members tend to live close to each other and where most extended family members tend to stay in one house. Through close proximity, children in Brunei homes engage in daily conversations with their families and have opportunities to receive knowledge and information, including one's cultural traditions and values from the older generation and with those who live together. It is also a common cultural practice that Brunei family members spend time together in the weekends and that parents bring their children to meet the older generation. Family gatherings at the dinner table and attending social events and weddings, for example, are some of the usual activities that are common amongst highly cultural societies.

Brunei is also one of the countries in the world with a history of monarchical system that has ruled the nation for the past 700 years. The country is ruled by an absolute monarchical system by the Sultan, who has descended from a past history of royal inheritance, and faces no political opposition from the people. In fact, the Brunei people are proud of the rule of His Majesty, the Sultan of Brunei and for being the world's oldest reigning monarchy and the only remaining Malay Islamic Monarchy.

After gaining independence in 1984, Brunei adopted the national philosophy of the Malay Islamic Monarchy (Melayu Islam Beraja, or MIB) as a state philosophy. It is a system that is indicative of strong Malay cultural influences, stressing the importance of Islam in daily life and governance, and having high respect and regard for the monarchy. Other cultures, however, are allowed to practice their own religion and their individual traditions. MIB forms the foundation of the social and political structure of Bruneian culture. According to Braighlinn (1992), Brunei is identified as being the only surviving independent Malay Islamic Monarchy in South East Asia. MIB is intended to uphold the rights and privileges of the Malay ethnic community, to uphold Islam as the national religion and to justify the monarchy as the governing system for the country.

Brunei's education system requires strict adherence to learning experiences and subjects that must be appropriate, culturally acceptable and aligned with MIB. In school, MIB is offered as a subject in the curriculum and introduced as early as Year 1 (for children aged 6 years) with the implementation of SPN21. MIB is also one of the nine learning areas (known as nationhood education) included into Brunei's revised curriculum for secondary education. MIB is also a compulsory module for students undertaking bachelor's programmes in Brunei universities.

Within the Brunei context, it is a requirement for children's learning and literacy that such experiences be aligned to MIB. In this aspect, as a sociocultural practice, I refer to *cultural literacy*—which is defined as acquiring knowledge of acceptable norms, traditions and cultural practices, and which identifies one as belonging to a particular culture. Some local examples of cultural literacy in Brunei are possessing knowledge of weddings, traditional dances, traditional games and local food, amongst others. Extensions on Islamic-based activities common among the Brunei culture are 'zikir' (ritual prayer practiced by the Muslim society), attending Quranic classes, recital of prayers before and after meals and praying together as a family. It is expected that Brunei children's literacy experiences are closely linked with their cultural experiences and thus gain high amounts of cultural capital (Bourdieu, 1991). In other words, the Brunei students' cultural literacy will remain high compared to other forms of capital. Any efforts in improving literacy in Brunei must therefore include elements of MIB, which focus on the teaching of Islam, customs and cultural practices that promote the Malay culture and respect for the monarchy.

In preparation for the demands expected in the 21st century, in September 2019, MOE has launched and developed the "Digital Literacy Standards and Cultural Literacy Standards" in the SPN-21 curriculum to strengthen the education of Science, Technology, Engineering, Arts and Mathematics (STEAM), and opportunities are given for teachers to utilise technology in teaching and to elevate competitiveness and raise standards in science and technology. These more recent initiatives are important to ensure that Brunei's education system will remain relevant and help prepare students with 21st century skills.

Personal research in literacy in Brunei

My research interest in literacy began after the completion of my doctoral research, which investigated the literacy practices of Brunei students that are linked with their socio-economic status and performance in the Cambridge GCE O level English Language. I pursued my research over the years to build an understanding of factors that affected Brunei students' literacy skills.

Generally, there are different forms of measurement for assessing Brunei students' literacy skills at various sectors of their education, mainly primary and secondary. At primary level, primary school children at present undergo literacy assessment through the Running Record A–Z (USA) for Year 1–6, and the Brunei Primary School Examination (PSR) administered to certify completion of primary education (Year 6 only). While the Running Record allows teachers to use a systematic record for gaining insights into a child's reading, the PSR is a written examination, administered face-to-face and delivered through paper-pencil tests. At the secondary level, students must obtain minimum credit passes (Grade A–C) for the Cambridge O level examinations as the national benchmark to mark completion of secondary education in all subjects for students aged 15–16 years old.

In one of my previous research studies, I interviewed 15 primary school children from different districts in Brunei; one rural and the other a semi-urban school. Out of the 15 students, eight participants were girls and seven were boys. From the interviews, all participants stated they agreed that reading was a fun activity, but girls have higher preference for reading than boys. The reading genre was gendered: the boys favoured reading comics, while girls generally read fairy tales and children's stories.

In the same primary school data study, I found similarity in the data with writing skills, which is also gendered. In my findings, all girls stated that writing was not only fun but that they also used new words in their writing. All boys were less enthusiastic about writing compared to girls. From the interviews, the girls stated they wrote about their family and friends, while the boys preferred to write about themselves. The boys enjoyed drawing masculine characters such as action figures, superheroes and cartoons, while girls drew feminine objects such as flowers, fairy tales and heroine characters. The drawing genre from my study, therefore showed a strong match between the materials that students read and the things that they drew. Another interesting finding was that girls had more experiences in literacy practices than the boys. For example, the girls were making personalised birthday cards and writing messages to express their emotions and feelings, but boys made no such effort in engaging in such literacy activities.

In my recent study, I conducted quantitative research to investigate literacy practices of students in two primary schools of similar geographical location and school composition, unlike the previous study, which concentrated on rural and semi-urban schools. From a total of 350 respondents (in upper and primary levels from Year 3 to Year 5), there were 214 participants (61%) of respondents who stated that they "sometimes" read English books at home, 94 participants (27%) responded "yes" and 42 participants (12%) responded "no" to reading. From the same question, there was an equal number of boys and girls (107 girls and 107 boys) or 31% who stated that they "sometimes" read English books. The percentage of "yes" to reading English books were also similar in that less than 20% of boys and girls agreed they read English books, with less than 10% of boys and girls who stated "no" to reading English books.

In terms of literacy practices, 65% of respondents in my study also stated "no" to reading bedtime stories, but both genders showed a similar percentage of responses, with 36% disagreement from boys and 29% from girls. There were only less than 6% of boys and 9% of girls who stated they read bedtime stories with their families. Writing letters was also less common among participants, with 33% of participants responding "yes", 27% who responded "no" and 40% who responded "sometimes". From the same question, it was found that less than 20% of the boys stated they did not write letters to their friends, with only 10% of girls who made the same statement.

The research findings in the studies so far indicated that female participants have more positive feelings about reading than male participants and that the reading and reading genre is gendered. The same pattern was also observed with writing in that female respondents enjoyed writing more than boys. In literacy practices, I found that both boys and girls do not engage in bedtime stories, but boys also participated less in writing tasks such as letter writing or writing cards. Girls generally wrote about others, while boys were content about writing about themselves.

From students' responses in my study, the practice of bedtime reading is not common in Brunei homes. About 36% of the boys and 29% of the girls responded "no" to bedtime reading; 9% of boys and 12% of girls responded "sometimes" and with less than 10% (6% of boys and 9% of girls) who responded "yes" to bedtime reading. In terms of owning books (including storybooks, magazines and comics), 57% of the boys and 52% of girls own these reading books. About 75% of the participants in my primary school research stated they own reading books (for leisure).

Overall, more than half of the respondents (with more boys than girls) in these two studies indicate that there are sufficient literacy practices to enhance reading and writing skills, in addition to owning books. Of particular interest is the infrequency of the practice of reading and reading bedtime stories and writing that are not common among the participants in my study. In Western culture, reading bedtime stories to children is indicative of good literacy practices at home, while reading is one of the most essential literacy skills, in which students should participate as early as primary school.

The results are indicative that girls in Brunei are more "literate" than boys. My studies have also shown that girls' attitudes and preference for reading and writing start to develop in the primary school years and that similar attitudes continue to grow and affect students' educational attainment right through secondary education. This leads to gendered reading attainment at secondary education and low performance in academics, as observed in the Brunei PISA 2018 results. This research has been addressed in similar work that focuses on core academic skills (Snow & Uccelli, 2009; Uccelli, Galloway, Barr, Meneses, & Dobbs, 2015; Uccelli & Galloway, 2016).

Biographical stance: my literacy background

I first started teaching as a primary school teacher when I was 19 years old. I continued into the teaching profession and completed my tertiary education with a doctorate in English language and literacy. My parents were both language teachers before retiring. My mother completed her bachelor's degree in Teaching English as a Second Language (TESL) at a local university in Brunei, while my father completed his Diploma in Teaching overseas and taught Malay. Ethnically, I am Malay, as both my parents are Malay, but my father has mixed Arabic blood. My siblings and I grew up in a literate environment surrounded by various print materials, as our parents were teachers. My siblings and I are bilingual and proficient in two languages, Malay and English. I define "proficient" as being able to communicate and speak fluently, use simple to complex and sophisticated vocabulary and produce grammatically correct sentences.

Being a bilingual parent myself, I passed on the same language practices and skills to my children. When I was young, I recalled that my mother supervised my homework at the dinner table. I found evidence of this in a photo of one of my encounters with paper and pencil (see Figure 11.1)

I compared my own photo (see Figure 11.1) with my toddler's photo (see Figure 11.2) at the time of writing this chapter. Both photos showed that the use of pencil and paper are early indicators of contact and evidence of literacy practices. Children instinctively hold objects such as pencils/pens and express their thoughts through actions and through writing. I make a connection that when children interact with daily objects during play, these are the best times to encourage reading and writing activities, as it indicates their receptiveness towards learning. Combining writing practices with early reading exposure such as bedtime reading and frequent reading experiences are most likely to lead to positive reading and writing activities to enhance children's literacy skills.

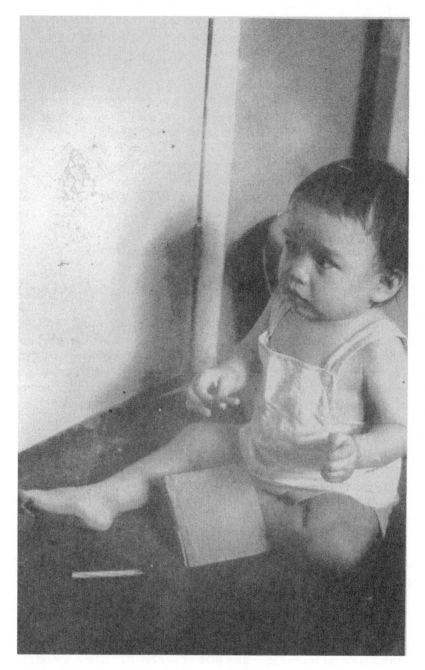

Figure 11.1 Zeiti Hamid holding a pencil, at 2 years old

Figure 11.2 Ariz Nasiruddin holding/using a pencil, at 2 years old

Conclusion: what should be retained and what should be changed for literacy in Brunei

In summary, the previous bilingual education policy and SPN21 system has maintained the main goals of Brunei's education system. With the bilingual policy, the system aimed to ensure students are taught most school subjects in Malay first (except English Language) in early primary years, but English gains relative importance at upper primary upwards (Year 4). Through SPN21, it is hoped that significant early exposure to English-based subjects from Year 1 will benefit Bruneian students in acquiring proficiency in English at a much earlier age.

Taking into perspective that literacy is viewed as a sociocultural practice, the language and everyday experiences of Brunei children are largely done in their first language, Malay. However, there is a mismatch in terms of what students require and what students are capable of achieving. Some factors are externally driven and beyond the scope of the education system, including cultural and societal factors. One suggestion is to allow for sensitivity and inclusion of the local context in the school curriculum and localised examinations that are catered to meet Brunei students' capabilities. In this way, students do not necessarily require proficiency in a second language to pass public examinations. Instead, a carefully designed international testing system that assesses broader dimensions of learning could provide a fairer testament of students' achievements in school subjects, which are not only culturally sensitive and relatable but must also be aligned to Brunei's state philosophy, MIB. A second bolder move is to propose for government/state schools to emulate private schools settings and opt for teaching to be conducted through an all English curriculum (or total immersion) from as early as Kindergarten for every school subject (primary to secondary education). The exceptions will be on Malay-based subjects that must be taught in the first language, Malay.

Literacy studies in Brunei in my chapter so far have shown Bruneian children, particularly girls, are more literate and have more preference for reading and writing compared to boys. Reading is also gendered as early as primary schools. From my ongoing research, I observed that Brunei children's spoken and home literacy experiences play a crucial role for enhancing their proficiency in English. Yet, there is a severe lack of an `English *literate-friendly*' environment in Brunei homes to encourage natural acquisition of English. In formal schooling, there is a very high expectation for Brunei children to speak, read and write fluently in both languages. However, the reality is that Malay **remains** as the main language of the society and the dominant language in formal and public settings due to the high population of the Brunei community. Despite the role of English as Brunei's second language, Malay is still the main language for communication with the highest cultural and societal impact among the local community, so this language situation is unlikely to change in the foreseeable future.

This chapter also described some literacy initiatives conducted by various parties, particularly MOE, to raise standards of English through SPN21 amongst other initiatives. The limitations of this chapter are acknowledged, as there is far too little research in literacy in Brunei and not much is available on the future direction of literacy teaching in Brunei. Further detailed research and nationwide studies could be pursued to produce more detailed information on the literacy skills of the Bruneian society.

Finally, I have described the dominance of the Islamic religion, Malay language, Malay culture and loyalty to the Monarch (MIB), that has some influence on literacy teaching and literacy standards. In other words, the amount of exposure to English input (since the implementation of SPN21) and societal and cultural issues must be addressed if Brunei is to achieve these targets in improving literacy. Using the first language, Malay in Brunei also means that one is also learning and having awareness and an understanding of the Malay cultural values and practices of the Malay people. In this sense, literacy is a sociocultural practice. More importantly, literacy in Brunei entails that a person must show respect and solidarity of the Brunei society, that is aligned closely with Brunei national's philosophy, MIB.

References

Azaraimy, H. H. (2003, October 10). Official chides teachers over lenient marks. *Borneo Bulletin*.

Barton, D. (2007). *Literacy: An introduction to the ecology of written language* (2nd ed.). Oxford: Wiley-Blackwell.

Bourdieu, P. (1991). *Language and symbolic power* (G. Raymond & M. Adamson, Trans.). Cambridge, MA: Harvard University Press.

Bourke, J. (1999). Assessing the English language proficiency of form 5 students in Brunei Darussalam and the problem of O-level English. *Journal of Applied Research in Education*, *3*(1), 11–25.

Braighlinn, G. (1992). *Ideological innovation under monarchy: Aspects of legitimation activity in contemporary Brunei*. The Netherlands: VU University Press.

Coluzzi, P. (2011). Majority and minority language planning in Brunei Darussalam. *Language Problems & Language Planning*, *35*(3), 222–240.

Cook—Gumperz, J. (Ed.). (1986). *The social construction of literacy*. Cambridge, MA: Cambridge University Press.

Department of Economic, Planning and Statistics (DEPS). (2019). *Ministry of finance and economy, Brunei Darussalam*. Retrieved from www.deps.gov.bn/SiteP ages/Population.aspx

Garcia, O. (2009). *Bilingual education in the 21st century: A global perspective*. West Sussex: Wiley- Blackwell.

The Government of Brunei Darussalam. (1985). *Education system of Negara Brunei Darussalam*. Curriculum Development Centre, Ministry of Education. Brunei Darussalam.

Hamid, M. Z. S. A. (2020). Gender differences in learning English as a second language among Brunei primary students in Brunei Darussalam. *International Journal of English Language Education*, *8*(2), 16–28.

Izah Azahari. (2019). Brunei stands third among ASEAN in PISA. *Borneo Bulletin*. Retrieved from https://borneobulletin.com.bn/2019/12/brunei-stands-third-among-asean-pisa/

Lim, C. S. (2000). The English language syllabus 2001: Change and continuity. *TELL, 16*(2), 9–14.

Martin, P. W., & Abdullah, K. (2004). English language teaching in Brunei Darussalam. In Ho Wah Kam & R. Y. L. Wong (Eds.), *English language teaching in East Asia today: Changing policies and practices* (2nd ed.). Singapore: Eastern Universities Press.

Ministry of Education, Brunei. (2018). Retrieved from http://moe.gov.bn/DocumentDownloads/Education%20Statistics%20and%20Indicators%20Handbook/Brunei%20Darussalam%20Education%20Statistics%202018.pdf

Ministry of Education, Brunei. (2019). Retrieved from www.moe.gov.bn/spn21dl/SPN21%20ENG%20(2013)%20COMPLETE.pdf

Nicol, M. F. (2004). Some problems experienced by Bruneian students with the Cambridge O level English language reading comprehension paper. *Southeast Asia: A Multidisciplinary Journal, 5*(1 & 2), 47–70.

OECD. (2017). *PISA 2015 assessment and analytical framework: Science, reading, mathematic, financial literacy and collaborative problem solving.* Paris: OECD Publishing. https://doi.org/10.1787/9789264281820-en

Running Record, A—Z (USA). Retrieved from www.readinga-z.com/helpful-tools/about-running-records/

Simmons, P., Davis, S., Bakkum, L., Hessel, G., & Walter, C. (2014). *Bilingual education in Brunei: The evolution of the Brunei approach to bilingual education and the role of CFBT in promoting educational change: Summary report.* CFBT Education Trust 2014.

Snow, C. E., & Uccelli, P. (2009). The challenge of academic language. In D. R. Olson & N. Torrance (Eds.), *The Cambridge handbook of literacy* (pp. 112–133). New York: Cambridge University Press.

Teaching for English Literacy. Teaching for English Literacy Mastery Framework. (2017). *Ministry of education, Brunei Darussalam.* Brunei: CFBT.

Uccelli, P., & Galloway, E. P. (2016). Academic language across content areas: Lessons from an innovative assessment and from students' reflections about language. *Journal of Adolescent & Adult Literacy, 60*(4), 395–404. https://doi.org/10.1002/jaal.553

Uccelli, P., Galloway, E. P., Barr, C. D., Meneses, A., & Dobbs, C. L. (2015). Beyond vocabulary: Exploring cross-disciplinary academic-language proficiency and its association with reading comprehension. *Reading Research Quarterly, 50*(3), 337–356. https://doi.org/10.1002/rrq.104

Wagner, D. A., Venezky, R. L., & Street, B. V. (Eds.). (1999). *Literacy: An international handbook.* Boulder, CO: Westview Press.

12 Broadening meaning-making

Towards a Framework for Respect in Literacy Education (FRiLE) in Malaysia

Su Li Chong

Background

Mackey (2016) very eloquently traced her own lived experience of being literate through her auto-bibliographical account of her childhood in St. John's, Newfoundland. As she clarifies, her account serves not as a memoir but instead as a theorised summation of how an individual reader is constructed. Chiming with Mackey (2016), I begin my chapter by locating my literacy journey within my biographical and bibliographical trajectory. Growing up in one of the cities along the west coast of Peninsular Malaysia, I am considered to hail from a typical lower-middle-class family in urban Malaysia. In families like ours, education is prized and literacy highly valued. As teachers, both my parents inherently understood the importance of reading and acted upon that belief. For reasons unclear even to me, I seem to be able to remember the exact moment when I knew I could read. Sitting on the floor with the local broadsheet English newspaper spread out in front of the 6-year-old me, I struggled to phonetically sound out a rather strange looking word that my father (whom I remember to be my earliest reading teacher) was pointing to. "E-e-en-eng-li-lish", I ventured. "E-eng-eng-lish", I carried on. "Eng-lish", I said. Oh! ENGLISH!" I proclaimed with astonishment. The astonishment came from the realisation that I had stepped across a threshold and had entered into a new world of meaning-making. I do not seem to remember much else after that, but I have since then been an ardent, biliterate reader.

My parents could not always afford to buy new books, as books were and still are costly in Malaysia. Therefore, library books borrowed during library visits and second-hand books gratefully received from friends and extended family were a major part of my environment. Torn and worn books that held wondrous stories about Grumbling Grace (Tales after Supper, Enid Blyton), and Julian, Dick, Anne, George and Timmy with their adventures of mystery and intrigue (The Famous Five, Enid Blyton) and Charlie and his winning, golden ticket (Charlie and the Chocolate Factory, Roald Dahl) surrounded me.

Although when I was growing up many of my books were not new, holding pride of place in our house was a brand-new collection of *Children's Britannica Encyclopaedia* (Figure 12.1), which my parents purchased circa 1985, paid

Figure 12.1 Children's Britannica Encyclopaedia

painstakingly through 12 monthly instalments. At the time of purchase, the collection was considered a luxury that the family could hardly afford. However, the immense pleasure which my sibling and I received from hours of poring over the books more than made up for the financial expenditure. My own account of becoming literate and sustaining literacy strongly suggests that I came from a literacy-rich home.

Today, my much-loved set of Encyclopaedia have been passed on to my 12-year-old son who has turned out to be equally, if not more ardent in his pursuit of reading (Figure 12.2).

While aesthetic reading was pursued at home for me, in stark contrast, the act of reading in school took on a largely functional, academic role with there being heightened focus on reading in order to do well in school. Despite my freedom to pursue aesthetic reading at home, our home-centric ways with words (Heath, 1983) would also chime with the school's academic trajectory. Doing school was key to doing well in life. The school forbade us from bringing books that were unrelated to the school's academic aims. To be found in possession of a non-academic, non-school-prescribed book was a punishable wrongdoing. More than that, the notion of reading was often couched in terms of language learning. Thus, reading was seldom done for its own sake but was a means to learn yet another language. Because Malaysia is a multilingual country, its education system shows consideration for multiple languages. I learnt to read in English and Malay, and to a much lesser extent, Mandarin. This went on to shape my professional career. I trained to be an English teacher. Spanning more than 20 years, I have taught in various universities and colleges in Malaysia. In my teaching experience, I have sensed that reading seemed to be burdensome

Figure 12.2 My then-6-year-old son scanning through the local Cambridge newspaper, circa 2014

and even challenging to my undergraduates. This impression was formed when I consistently encountered undergraduates demonstrating what appeared to be incomplete reading assignments. My informal discussions with other colleagues also brought forth similar notions. It was this realisation that spurred me to pursue this line of research.

The confluence of my biographical stance and my professional career has raised important questions about how reading has been understood, researched, socialised and lived in this country. Central to this chapter are the following questions: In what ways do readers of different ages live their reading experience? Through which research paradigms should reading be understood? How can national literacy policies better inform literacy practice? The paradoxes and clashes as well as the triumphs and victories that Malaysians confront in terms of their attempts to read and make meaning deserve to be juxtaposed and understood. Thus, bringing together my own biographical background and my current research work, in this chapter, a systematic comparison of six Malaysian-based literacy research projects that I conducted across 15 years (2006–2020) is carried out. The rationale for this comparison is to produce a critical review of research projects that examined the literacy lives of Malaysian students from primary schools to higher learning institutions. Contrasting across the aspects of participant selection, methodology, findings and implications of the research projects, I combine the phenomenological principle of lived experience and perform a comparison in order to take stock and connect the dots across the projects. Conclusions from this chapter will provide historical and practice-based empirical findings to inform Malaysia's national policy on education, language and literacy.

What can we learn from the past?

Before moving further, it is at least important for me to briefly explain the socio-cultural milieu that underpins Malaysia's cultural landscape. In terms of modern Malaysia, its present is heavily influenced by British colonisation that spanned across the 18th and 19th centuries. Imperial might saw the migration of peoples from China and India into what was then Malaya, so that its land and natural resources could be worked upon. As a direct result of this, Malaya took on a multi-cultural, multi-ethnic composite of people. Today, its ethnic and linguistic diversity runs along four large divisions, with the Malay language seen as originating from the Malay ethnic group, the Mandarin language from the Chinese ethnic group, the Tamil language from the Indian ethnic group and a variety of indigenous languages (oral and written) belonging to indigenous communities in Peninsular and East (Borneo) Malaysia. There has also been the more recent migration of people from Pakistan, Nepal, Indonesia, Myanmar and Bangladesh into Malaysia in the 1990s that makes the Malaysian landscape, like in many parts of the world, super-diverse (Meissner & Vertovec, 2015). In such a landscape, the way reading and writing are experienced, taught and lived will necessarily take complex forms.

Official data about Malaysia's literacy rate can only be found from 1981 onwards (United Nations Development Programme (UNDP), 2018). This data shows that from 1981, the national literacy rate rose steadily and today stands at 98% for youths between 15 and 24 years of age (United Nations Development Programme (UNDP), 2018). Despite official data being found only in the latter part of the 20th century, from as early as 1928, evidence of academic research on reading and education in what was then British Malaya has been in existence. Nagle's (1928) work on literacy in Malaya broadly sketched the educational landscape of the land while pinning down important aspects of learning objectives, school attendance, finance and curriculum in order to provide a cross-sectional facts-and-figures view of the Malayan context. In his recommendation for encouraging reading amongst children, Nagle (1928) called for further studies to look into "the interests of individual pupils" so as to provide "the only safe guide" (p. 157) for teachers to help promote reading interest. However, because the dominant approach to research during that time was heavily informed by the positivist paradigm, it followed that Nagle's recommendation for helping Malayan children cultivate the reading habit would be underpinned by methods that were "determined scientifically" (p. 156) and based on laboratory experiments. Specifically, Nagle referred to Vogel and Washburne's (1928) work which took on a mechanistic and statistical approach from surveying 36,750 children's ballots of book titles they were reading or interested to read, resulting in "The Winnetka Graded Book List". Nagle proposed a Malayan version of the graded book list. Nagle also strongly recommended the adherence to W. S. Gray's summarised recommendations of scientifically based reading instruction programmes as a way to design reading classes in schools (Gray, 1932, 1933). It is important to note that by *positivist* I am referring to the influence of the natural science research paradigm.

Soon after, in the 1930s, Buchler (1932) reported on the Malayan reading public in very generalised terms. Tracing his analysis along ethnic lines, Buchler commented on how the Chinese in Malaya made up the largest portion of the reading public, while indigenous Malays showed the least interest. According to Buchler, Indians in Malaya were largely illiterate. However, Buchler's assessment was not accompanied by any explication about how he had arrived at such generalised conclusions. In juxtaposing Nagle's (1928) call for in-depth investigations into school children's reading interests with Buchler's (1932) generalised conclusions about the reading public, the question of the usefulness of statistical surveys and laboratory experiments in drawing out the complexities arises. These early works make for powerful historical documents that demonstrate at least two points. First, the push for eradicating illiteracy among Malayan children was already put in motion. This could partly explain why literacy and the overall education system in Malaya and later, Malaysia, could progress relatively well during the 1960s and into the 1980s. Second, research projects that were in published forms seemed to be driven and viewed not through local eyes but through the perspective of the "other". Nagle was a colonial officer to Malaya and would have only been able to view the educational landscape through an outsider's perspective. This perspective was also underpinned by a prevailing positivist paradigm.

As if in deference to these early studies, current research work on reading in the 21st century continues to adopt the positivist stance when setting out to draw conclusions about Malaysians and reading. In more recent times, the participant selection of this research began to expand from primary and secondary schools to include students in higher learning institutions. In his series of studies using the survey method, Pandian and his associates (Pandian, 1997, 1999; Pandian & Moorth, 2001) identified what they termed as reading reluctancy amongst undergraduates in universities across Malaysia. Findings from their quantitative studies showed that these undergraduates appeared to be practising minimal reading. This meant that beyond institutional requirements, reading for pleasure seemed absent. By association, conclusions from these research efforts suggested that reading motivation amongst pre-university and university students in Malaysia was unsatisfactory. Elsewhere, Eakle and Garber (2004) in an international report on literacy highlighted another statistical study which found that a sample group of Malaysian undergraduates read only for examination purposes. Although that study was quantitative in nature, its generalisability is questionable due to its small sample size. In another survey, Kaur and Thiyagarajah (2000) discovered that Malaysian undergraduates who were studying for their degree in English language and literature were not strongly motivated to read. This seemed counter-intuitive in that undergraduates who were reading for a degree in language or literature would presumably be highly motivated readers. Instead, those undergraduates were found to be unprepared for their course expectations.

This is not to say that there were no qualitatively based research projects. Amongst the qualitatively informed research projects that were fewer and further between, Pillai (2007) investigates what she terms the "tertiary learner's world" by drawing together her literature undergraduates' written responses to selected literary texts. Pillai highlights that Malaysian undergraduates may be seen to lack in the ability to read and write critically. I argue that while the insights may be useful in providing a more detailed and descriptive stance of the undergraduates' reading experience, these insights may still be based on what the undergraduates construe to be "right answers" to the questions regarding their literary texts. Also, there is rarely any longitudinal review carried out on these studies. Apart from Pandian's collection (Kalantzis & Pandian, 2001; Pandian, 1997, 1999, 2000, 2001, 2008; Pandian & Baboo, 2002), the other mostly piecemeal projects do not allow for deep, critical analysis based on connected work.

As a result, snapshots of Malaysians and what appear to be their levels of poor reading motivation have become a recurring picture. This also resonates with the general perception that despite having a high literacy rate and possessing multilingual abilities, Malaysians in general are not motivated readers (Azizan & Tan, 2006; Siti Aishah, 2003; Small, 1996). More importantly, this brief synthesis shows that in all this time, reading research in Malaysia has been dominated by positivist views. While the positivist view in and of itself can be an important means of shedding light on an issue, an imbalanced stance could result if counter perspectives are absent. In the case of reading research in Malaysia, the dominance of positivist views meant that real individual voices of readers may have been drowned out.

In the rest of the chapter, a meta-analysis of my research work will interrogate how my own thinking about reading and literacy—as well as the way this connects with a number of theoretical positions in reading motivation (Ajzen & Fishbein, 2005; McKenna, 2001; Verhoeven & Snow, 2001), multiliteracies and reading as a social practice (Gee, 2008; Street, 1995; The New London Group, 2000) and transactional theory of reading (Rosenblatt, 1938, 1978) —has shifted in order to newly propose a broad framework for literacy education in Malaysia.

Broadening meaning-making: comparing and contrasting six projects

In the following section, literacy research from 2006 through 2020 will be critically reviewed in terms of four aspects. The aspects are participant selection, research paradigm (methodology and methods), research findings and implications. These four aspects chime with conventional requirements that fundamental academic research is based on.

Project 1

In 2006, I undertook a quantitatively designed research project in which it was hypothesised that the right reading attitude will lead to the desired reading behaviour. Based on Fishbein and Ajzen's Theory of Planned Behaviour (Fishbein & Ajzen, 1975), Project 1 was a survey study which set out to test the hypothesis about how a group of undergraduates' awareness of the importance

Table 12.1 Project 1

Project 1	
Participant selection	Random sampling: 214 undergraduates in a Malaysian university.
Methodology and method	Quantitatively informed: survey.
Findings	There is a statistically significant but weak correlation between the students' belief in the importance of reading and their practice of reading.
Implications	This project showed that the act of reading is much more complex than a correlational relationship.

of reading was associated with their reported practice of reading (Chong & Lai, 2007). This survey utilised a seven-point Likert scale (strongly agree to strongly disagree) and set out to measure two constructs (i.e. perception of reading and practice of reading). The perception of reading was represented by variables that gauged the undergraduates' impression of reading in academic and non-academic contexts. However, the scope of this study was narrow in that the notion of reading was, at that time, assumed to be reading via the English language. This in itself causes a disjuncture because in the Malaysian context, any reader is almost always reading through more than one medium of language. In fact, the bifurcation of languages is also a contentious issue. On the other hand, the practice of reading was operationalised via variables related to materiality (text), reader disposition (preferences, interest, choice) and reader's context (physical surrounding, environment). Findings from that statistical study showed that while the undergraduates demonstrated strong awareness of the importance of reading, their reported practice of reading did not seem to match. Table 12.1 summarises Project 1.

This first empirical project indicated that broad-based research that is quantitative in paradigm can, at best, yield a generalised understanding of patterned opinions. However, these patterned opinions cannot furnish an in-depth understanding that explains behaviour. In the case of this study, the statistics could not explain why highly literate young adults who clearly acknowledged the importance of reading did not follow it up with meaningful reading.

Project 2

Project 2 was the result of a follow-up study to Project 1. In this second project, I carried out a qualitatively informed study to draw out the descriptions of undergraduates who considered themselves ardent readers (Chong & Renganathan, 2008). In this project, the undergraduates talked about what they read, when and how often they read and most importantly, why they chose to read. However, because this study was narrow in scope, it could only shine a light on the reasons for a young adult engaging in reading fiction. It is important to highlight the responses that attribute the reading journeys to one important influence or turning point:

> It started with my parents. They would get me simple books with pictures. . . . Initially it was for the pictures that I read, but later on it was for the words and the story . . . my parents slowly brought me along the path for reading.
>
> (Chong & Renganathan, 2008)

Table 12.2 denotes Project 2.

Significant to this study is the subversion of the hypothesis in Project 1. It is not in how much the importance is acknowledged at the onset of reading but in how far the reader identifies with reading. In this study, however, reading was still considered to be a behaviour that was shaped by attitude (Ajzen & Fishbein, 1977, 2005; Fishbein & Ajzen, 1975, 2009; McKenna, 2001).

Project 3

In this project, I set out to understand the thoughts of highly literate undergraduates with regard to their experience of reading across genres. Particularly, the phenomenon of aliteracy was explored because the occurrence of the reluctance in reading seemed relentless. The qualitatively informed paradigm underpinned this study. In this project, the underlying substantive theory began to shift. Although it began with the understanding that reading is a behaviour that was shaped by attitude, it developed to include the sociocultural perspective of multiliteracies (Gee, 2008; Kress, 2000; Street, 2001; The New London Group, 2000). This project captured fascinating titles of reading material that ranged across the genres of fiction, self-help, history, business and religion, to name a few (Chong, 2011). Table 12.3 is a summary of Project 3.

Table 12.2 Project 2

Project 2	
Participant selection	Purposive sampling: eight undergraduates in a Malaysian university.
Methodology and method	Qualitatively informed: semi-structured interview.
Findings	Each of these ardent readers experienced significant turning points that have served to transform and consolidate their love of reading as undergraduates.
Implications	For an ardent reader, sustained reading has very little to do with the belief that reading is important.

Table 12.3 Project 3

Project 3	
Participant selection	Purposive and snowball sampling: nine Malaysian undergraduates in a Malaysian university.
Methodology and method	Qualitatively informed: semi-structured interview and diary-writing.
Findings	Reading is an experience that is relative to the reader's relationship with significant surrounding space (institution, home) which affect reading choice.
Implications	Aliteracy is not about isolated decisions but occurs in complex spaces that relate especially to a powerful other. Reading is not neutral.

The significance of this project lay in how I began to see reading as a co-constructed phenomenon. No longer an activity in isolation, reading is an ongoing experience for anyone who is literate (Chong, 2011, 2016).

Project 4

In this project, I extended my investigation on the occurrence of aliteracy to understand the circumstances within which young adults chose to read and not to read. The scope of this project was further broadened to account not only for unbounded genres but for the way Malaysians are multilingually literate. This project also made room for new literacies, which meant that features like the participant's electronic footprint of their internet browsing activity was captured. At this point in time, the internet and technological advancement had brought a wave of change that was to transform the way semiotic meaning is made by those who are literate. Thus, the electronic text formed a major part of this study's considerations. At this point of the project, Rosenblatt's (1969, 1978, 2005) transactional theory of reading became an integral theoretical backbone. This theory chimed with the theory of reading as a sociocultural practice because of the way the former acknowledged the phenomenologically informed lived experience of reading. Table 12.4 is a summary of Project 4.

By this fourth project, the scope of research was extended to consider meaning-making from new angles. It was found that the essence of reading revolves around meaningful meaning-making (Chong, 2014, 2018a, 2018b). When I was investigating why Malaysian undergraduates seemed to be averse to wider reading despite their wider linguistic access and expanding multimodal and media contexts, I found that I had to first understand how they negotiated academic and non-academic reading. As I began to talk to the undergraduates, I discovered that their accounts of their reading experiences reflected not just the obvious separation in the academic/non-academic domains but unexpectedly, largely featured

Table 12.4 Project 4

Project 4	
Participant selection	Purposive and snowball sampling: eight Malaysian undergraduates in a British university.
Methodology and method	Qualitatively informed: Phenomenological (in-depth) interview, diary-writing and document analysis.
Findings	The reader's physical, epistemological and ontological environment critically shapes the reading choice, which is the driver behind either the sustenance or suspension of the reading experience.
Implications	The essence of reading lies at the heart of *meaningful meaning-making*.

the crossings-over. This refers to the way some of the participants experienced discipline-bound textbooks to be highly enjoyable and also highly functional. This is, as Rosenblatt (1993) herself would have pointed out, the misleading "dualism" of the aesthetic/functional texts which can in fact, collapse upon itself. The participants of this study used expressions like "one big blob" to describe their reading experience. The reader's stance and frames of reading flagged up how some of these undergraduates were not so much averse to wider reading than they were formulating reading choices as the choices related to their texts and contexts. Refer to Figure 12.3 for the *Embodied Reading Choice*.

Exploring the way these undergraduates chose to read or not read provided an avenue to tap into a wider notion of reading in the 21st century.

Project 5

In this project, the focus was shifted to examine primary school children's negotiation with new materiality in terms of multimodal and multimedium reading. Taking stock of technological advancements and experiences in new literacies, this project aimed to capture the comparisons and contrasts of emergent readers' negotiation with print and screen-based texts. Departing slightly from the previous projects, Project 5 utilised visual methods that included video footage and art (drawings) as means of data collection. This was done because the participants were 8-year-olds, some of whom were struggling with reading. Therefore, methods that assumed basic literacy like surveys or diary-writing were unsuited for a small number of these participants.

In this project, the transactional theory of reading and reading as a social practice continued to provide important theoretical underpinnings. These theories allowed for possible ways to understand the participants' contexts even and especially for those who lagged behind in being alphabetic-literate. In addition to

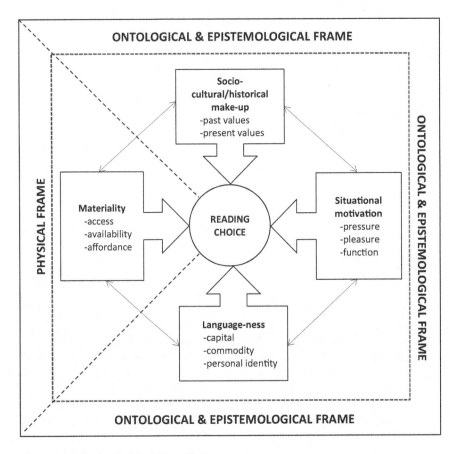

Figure 12.3 Embodied Reading Choice
Source: Chong, 2014.

these theories, the theory of the (im)materiality of literacy (Burnett, Merchant, Pahl, & Rowsell, 2014) was important to show up the implicit but powerful ways in which we relate to materiality and how that shapes reading opportunities which are most critical, especially for marginalised children. Table 12.5 summarises Project 5.

In Project 5, the consideration of the opportunity gap in terms of reading experience among mainstream and marginalised children formed an important factor of the study. Here, the significance of sociocultural (family/parents' background, home environment) and geopolitical (urban/rural, excellent/poor performing school) factors added on to the perspective of how meaning-making can be controlled and determined by powerful others.

Table 12.5 Project 5

Project 5	
Participant selection	Purposive sampling: 64 primary school students in an urban and rural Malaysian national school respectively.
Methodology and method	Qualitatively informed: informal conversations, visual methods and document analysis.
Findings	The gap between urban and rural students lies not only in the difference in physical infrastructure but in the way the children live their literate lives in school and at home.
Implications	The opportunity gap can best be addressed through localised solutions that take into account the immediate contexts of the children, especially the marginalised.

Project 6

In Project 6, the research broadens to glean empirical data from 8-year-olds and 11-year-olds in primary schools across urban and rural schools within the Perak state, in Malaysia. In Phase 1 of the project, out of a total of 850 primary schools in the state, 15 schools, stratified along the rural/urban and national/vernacular categories were randomly selected. More than 500 Primary 2 and Primary 5 students took part in a literacy practice survey that set out to provide a glimpse of urban and rural school children's self-reported motivation, attitude and perceptions of what reading may mean to them. Surveys were also distributed to their parents and the language teachers in the respective schools. More than 260 parents and 30 teachers responded to the survey.

Distinct to this project was my shifting perspective that had begun to locate reading on the broader spectrum of meaning-making. In this regard, the conventional sense of "reading" will have to give way to new ways, means and modalities of meaning-making in order for there to be more room to create new ways of reading. However, it was found that within the walls of schools, reading was still defined and regarded as decoding skills which were constantly assessed and measured across multiple writing systems. More alarmingly, early findings indicate that the most marginalised children in rural Malaysian schools face difficulty in reading and meaning-making even in the language that is native to them.

In Phase 2, three schools considered to be "under-performing" in terms of reading seen through their language school subjects were selected so that Reading and Meaning-making Workshops could be carried out. The emphasis was on the exploration of using non-alphabetic, non-linguistic modalities to access literacy, especially if alphabetic means have all but failed the children. Such new ways, as they are shaped and dictated by the very students we worked with, showed up an unexpected but much-welcomed trajectory that allowed for autonomy

Table 12.6 Project 6

Project 6	
Participant selection	Stratified random sampling: Approximately 550 Primary 2 and Primary 5 school students in 15 urban and rural, national and vernacular Malaysian schools in the state of Perak. Approximately 250 parents of Primary 2 and Primary 5 school students.
Methodology and method	Two-phased: Quantitatively informed: survey questionnaires. Qualitatively informed: informal conversations, semi-structured interviews, visual methods and document analysis.
Findings	School-based definitions and culture of what it means to read is still entrenched along largely academic and to a lesser extent non-academic boundaries, particularly through the dominant definition of decoding as reading.
Implications	Continued definitions that are narrow will delimit literacy policy and practice.

and control from the position of the students to drive their literacy experience. Table 12.6 denotes Project 6.

In this latest project, the theoretical perspective shifted to include Freire's (1984) notion of critical pedagogies which question the way the literacies are situated, especially in terms of how much agency lies in the hands of the reader.

Retaining and reviewing policy and practice: Framework for Respect in Literacy Education (FRiLE)

In sum, longitudinal findings from this at least 15-year research initiative show that the changes across the projects flag up how I critically understood my own shifting definitions of the phenomenon of literacy and reading over time. Particularly, this review shows up subtle but important changes in terms of how overarching theories, paradigm, scope and context have occurred. Table 12.7 captures the changes across the projects.

The writing of this chapter has been instructive in ways that I had not initially imagined. First, the shift in my research focus across the decade has forced me to broaden the definition of reading in order to capture meaning-making through new mediums and modalities. Second, the shift in my research perspective particularly through the lens of research methodologies signals how the limitation of my own research ontological standing is unable to capture the phenomenon of literacy. For example, despite having the benefit of exploring a range of research paradigms from post positivist to constructivist perspectives, I have found that

Table 12.7 Changes across the projects

META-ANALYSIS	PROJECT 1	PROJECT 2	PROJECT 3	PROJECT 4	PROJECT 5	PROJECT 6
OVERARCHING THEORY	Theory of planned behaviour.	Reading Attitude Acquisition Model.	Reading Attitude Acquisition Model. Reading as a sociocultural practice.	Reading as a sociocultural practice. Transactional theory of reading.	Reading as a sociocultural practice. Transactional theory of reading. Theory of human-material relationship.	Reading as a sociocultural practice. Transactional theory of reading. Critical pedagogies.
PARADIGM	Post positivist.	Constructivist.	Constructivist.	Constructivist.	Constructivist.	Post positivist & Constructivist.
DEFINITION	Reading as decoding texts.	Reading as decoding texts.	Reading as decoding across genres.	Reading as meaning-making across print, screen and genres.	Meaning-making across multimodal/multimedia materials and genres.	Meaning-making across multimodal/multimedia materials and genres located in sociocultural contexts.
CONTEXT	Individual act.	Individual experience.	Individual experience located within sociocultural space.	Co-constructed experience located within sociocultural, historical milieu.	Co-constructed phenomenon located within sociocultural, historical, geopolitical milieu.	Co-constructed phenomenon located within sociocultural, historical, geopolitical milieu as legitimate principle.
IMPLICATION	Reading is seen mainly as a skill to be learnt.			Reading is lived experience of meaning-making in a variety of contexts.		

these perspectives are unable to accommodate the lived experience of those whose lifeworlds are markedly different from my own. Allowing space for what Smith (2012) refers to as understanding local problems through using local settings and local ways, I can appreciate how my research perspectives will be further altered. Methodologies that emerge from the ground up and are indigenous to the land will form a powerful foundation for new perspectives of literacy to be shaped. In this way, future trajectories may show up facets of the phenomenon that speak for readers whose world views have not yet found traction.

I began this chapter with my biographical stance that accounts for one person's (mine) trajectory of reading and meaning-making. In following that trajectory, the almost five decades of my own experience both as a reader and as a researcher in reading shows up one unwavering point: in the Malaysian context, reading is still regarded as a skill to be learnt and that can be trained for. While this notion, in and of itself does bear significance in the argument for learning how to decode (for languages like English and Malay) and to negotiate complex iconographic characters (for languages like Chinese and to an extent, Tamil), it is the way in which this skill has been pursued so relentlessly in schools that may have elbowed out the potentially more powerful way of meaning-making which is the real loss to the pursuit of reading.

Freire (1984) made accessible the powerful notions of critical pedagogies in his advocacy of liberalising literacy education by dislocating it from the powerful other and placing it in the hands of the oppressed. For him, literacy cannot be about the "syllabification of *ba-be-bi-bobu*", but should, indeed, *must*, be about meaningful exchanges located in real contexts that work to raise life standards, rights and liberties (Freire & Macedo, 1987, p. 44). In advocating this, Freire unhinges reading from the narrow assumptions of decoding (often the language of a powerful other) in order to appropriate it within localised contexts. Under-pinning Freire's work is the fundamental value of respect.

In examining what to retain and what to review, my data and its analyses suggest that it is crucial that the Malaysian education system brings into its landscape this same value of respect. From my trajectory of the biographical, bibliographical and empirical, I urge Malaysia to retain its strong focus on schooling and even "doing school" whilst reconsidering the way reading is narrowly treated as a linguistic skill to be taught.

Here, I forward the idea of a Framework for Respect in Literacy Education (FRiLE) so that broader notions of meaning-making can be laid out. The findings presented earlier show that at least three broad overarching agendas are important to be considered. I name them the *Stakeholder agenda*, *National agenda* and *Research agenda*.

First, the Stakeholder agenda takes into account the consideration of the students and their immediate community (family, friends, society) as stakeholders of the literacy education system. In borrowing Freire's (1984) principles of critical pedagogies, FRiLE must account for how the reader is positioned in their social, economic and cultural context. This position must be examined and defined for how the reader is (dis)empowered and how any systematic inequity should be resolved. Critical questions in the Freire-an sense like "Why should I learn how to read and write?" "How can I become a better person if I have the ability to make meaning?" and "How does my sociocultural background shape my understanding of my world?" must be asked. It is crucial to note here that as in the Freire-an sense, the centrality of the individual reader (as referenced by the pronouns "I" and "my") is key to this agenda.

Secondly, for the National agenda, critical and honest questions must be posed to the powers-that-be that take into account the historical, linguistic and sociocultural factors that shape the past, present and future of the nation. Again, critical Freire-an questions like "How does national policy shape individual linguistic and literacy experience?", "How can any government exercise executive power and be purposefully inclusive and culturally sensitive in literacy education?" These questions have important implications towards policy change predominantly in terms of how policy makers and implementers understand new boundaries of literacy education. For example, if multimodality in reading is only accepted in marginalised spaces, authorities in schools and higher learning institutions will still be reluctant to accept non-alphabetic symbolic representations (i.e. pictures, drawings, numbers, colours, sounds) as legitimate ways of meaning-making. This means that even as young people begin to make meaning through new, non-mainstream, non-alphabetic-symbolic representations, the conventional and narrowly accepted understanding of reading may be a stumbling block to creative transformations of meaning-making.

The third agenda is the Research agenda. Within this scope, consideration needs to be given to the epistemological grounding of literacy research. The epistemological lenses that are brought to bear within such research projects have immense influence on the way research results are (mis)understood. This feeds back into the research loop and can potentially perpetuate entrenched ways of understanding phenomena. Critical questions like "From whose perspectives is this research conducted?", "How involved are the human participants in this research?" and "How will this research change the lived experience of those involved?" can be asked so that researchers remain cognisant of their influence in their reporting and writing.

Based on these three agenda in FRiLE, Malaysia should first move forward with literacy education as having its own space within the education system. This means that instead of being understood as an offshoot of language education, literacy initiatives should be carried out over and above language education. In so doing, literacy educators can focus on creating a culture of reading which can encompass a variety of meaning-making methods. Importantly, this allows for a shift in the way alphabetic reading may monopolise the sphere of meaning-making. Such a move will help in providing room for those who may struggle with alphabet decoding and phonics, and for whom life is lived in marginalised spaces. Second, teacher training should include within its scope cutting-edge pedagogical methods that optimise the vast amounts of multimodal and multimedia resources through advanced technological means. These methods will benefit literacy educators in terms of assisting them to create and curate for resource.

With a broader scope in training, literacy educators can accommodate students, especially those who may come from underprivileged backgrounds. Finally, partnerships should be formed across the triadic spaces of school, home and university so that a symbiotic relationship can emerge. This relationship, if meaningfully nurtured, can be critical in creating a forward-looking society that does more than read. This society engages in meaningful meaning-making.

As a co-constructed phenomenon located within a sociocultural, historical and geopolitical milieu, this ideation of reading provides not only new but *more* ground for researchers and literacy educators to negotiate upon. When those at the forefront of literacy education have a deep understanding of the main stakeholders who are the readers themselves, these educators make for better and more effective counterparts.

Acknowledgements

The work in this chapter was made possible by the generous funding received from Ministry of Education's Fundamental Research Grant Scheme (FRGS/1/2018/SS109/UTP/02/01).

References

Ajzen, I., & Fishbein, M. (1977). Attitude-behavior relations: A theoretical analysis and review of empirical research. *Psychological bulletin, 84*(5), 888–918.

Ajzen, I., & Fishbein, M. (2005). *The influence of attitudes on behavior. Handbook of attitudes.* Mahwah, NJ: Lawrence Erlbaum Associates, Incorporated.

Azizan, H., & Tan, E.-L. (2006, August 13). Low volume reason for high book prices. *The Star.*

Buchler, W. (1932, August). The Malayan reading public. *British Malaya, 7,* 89–90.

Burnett, C., Merchant, G., Pahl, K., & Rowsell, J. (2014). The (im)materiality of literacy: The significance of subjectivity to new literacies research. *Discourse: Studies in the Cultural Politics of Education, 35*(1), 90–103.

Chong, S. L. (2011). *A study of Malaysian undergraduates' motivation for reading* (Master in Philosophy unpublished thesis). University of Cambridge, Cambridge.

Chong, S. L. (2014). *Understanding reading choice: An investigation of multilingual Malaysian undergraduates' print-based and computer-mediated reading experiences* (PhD). University of Cambridge, Cambridge.

Chong, S. L. (2016). Re-thinking aliteracy: When undergraduates surrender their reading choices. *Literacy, 50*(1), 14–22.

Chong, S. L. (2018a, July 9). The changing face of literacy. *New Straits Times.* Retrieved from www.nst.com.my/opinion/letters/2018/07/388957/changing-face-literacy

Chong, S. L. (2018b). Pressure, pleasure and function: Malaysian undergraduates reading across boundaries in a university in England. In E. Arizpe & G. C. Hodges (Eds.), *Young people reading: Empirical research across international contexts* (pp. 166–180). Abingdon and Oxford: Routledge.

Chong, S. L., & Lai, F. W. (2007). *Perceptions and practices of reading: An investigation of readers' belief system.* Paper presented at the Language, Education and Diversity Conference (LED) 2007, University of Waikato, New Zealand.

Chong, S. L., & Renganathan, S. (2008). Voices of ardent readers: One in concert. *The English Teacher, XXXVII*, 1–14.

Eakle, A. J., & Garber, A. M. (2004). International reports on literacy research: Malaysia, sultanate of Oman. *Reading Research Quarterly, 39*(4), 478–481.

Fishbein, M., & Ajzen, I. (1975). *Belief, attitude, intention, and behavior: An introduction to theory and research*. Reading, MA: Addison-Wesley Pub. Co.

Fishbein, M., & Ajzen, I. (2009). *Predicting and changing behavior: The reasoned action approach*. New York: Psychology Press.

Freire, P. (1984). *Pedagogy of the oppressed*. New York: Continuum.

Freire, P., & Macedo, D. (1987). *Reading the word and the world*. Great Britain: Routledge and Kegan Paul Ltd.

Gee, J. P. (2008). *Social linguistics and literacies*. Abingdon, Oxon: Routledge.

Gray, W. S. (1932). Summary of reading investigations (July 1, 1930, to June 30, 1931). *The Elementary School Journal, 32*(6), 447–463.

Gray, W. S. (1933). Summary of reading investigations (July 1, 1931 to June 30, 1932). *The Journal of Educational Research, 26*(6), 401–424.

Heath, S. B. (1983). *Ways with words: Language, life, and work in communities and classrooms*. Cambridge: Cambridge University Press.

Kalantzis, M., & Pandian, A. (Eds.). (2001). *Literacy matters: Issues for new times*. Melbourne: Common Ground Publication.

Kaur, S., & Thiyagarajah, R. (2000). The English reading habits of ELLS student in university science Malaysia. *Ultibase*.

Kress, G. R. (2000). Multimodality. In B. Cope & M. Kalantzis (Eds.), *Multiliteracies: Literacy learning and designs of social futures* (pp. 182–202). London: Routledge.

Mackey, M. (2016). *One child reading: My auto-bibliography*. Edmonton, Alberta, Canada: The University of Alberta Press.

McKenna, M. C. (2001). Development of reading attitudes. In L. Verhoeven & C. Snow (Eds.), *Literacy and motivation: Reading engagement in individuals and groups* (pp. 135–158). London: Lawrence Erlbaum Associates.

Meissner, F., & Vertovec, S. (2015). Comparing super-diversity. *Ethnic and Racial Studies, 38*(4), 541–555.

Nagle, J. S. (1928). *Educational needs of the straits settlements and federated Malay states*. (PhD). John Hopkins University, Baltimore.

The New London Group. (2000). A pedagogy of multiliteracies. In B. Cope & M. Kalantzis (Eds.), *Multiliteracies* (pp. 9–37). London: Routledge.

Pandian, A. (1997). Literacy in postcolonial Malaysia. *Journal of Adolescent & Adult Literacy, 40*(5), 402–404.

Pandian, A. (1999). Whither reading in Malaysia: Confronting reading reluctancy among pre-university students. In A. Pandian (Ed.), *Global literacy—vision, revision and vistas in education*. Serdang: University Putra Malaysia Press.

Pandian, A. (2000). A study on readership behaviour among multi-ethnic, multilingual Malaysian students. *The International Journal of Learning*, 5–9.

Pandian, A. (2001). Advancing literacy in the new times. In M. Kalantzis & A. Pandian (Eds.), *Literacy matters: Issues for new times* (pp. 11–18). Australia: Common Ground Publishing Pty. Ltd.

Pandian, A. (2008). Literacies: Languages, mathematics and the sciences. In I. A. Bajunid (Ed.), *Malaysia from traditional to smart schools* (pp. 197–220). Shah Alam: Oxford Fajar.

Pandian, A., & Baboo, S. B. (2002). Literacy behavior, social interaction and performance of TESOL in Malaysia. In A. Pandian & S. B. Baboo (Eds.), *Learning to communicate* (pp. 7–24). Victoria, Australia: Common ground publishing.

Pandian, A., & Moorth, S. T. (2001). Literacy practices among TESOL trainee teacher. In M. Kalantzis & A. Pandian (Eds.), *Literacy matters: Issues for new times* (pp. 131–144). Victoria, Australia: Common ground publishing.

Pillai, S. (2007). The reality of reading in the tertiary learner's world. *The English Teacher, 36*, 101–118.

Rosenblatt, L. M. (1938). *Literature as exploration.* London: D. Appleton-Century Company Incorporated.

Rosenblatt, L. M. (1969). Towards a transactional theory of reading. *Journal of Literacy Research, 1*(31), 31–49.

Rosenblatt, L. M. (1978). *The reader, the text, the poem: The transactional theory of the literary work.* Carbondale: Southern Illinois University Press.

Rosenblatt, L. M. (1993). The transactional theory: Against dualism. *College English, 55*(4), 377–386.

Rosenblatt, L. M. (2005). *Making meaning with texts: Selected essays.* Portsmouth, NH: Heinemann Educational Books

Siti Aishah, S. (2003). Experience and efforts in literacy programmes: Brief country report, Malaysia.

Small, F. (1996). *Reading profile of Malaysians.* Kuala Lumpur: Perpustakaan Negara Malaysia.

Smith, L. T. (2012). *Decolonizing methodologies* (2nd ed.). New York: Zed Books Ltd.

Street, B. V. (1995). *Social literacies: Critical approaches to literacy in development, ethnography and education* London: Longman.

Street, B. V. (2001). *Literacy and development.* London: Routledge.

United Nations Development Programme (UNDP). (2018). *Human development indices and indicators.* Retrieved from http://hdr.undp.org/en/2018-update/download

Verhoeven, L., & Snow, C. (2001). Introduction-literacy and motivation: Bridging cognitive and sociocultural viewpoints. In L. Verhoeven & C. Snow (Eds.), *Literacy and motivation* (pp. 1–22). London: Lawrence Erlbaum Associates.

Vogel, M., & Washburne, C. (1928). An objective method of determining grade placement of children's reading material. *The Elementary School Journal, 28*(5), 373–381.

Index

Note: page numbers in *italic* indicate a figure and page numbers in **bold** indicate a table on the corresponding page.

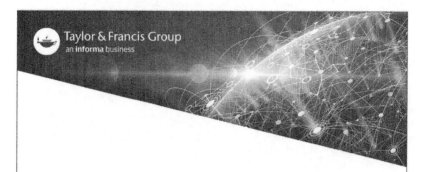